Sounding Modernism

Sounding Modernism

*Rhythm and Sonic Mediation in
Modern Literature and Film*

Edited by Julian Murphet,
Helen Groth and Penelope Hone

EDINBURGH
University Press

Edinburgh University Press is one of the leading university presses in the UK. We publish academic books and journals in our selected subject areas across the humanities and social sciences, combining cutting-edge scholarship with high editorial and production values to produce academic works of lasting importance. For more information visit our website: edinburghuniversitypress.com

Edinburgh University Press Ltd
The Tun – Holyrood Road, 12(2f) Jackson's Entry, Edinburgh EH8 8PJ

Typeset in 10.5/13 Adobe Sabon by
Servis Filmsetting Ltd, Stockport, Cheshire,
and printed and bound in Great Britain by
CPI Group (UK) Ltd, Croydon CR0 4YY

A CIP record for this book is available from the British Library

ISBN 978 1 4744 1636 8 (hardback)
ISBN 978 1 4744 1637 5 (webready PDF)
ISBN 978 1 4744 1638 2 (epub)

Contents

Part Three: Difficult Voices

Part Four: Modern Rhythm: Writing, Sound, Cinema

Acknowledgements

The seeds of this volume were sown by a conference, *Modern Soundscapes*, which was held at the University of New South Wales in 2012. We are indebted to the Australasian Association of Literature and the Centre for Modernism Studies in Australia, and the University of New South Wales for supporting this event. Professor James Donald, then Dean of the Faculty of Arts and Social Sciences, deserves particular thanks for his support. We would also like to acknowledge the Australian Research Council, which has supported the research of a number of contributors in this volume, including our own. Finally, we would like to thank our families for their patience and support.

Chapter 1

Introduction: Sounding Modernism 1890–1950

Helen Groth, Julian Murphet and Penelope Hone

Did modernism sound differently from its predecessor aesthetic domi-
nants, realism and romanticism; and if so, how? Was it louder, or
quieter, or were the ears of its subjects simply that much more sensitive,
or deadened? What were its organs of projection and of audition, and
how may these have been reshaped, retrained by technologies capable
for the first time of retaining and replaying sonic phenomena? How did
the older arts adapt to make sense of these new sound media, or reme-
diate them into their own traditional substances: paint, sculpted wood
and metal, or letters printed on a page, let alone those more privileged
instruments of the orchestra proper? Were the sounds sacred to aesthetic
and cultural traditions to be protected from or shattered by the growing
din of an industrial economy driven by colossal mechanical engines
and a plethora of new and noisy consumables (cars, motorbikes, train
journeys, vacuum cleaners, aeroplanes, and so on, let alone the directly
mediatic everyday instruments: telephones, radio sets, gramophones
and dictaphones)? Let Edvard Munch's great painting *The Scream* stand
as an indicative aesthetic testimony to the prodigious affective impact
of auditory phenomena wound to the pitch of mental crisis across this
entire period; those great luminous whorls etched into the vivid evening
like the palpable traces of a subjective thermonuclear explosion: the
inscription of a radical sonic Real on the firmament itself.

If, at the very outset of the period considered by this volume, Walter
Pater had advised that all art constantly aspires 'to the condition of
music', then that late-romantic reaching toward some musically harmonious aesthetic apotheosis would perforce, in the decades that
followed, be violently rerouted through the disreputable noises of a
transformed public sphere and its underlying economic mode of production. Undoubtedly the very concept of 'music' was altered beyond
recognition by way of this unprecedented passage, as first the various
experiments with serialism and dodecaphonic scale, and later *musique*

concrète, make palpable at the level of composition. Ezra Pound certainly detected untold potential for the sonic arts in the rhythms and thunder of industrialisation; his efforts (in tandem with George Antheil) to forge a pathway through the noises of the labour process toward a 'machine art' of sound, remain intriguing:

> Three years ago [in 1924] Antheil was talking vaguely of 'tuning up' whole cities . . . With the performance of the Ballet mécanique one can conceive the possibility of organizing the sounds of a factory, let us say of boiler-plate or any clangorous noisiness, the actual sounds of the labor, the various tones of the grindings; according to the needs of the work, and yet, with such pauses and durées, that at the end of the eight hours, the men go out not with frayed nerves, but elated.[1]

Pater's idealist imperative lingers on here as a fugitive (even 'mad') utopian aspiration to transfigure the most hideous cacophonies in the history of humankind into innervating aesthetic experiences.

Is there any more potent image of the sonic intensities of the various modernisms than that of Filippo Tommaso Marinetti, bringing his Futurism to London not with a whimper but a performative Big Bang? Describing his 'second dynamic and synoptic declamation' to an astonished English gathering at the Doré gallery on 28 April 1914, Marinetti recalls:

> I declaimed several passages from my *Zang tumb tumb* (the Siege of Adrianople). On the table in front of me I had a telephone, some boards, and special hammers, all of which permitted me to imitate the Turkish general's orders and sounds of artillery and machinegun fire.
> . . .
> In another room a bit away, there were two big drums on which my collaborator, the painter [Christopher] Nevinson, produced the rumbling boom of cannon whenever I told him to do so over the telephone.
> The growing interest of the English audience became frantic enthusiasm when I achieved the greatest dynamism by alternating the Bulgarian song 'Sciumi Maritza' with the dazzle of my images and the roar of the onomatopoetic artillery.[2]

Two months later, Marinetti was back with his collaborators, Ugo Piatti and Luigi Russolo, at the London Coliseum, this time with Noise Tuners and a veritable symphony of unpalatable noises. Indeed, few artists or intellectuals at the time were as clued in to the abiding importance of new sound technologies as Marinetti, who embraced all of them as potential portals to a new cultural order of things. Radio, for Marinetti and his fellow futurist Pino Masnata, dissolved formal limits, generating an 'art without time or space without yesterday or tomorrow'.[3] The ear tunes in, captures a sound or a voice, before it dissolves once again into nothingness.

Picking up on Marinetti and Masnata's stress on formal dissolution and dislocation, Steven Connor has written of the text of Beckett's radio play *All That Fall* that it emerges 'from nothing and nowhere'.[4] It is in radio, Connor continues, 'that Beckett seems to have found the possibility of writing without ground – that is to say, writing in which the spoken words are at once figure and ground' (67). Sounds surge, jarr and reverberate through Beckett's text, sometimes to the point of excess, of noise – bells ring, whistles blow, dogs bark, sheep baa, and music plays. Material traces of Irish colloquial speech are transcribed and transformed into rhythmic refrains that cue the listener to attend to the acoustic minutiae of the central characters', the Rooneys' everyday life: 'Nice day for the races', 'Divine day for the meeting', 'Lovely day for the fixture'.[5] Writing mediates the process of making sound for Beckett, an acoustic experiment that exults in its own destructive energy. He insisted that *All That Fall* was a 'radio text, for voices, not bodies', while the visible printed text was a simple static thing that threatened the quality of the event of vocalisation and listening 'which depends on the whole thing's *coming out of the dark*'.[6]

All That Fall, as Beckett insists, demands attention to mediation, to how words sound and how writing, in turn mediates sound. Sounding the limits of modern media – of writing and radio – Beckett's radio plays have and still do challenge scholars to explore the various ways modernist writing met the new challenge of capturing the sounds of modern life at a critical transitional moment when an array of entirely new storage devices emerged that simultaneously did what literature could not: namely, record them. And yet, as the essays in this collection show, it was precisely this challenge that drove writers to engage as never before with what the symbolic apparatus of written language had never yet properly grasped: the vocal textures, rhythmic mechanisations and stochastic accidents of real, socially embodied sound. Synchronously, the multiple sonic variations in the cinema of this period, as Laura Marcus and Steven Connor variously demonstrate in what follows, materialise cinema's unprecedented capacity to record and structure the specific rhythms of modern acoustic experience.

The explosion in sound studies across many disciplines – including music, anthropology, ethnology, historical studies, architecture, cultural studies and gender studies – has touched literary studies at various points, particularly in restricted national and periodised case studies. Likewise seminal studies of cinema, sound and modern literature by Garrett Stewart, Steven Connor and Laura Marcus have raised equally urgent questions about the matching of motion picture images to optical soundtracks, and the implications of that suturing of sound and vision for literary forms.[7] The rich nexus of new sound-recording technologies, new vocabularies of and for sonic phenomena, new standardisations of rhythm and speed, and the weird displacements of 'voice' peculiar to modernity offer unparalleled resonators for the period in literary history known as modernism. In elaborating these resonances *Sounding Modernism* addresses two simultaneous needs: in sound studies, for more explicit engagements with the symbolic registrations of sonic modernity on textual forms; and in modernism studies, for more various and systematic analyses of modernist forms in terms of their capacities to mediate rhythms, sonic textures and vocal derangements.

This introduction considers what it means to attend to the dynamics and aesthetics of sonic mediation in modern writing, acoustic and cinematic forms produced from the 1880s through to the mid-twentieth century. Tracking the various, yet particular, transformations of the rhythmic or metrical patterning of sound across a range of modern literary and cinematic forms opens up a space for new ways of understanding both the specific sonorous qualities that different modern media are capable of registering, and how sonic transpositions and transferences across media affect the techniques with which human subjects respond to modern soundscapes. We begin by laying down some methodological groundwork for the analysis of literature's historically complex relationship to extra-literary sounds, and the identification of parallels and divergences with other modern media, such as the phonograph, radio and cinema. Building on work by Garrett Stewart, Jonathan Sterne, Steven Connor, Melba Cuddy-Keane, and others, we elaborate some of the conceptual means recently developed through sound studies and other cognate disciplines for 'listening' to the sounds embedded in modern media. We then consider how this theorisation of 'listening' can be applied to the training of the modern ear to hear, recognise and reproduce rhythmic acoustic patterns that alternately registered and filtered out unwanted noise. While recognising the seminal work on sound in this period by both media and film historians, including two contributors to this volume, we argue that there still remains a large amount of work to be done on the specific cultural and technological conjuncture of 'modernism' as a period dense with unprecedented acoustic messages and noise.

Inscriptions of sound

There are several long-standing mimetic conventions for stabilising the relationship between literary textuality and sonic phenomena, and several more specific to the period of modernism proper (roughly

1880–1940); and naturally enough these latter radically refashioned the former in unpredictable ways. So, the fact of alphabetisation itself, the conquest of a fixed series of correspondences between conventional glyphs and phonemic sound patterns, which is generally traced to the innovations of the Phoenicians with the Proto-Sinaitic scripts of the Egyptian Bronze Age around 1050 BCE, and extended through the Greek and Roman alphabets into all Romance languages, looks profoundly different after the invention of the typewriter. The long-established notion that written words enjoyed more or less stable phonetic pronunciations in their spoken languages was secretly (perhaps occultly) undergirded by a stubborn logic of 'phonocentrism' that subordinated thought to inspiration, speech to thought, script to speech, and print to handwriting. It was this phonocentric logic that faced a crisis of legitimacy once typewriters emerged as mass-producing machines of typescript in business affairs and government records after 1880. Now, it appeared that 'voice' had been subtracted from the entire complex; typescript appeared as if of its own accord, shorn of the breath and inspiration that had still vouchsafed what Friedrich Kittler has called the discourse network of romanticism, where the 'Mother's Mouth' had issued a stream of primary orality whence the strivings of genius might draw their articulate webs of text.[8] The typewriter with its mechanical clatter at once silenced the echo-chamber of virtual speech that had underwritten centuries' worth of printed material; for the sudden obsolescence and redundancy of handwriting within the living tissues of literature, thanks to the intervention of 'something in between tool and machine', was also a final supersession of the 'spiritual' linkages between hand, mouth and central nervous system that had vouchsafed the grudging Socratic approval of print in the first place.[9]

When a poet commits to print something on the order of this:

                                            r-p-o-p-h-e-s-s-a-g-r
                          who
a)s w(e loo)k
upnowgath
            PPEGORHRASS
                                eringint(o-
aThe):l
            eA
                    !p:
S   a
                          (r
rIvInG   .gRrEaPsPhOs)
                                                              to
rea(be)rran(com)gi(e)ngly
,grasshopper;[10]

the entire tradition of Romantic literature, in which the sonic echoes of traditional song forms, ballads, speech patterns, the 'language really used by men', and so on, ramify the socially rebarbative ideology, is up in smoke. The typewriter silences this primary orality at a keystroke and commits the poem to a visuality and a materiality specific to print as such, in which 'sound' appears merely as a dim vestige. This poem does not *sound*; it is bereft of vocality, as it is of tradition; delivered of the new machine age, its striking silence disposes of the alphabet as so many visual forms bent on unprecedented itineraries across the page.

If so much can be said for the typewriter, how much more significant will have been the impact of new media technologies capable of recording, storing and replaying actual sound waves in isochronic, analogic forms? The gramophone and its various derivatives and prototypes marked an epoch not just for culture in general, but specifically for literature which, for the first time, lost the monopoly on sonic recording it had enjoyed for millennia. Hitherto, amongst media, only writing had been capable of sufficient symbolic sophistication and variety to transcribe and preserve the soundscapes of various lifeworlds. Its complex descriptive and mimetic functions were tasks not suited, for instance, to the live arts of theatre or music, nor to the plastic arts of sculpture and painting. Gilbert White, who complained frequently of his fits of deafness, could write as follows of the multifarious birdsongs that were his special delight:

> The notes of the eagle-kind are shrill and piercing . . . Owls have very expressive notes; they hoot in a fine vocal sound, much resembling the vox humana, and reducible by a pitch-pipe to a musical key. This note seems to express complacency and rivalry among the males: they use also a quick call and an horrible scream; and can snore and hiss when they mean to menace.[11]

Some sixty years later, Henry David Thoreau would perform much the same function for the woods around Walden Pond, throwing in dashes of onomatopoeia and prosopopoeia for good measure:

> I seldom opened my door in a winter evening without hearing [the forlorn but melodious note of a hooting owl]; *Hoo hoo hoo, hoorer, hoo*, sounded sonorously, and the first three syllables accented somewhat like *how der do*; or sometimes *hoo, hoo* only. One night in the beginning of winter, before the pond froze over, about nine o'clock, I was startled by the loud honking of a goose . . . *Boo-hoo, boo-hoo, boo-hoo!* It was one of the most thrilling discords I ever heard. And yet, if you had a discriminating ear, there were in it the elements of a concord such as these plains never saw nor heard.[12]

Such lavish and extended stretches of sonically sensitive prose were unique to the writer's craft, the more valuable for their distinction: the only record posterity will ever have of what Walden Pond in the winter of 1852, or Selborne at high summer, 1778, actually sounded like. But with the advent of a machine that could record 'the physiological accidents and stochastic disorder of bodies', such efforts were rendered, if not redundant, then at least mute in their suddenly exposed symbolic nature.[13] Once the eight-year old Ludwig Koch had used his Edison cylinder phonograph to record the fleeting trills and flutters of an Indian white-rumped shama bird in 1889 – the first known recording of any bird[14] – a century of avian-inspired romantic verse, from Shelley's 'To a Skylark' and Keats's 'Ode to a Nightingale' to Dickinson's bobolinks and robins, began to appear anachronistic. The poetic nomination of a sound, the graceful positioning of a musical adjective, the drive of a dynamic adverb, none of them could hope to compete with the scratchy impressions left in wax or shellac of vibrations in the very medium of sound.

Onomatopoeia itself assumed the appearance of so many dead letters, left cold on the doorstep of phonography, unless it was pressed beyond the limits of convention. When Joyce came to inscribe the sounds made by the Blooms' domestic cat in *Ulysses* (1922), what mattered (for the first time in literary history) was not the settled national conventions of a 'meow', 'miaow' or 'miau', but the infinitesimal intra-textual distinctions between a 'Mkgnao!' a 'Mrkgnao!' and a 'Mrkrgnao!', not to mention an irregular 'Gurrhr!'.[15] The pebbles at Dignam's funeral strike Bloom's ear with a 'Rtststr!' (6.970), while the printing press at the newspaper registers with him as a 'Sllt' (7.174). Stephen Dedalus's ashplant strikes the gasjet at Bella Cohen's with a 'Pooah! Pfuiiiiiii!' (15.2280); and more extravagantly still, the hungry young poet allows the surf to speak to him with a 'fourworded wavespeech: seesoo, hrss, rsseeiss, ooos' (3.456). And it is far from an exegetical stretch to insist that all of this fanatical attention to the letter-by-letter specificity of onomatopoeia's exquisite new pedantries in Joyce's hands can be traced to the impact of a machine that was automatically recording sounds *as sounds* and not as alphabetical glyphs. For it is also the case that *Ulysses* imagines what it might be like to communicate with the dead through the haunted medium of their posthumous recorded voices, and does so with a peculiar onomatopoeic relish for the crackles and scratches of the new medium:

> Have a gramophone in every grave or keep it in the house. After dinner on a Sunday. Put on poor old greatgrandfather. Kraahraark! Hellohellohello amawfullyglad kraark awfullygladaseeagain hellohello amawf krpthsth. Remind you of the voice like the photograph reminds you of the face. (6.962–7)

In 'Circe', the gramophone 'speaks' with a marked difficulty that can only register as the ribald and satirical laughter of a symbolic medium at the limits of an analogue recording medium: 'Whorusaleminyourhighhohhhh ... (*the disc rasps gratingly against the needle*)' (15.2211–12).[16]

Sounding modern

Friedrich Kittler has been paraphrased as arguing that, 'in the modernist landscape of medial specialization, writing is one medium among others, with its own limitations and possibilities, and the writer a media specialist, a professional of the letter'.[17] This self-conscious humbling signifies a dramatic reversal of fortunes for a means of communication that had, not long before, enjoyed such command over the domain of knowledge that it had conjured away its very materiality in myths of phonocentricity and romantic dreams of genius, organic form and the creative imagination – none of which gave much thought to the materiality of the letter.

Writing in the wake of the epistemological crisis inspired by Kittler's precursors, Michel Foucault and Jacques Derrida, Garrett Stewart argued in *Reading Voices* for a different understanding of literary reading as a form of silent voicing or 'textual sounding' driven by a simple question: 'Where do we read?'[18] The place of reading for Stewart is located in the receptivity of the body to phonic and graphic mediations – from the brain's cognitive rhythms to the reverberating surfaces of the diaphragm, throat, tongue and palate. In the late 1980s when Stewart was writing *Reading Voices*, to read 'aurally', or practice what Stewart dubbed 'phonemic reading', seemed to jar with the pervasive 'phonophobia' inspired by Derrida's demystification of the divinely inspired Logos. But Stewart argued that the converse was true. Attending to the phonemic counterpart to printed text or the dynamics of 'inner audition', as he calls it, did not mean reanimating the myth of the 'originary Voice' before the letter: instead it created a space to develop a more responsive approach to the 'phenomenality' of literary reading (3). Central to this 'phenomenal' approach was a privileging of listening over hearing, as Stewart succinctly observes: 'When we read to ourselves, our ears hear nothing. Where we read, however, we listen' (11). Stewart derived this distinction from Barthes's insistence in *The Responsibility of Forms*: '*Hearing* is a physiological phenomenon; *listening* is a psychological act.'[19] Listening in this sense is a self-consciously critical process, requiring far more of the reader than the automatic internalisation of an aesthetic ideal.

Variants of Barthes's distinction between hearing and listening

– including Jean-Luc Nancy's focus on listening and subjectivity in *Listening* (2002) – echo through critical work on sound in literature and cinema. Sometimes this distinction is characterised as a form of 'ear-witnessing', a term which R. Murray Schafer mobilised to describe, amongst other things, the acoustic precision of writers from Swift, Tolstoy, Hardy, Mann to Faulkner.[20] For Schafer there was something particular in the ways all of these writers were able to bear witness to and archive the soundscapes of different times and cultures that supplanted the counterfeit descriptions of less attuned ears with an authentic repro-ducible record. Attending more specifically to the time of Faulkner than Swift, Douglas Kahn, in *Noise, Water, Meat* (1999), describes the act of 'listening through history' in the context of the sound-saturated modern arts.[21] Kahn writes that the twentieth century becomes 'more melliflu-ous and raucous through historiographic listening' and 'just that much more animated with the inclusion of the hitherto muffled regions of the sensorium' (2). Muffled is a loaded term here, indicating a critical drive to listen to the silenced and peripheral, to investigate issues of cultural history and theory that reveal the 'selective audition' of established traditions of attending to the sounds of the past and present. In con-trast to Stewart's ultimately a-historical focus on the phenomenology of phonemic reading then, Kahn's method of 'historiographic listening' examines how the 'auditive states' generated by a modernist experimen-tal avant-garde drowned out 'the social in sound – the political, poetical and ecological' (4).

Claims for the modernist avant-garde inaugurating new auditive states imply the possibility of a distinctive, identifiably modern sound-scape or modes of sounding, a conclusion that Sam Halliday has recently cautioned against. Halliday rightly argues that we should not limit our-selves to the assumption that modern sounds are 'simply those made by all "modern" things, including typesetting machines – and, of course, phonographs themselves'.[22] Instead, he continues, both pre-modern and modern sounds should 'feature or even help define the modern "sound-world"' (15). Jonathan Sterne also resisted the problematic association of modernisation and modernity in his influential study *The Audible Past*, while conceding the formative influence of the cultural construc-tion of an identifiably modern soundscape.[23] Emily Thompson makes a similar point in her history of aural culture in early twentieth-century America by clarifying the distinction between 'the physical aspects of a soundscape' and the ways in which cultures construct particular 'sci-entific and aesthetic ways of listening', both of which, she argues were radically transformed in the 'years after 1900'.[24] Indeed, few would contest that 'representing' sound becomes a more complex process in the wake of the invention of 'modern things' such as the phonograph, the telephone, radio and the talkies; a process that means that it is impossible to separate the representation of sound from the mediation of sound.

David Trotter has recently argued in *Literature in the First Media Age* that placing too much emphasis on old media and new media, 'on remediation and dialectical system building' distracts from a 'further' and in many ways more intense 'rivalry' of 'the new against new': rivalries driven by 'political and aesthetic principles' or varying economic or social functions.[25] To understand and map these rivalries we need to distinguish between 'the representational and the connective', according to Trotter (7). Representational media – such as photography, phonography and cinematography – '*writing* in light, sound or movement' – records and stores images and sound, while connective media – the telegraph, telephone, teleprinter/fax – communicates information instantly and efficiently (7–8). While conceding Lisa Gitelman's point, that no medium is solely representational or connective, Trotter contends that an explicit set of conflicts between these two modalities emerge in Britain at the moment when the boundaries of empire and nation were being radically reconfigured by global telecommunication networks (8).[26] In this account, modern literature and cinema are allied against telephony, and radio is shaped by an internal tension between its representational capacities as a medium for reportage, chronicling and storytelling and its connective functions, as a medium of information and mass-communication. Whether one agrees or not with this dialectical account of modernism's inter-medial networks, Trotter's quest for specific distinctions between media parallels the work of modernist scholars, such as Melba Cuddy-Keane, Steven Connor and Garrett Stewart, whose work has sought in very different ways to read and theorise the particular ways in which sound reverberates through modern literary and cinematic forms.

Listening to the sounds of literary modernism, Cuddy-Keane has argued, requires the development of a specific 'critical methodology and a vocabulary for analysing narrative representations of sound'.[27] After identifying the traditional conventions for 'representing' sound – dialogue, metaphor, onomatopoeia – Cuddy-Keane turns to the descriptive repertoire of narratology to account for the concrete ways that modern narrative began 'to record a vast repertoire of sound, and to transcribe the actual process of listening' in response to the transformations wrought by modern sound technologies and the urban soundscape of early twentieth-century cities (383). While acknowledging precursors, such as Sara Danius's *The Senses of Modernism*, Cuddy-Keane argues that we need more technical precision in how we account for the new 'perceptual knowledge' that modern sound technologies enabled

(384). This involves the development of an 'auditory typology' to 'discriminate sense-specific elements' in a literary text (384). To this end, Cuddy-Keane proposes the acoustic terms – auscultation, auscultise and auscultator to parallel the existing optically biased narratological terms – focalisation, focalise and focaliser – and encourages us to draw upon empirical terminology mobilised by those studying the physiology of auditory perception, such as auditory streaming, stream segregation and integration, and auditory restoration (385). Her reading of Virginia Woolf's short fiction 'Kew Gardens' (1919) provides a striking exemplification of how an acoustically attuned critical methodology can reveal the way modern narrative forms experiment with the representation of sound. Inscription is a key term for Cuddy-Keane, another is representation, but surprisingly, she says little about mediation, although her compelling close reading of Woolf reveals how writing's capacity to mediate the sounds of modern life are challenged and transformed by new forms of sonic mediation:

> Diverse fragments of sound become the narrative thread: voices of people we see before we can hear what they are saying and which pass out of earshot before the conversations are over, the voice of the summer sky murmuring in the drone of an aeroplane overhead, and the voices of flowers heard by an old man who babbles on about a conductive machine that operated by a battery and uses a rubber-insulated wire to transmit the spirit voices of the dead. The effect is of narrative auscultised from the position of a stationary microphone, its membrane vibrating to the sounds of a summer day. (386)

What is striking about this reading is the way it recalls the phonograph's automatic registration of sound. Disembodied voices, the drone of an aeroplane, and the babbling of an old man summoning the spectre of radio transmission, are randomly registered in an associative flow that makes the dynamics of sonic mediation the focus. In many ways this reading reinforces David Trotter's and Lisa Gitelman's argument for the productive co-existence of representational and connective media. And yet, the apparently neutral scientism of narratological rhetoric also risks dematerialising the voice and sounds of modern life, removing them from bodies and spaces marked by class and race, a point that Julie Beth Napolin takes up in her chapter in this collection in the context of race and American modernism with specific reference to Cuddy-Keane's methodological focus on sound as an object. Napolin argues that 'neutrality defines the limits and scope of narrative theory in relation to audibility', making sound the object of our reading or viewing, she suggests, de-emphasises the fact that 'race determines in advance the field of audibility'.

Perhaps we can say that what 'sounds' in literature – poetic or narrative – after the inauguration of the 'discourse network of 1900' is the complex and negotiated passage of a newly materialised concept of sound itself across a number of competing institutions and media platforms, such that its ideological waves and radiation can be registered in a bewildering variety of discrete, even contradictory ways. There is henceforth no illusory 'perfect image' of a sonic phenomenon, only partial and provisional indications of its having been, having sounded, having passed by – the way waves themselves propagate their impulse at varying frequencies and intensity between and across the media that carry them. And perversely, as a number of our contributors below will point out, one of the most potent symptoms of this complex and negotiated signal transfer of sonic phenomena in literary modernity will be their encryption under the sign of silence itself; for what more typical, and enigmatic evidence is there of the new regime of sound in modernity than the cult and veneration of a newfangled and well-nigh metaphysical Silence, with no credible precursor in the annals of the sonic imagination?

The opening section of the volume – 'Writing Modern Sounds' – goes some way to answer this question, with its theoretical focus on the challenges encountered in capturing modern sounds. In a wide ranging discussion that ties together the poetry of Robert Duncan with the writing of Franz Kafka and Beckett, Julian Murphet considers modernist literature's treatment of sounds that cannot be heard – those, which exist within a 'utopian Silence beyond hearing'. Where Murphet asks us to think through the paradoxes that emerge within modernism's relationship to sonic phenomena that lie beyond hearing, Tom Vandevelde sets forth a theoretical framework that urges that we, as readers, become more attuned to the auditory dimension of narrative texts. Continuous with the work of Cuddy-Keane, Vandevelde underscores the critical insights found in attending to the dynamics and aesthetics of sonic mediation in modern writing.

Implicit in these theoretical approaches to thinking about the sonic imagination is an attention to the act of listening; they remind us of what it means to listen as we read. As this introduction has already discussed, modernism's interest in listening is, in part, a reflection of a newly material conception of sound that emerged with the invention of recording and play-back technologies. The second section of the collection – 'Mediated Voices' – responds to this shift, beginning with Lisa Gitelman's examination of the 'audile interiority' generated by the evanescent popularity of nickel-in-the-slot machines in the US. These public and commercial music players flourished in the 1890s, before home phonographs and gramophones moved the consumption of recorded sound into the private domain of the living room. Continuing this focus on the dynamics of listening to recorded voices, Helen Groth takes Christina Stead's disappointed response to James Joyce's gramophone recording of the 'Anna Livia-Plurabelle' section of *Finnegans Wake* as a representative instance of the uneven reception of early recordings of modernist texts. The disruptive acoustic affects, to Stead's ear, of Joyce's Irish brogue and the accelerated rhythms of his reading only amplified the *Wake*'s experimental interrogation of the limits of literary mediation while flouting C. K. Ogden's promise of an accessible auditory supplement. The effect of accent is also taken up in Debra Rae Cohen's examination of the mediation – if not ventriloquisation – of regional accents by the BBC in the 1930s and exemplified by the work of broadcaster and novelist, A. G. Street. Cohen argues that Street's supposedly 'neutral' Standardised English mediation of regional accents and dialect simultaneously unsettles and reinscribes institutionalised hierarchies and expectations of how voices should sound.

This section of the volume's focus on the effects of vocal mediation broadens with John Plotz's examination of how Willa Cather makes sense of a new sonic universe shaped by the transformative possibilities of live and recorded sound. Similar to Joyce's interest in the medial potential of the gramophone, Plotz reads Cather's embrace of the possibility of recording opera as continuous with her fictional invocation of opera as a means of testing the medial potential of the novel. Plotz's chapter highlights Cather's efforts to find a prose style that might elicit a similar degree of absorption from the reader to that which she experienced when listening to classical music. This intersection between the aesthetic affect of a writer's prose style and the acoustic experience of listening closely to voices also informs Julie Beth Napolin's analysis of how readers are implicitly trained to attend to the racial signifiers of voice in literary form. Corresponding with Murphet's theorisation of literary modernism's treatment of sounds that cannot be heard, Napolin's reading of Jean Toomer, Ralph Ellison and Ernest Hemingway reveals the elliptical narrative acoustics that indirectly mediate and reinforce the sounds of racially marked speech.

The third part of the collection – 'Difficult Voices' – examines the continuities between proto-modern and modernist writers' various experiments with the literary voice as an acoustic medium. This section begins with Penelope Hone's chapter on what she characterises as the intentionally 'harsh voice' of the late nineteenth-century novelist, George Gissing. While the discomforting effect of Gissing's literary aesthetics has long been attributed to his literary politics, Hone suggests that it also indicates a sensitivity to how the acoustic qualities of literary form shape meaning. Moving away from Gissing's earnestly crafted prose to the demanding acoustics of modernist poetry, Sean Pryor's chapter nevertheless identifies a shared preoccupation with the formal difficulties of mediating voice and sound. Pryor's chapter examines the relation of rhyme to metaphysics in modernist poetry, arguing that while the experimental rhythmic improvisations of modern poets, from Mina Loy to Wallace Stevens, H.D. to T. S. Eliot, may seem limited to the technical and ornamental, they were an integral element of literary modernism's interrogation of 'inherited conceptions of body and soul'. With a similar attention to acoustics in poetic form, Kristin Grogan examines the resolutely visual (for most anglophone readers) nature of Ezra Pound's use of Chinese characters in the late cantos. Reading sign as sound, Grogan reveals how Pound's use of ideograms is indicative of a formal – and acoustic – renovation in his late cantos.

With Helen Rydstrand's analysis of 'Miss Brill', the final section of the volume – 'Modern Rhythm: Writing, Sound, Cinema' – shifts focus to examine how modern literary and cinematic media experimented with forms of rhythmic mediation. Locating Mansfield within a broad network of writers who shared her interest in rhythm, Rydstrand's close reading of 'Miss Brill' reveals how, beyond evoking the sonic rhythms of voice and thought, Mansfield limns the complexity of a character's emotional state, if not being, through rhythmic mediation. The focus on what rhythm means for modernity, and modernist aesthetics, is continued in Laura Marcus's examination of rhythm and locomotion. Marcus tracks the analysis of rhythm from the mid-nineteenth century through to the mid-twentieth century. Her chapter draws from this history to consider how, across prose, poetry and silent film the railway renders rhythm audible in modern aesthetic form. In the concluding chapter to the volume, Steven Connor takes up a different kind of rhythm found in cinematic form: that which is conveyed by the acoustic patterns of tap. Connor's analysis of tap dance in cinema reveals how this acoustically bound dance form produces a 'sort of sonic surplus to the audiovisual composite' of film. More broadly, Connor's study of tap reveals modernity's interest in an art form that had the ability to render modern sounds – if not noise – purposively percussive.

Notes

1. Pound, *Ezra Pound and Music*, p. 315. These are thoughts later developed more fully in the Italian writings collected in *Machine Art and Other Writings*.

2. Marinetti, 'Dynamic and Synoptic Declaration' (c. 11 March 1916), in Rainey, *Futurism: An Anthology*, pp. 223–4.
3. Marinetti and Pino Masnata 'La Radia', p. 267.
4. Connor, *Beckett, Modernism and the Material Imagination*, p. 67.
5. Beckett, *All That Fall*, pp. 172–4.
6. Zilliacus, *Beckett and Broadcasting*, n. p.
7. Stewart, *Reading Voices*; Connor, *Beckett, Modernism and the Material Imagination* and *Dumbstruck*; Marcus, *Dreams of Modernity*.
8. Kittler, *Discourse Networks*, pp. 3–175.
9. Heidegger, *Parmenides*, p. 86.
10. Cummings, *Complete Poems*, p. 396.
11. White, *Natural History of Selbourne*, p. 216.
12. Thoreau, *Walden* (1993), p. 226.
13. Kittler, *Gramophone, Film, Typewriter*, p. 16.
14. See 'Ludwig Koch and the Music of Nature', available at: <http://www.bbc.co.uk/archive/archive_pioneers/6505.shtml> (last accessed 21 May 2016).
15. Joyce, *Ulysses* (1986), pp. 4.16, 25, 32, 38.
16. For more on this and much more, see Attridge, 'Joyce's Noises', pp. 471–84.
17. Wellbery, 'Foreword', in Kittler, *Discourse Networks*, p. xxxi.
18. Stewart, *Reading Voices*, p. 1.
19. Barthes, *Responsibility of Forms*, p. 245.
20. Schafer, *The Soundscape*, pp. 8–9.
21. Kahn, *Noise, Water, Meat*, p. 2.
22. Halliday, *Sonic Modernity*, p. 15.
23. Sterne, *The Audible Past*, p. 9.
24. Thompson, *The Soundscape of Modernity*, pp. 1–2.
25. Trotter, *Literature in the First Media Age*, p. 7.
26. Gitelman, *Always Already New*, p. 4.
27. Cuddy-Keane, 'Modernist Soundscapes and the Intelligent Ear', p. 382.

Part One

Writing Modern Sound

Chapter 2

On Not Listening to Modernism

Julian Murphet

At the heart of Robert Duncan's first great serial poem, *The Opening of the Field* (1960), is a fourfold lyric entitled 'Four Pictures of the Real Universe'. The poem strives to make mythic sense of the heat death of the universe, 'the death of stars' and 'emanations out of light perishing'.[1] The second verse reads as follows:

THE WALL
Crowned Beast of Pure Thriving!
You pass thru the wall of thot,
thru the stone wall, thru the walls of the body
gathering all into your strength,
altering nothing.

From your roar, legions fly thru the universe
ringing the suns, sounding flames of immediate victory
that we see as white flowers
lost in the waves of morning green. (34)

The universe's procreant urge is configured as a Beast of sound, whose 'roar' is not unlike cosmic radiation penetrating every wall, making everything immanent to it, but which we cannot hear, only 'see as white flowers'. The tune is taken up again in the final verse:

THE CLOSET
And does not the spirit attend secretly
the music that is hidden away from me,
chords that hold the stars in their courses,
outfoldings of sound from the seed of first light?

Were it not for the orders of music hidden
we should be claimd by the preponderant void. (35)

The Pythagorean music of the spheres persists, via Duncan's mythography, even into the age of the Big Bang, where the 'cosmic hum' of interstellar space was just then being taken as a sign of the infinite universe's singular origins. In 1947 George Gamow and Ralph Alpher had speculated that 'the existence of galactic background radiation [was] a remnant of that initially stupendous detonation of what [he] called "ylem", matter-in-readiness, and what Lemaître called "*l'atome primitif*" (these days, a "singularity")'.[2] But this speculated sound would not actually be heard, and then only by machines, until 1964, four years after Duncan's poem was published, 'when Arno Penzias and Robert Wilson of Bell Labs in Holmdel confronted a faint, ineliminable noise in the "ultra-sensitive microwave receiving system" of their radio-telescope', a dim 'fossil whisper' of creation, or 'outfoldings of sound from the seed of first light' (825).

The point for Duncan was that we do not, *cannot*, hear this radiant music of creation; while that music keeps us from the 'preponderant void' and holds 'the stars in their courses', it is 'hidden away from me', inaudible and unknown other than through spiritual intimations. Earlier in the collection, Duncan had written of 'footfalls in Noise which we do not hear but see as a Rose pushd up from the stem of our longing'.[3] What we cannot, must not hear, we can nevertheless sometimes see, expressed from 'the stem of our longing' as a multi-foliate white rose. The 'Real Universe' is an orchestral masterpiece, high notes and low, but unheard – become floral in the domain of Image.

This chapter is an attempt to come to some initial terms with a literary tendency, across modernism's long arc, to gesture toward sounds that cannot or should not be heard, or at a utopian Silence beyond hearing – to ask us not to listen, but to imagine sound transposed synaesthetically into image, or to hesitate anxiously on the threshold of audition. It will inevitably feel somewhat schematic, given how vast the territory is, and how limited the space. But we can at once say that the historicity of this modernist effort is over-determined. Four structural causes seem pertinent, all peculiar to the historical coordinates of modernism:

1. *The Symbolic cannot present sound's reality*: the crisis of what Kittler called literature's monopoly over data storage circa 1900 thanks to the emergence of technologies able to record and transmit sound in the dimension of its *real*. If print filtered everything through the 'bottleneck of the signifier' and the twenty-six letters of the alphabet, the phonograph catches 'the waste or residue that neither the mirror of the imaginary nor the grid of the symbolic can catch: the physiological accidents and stochastic disorder of bodies'.[4] Literature was henceforth obliged to accept its deficiencies with regard to sonic reality.

2. *The ear cannot hear the reality of sound*: the paradigm shift in the natural sciences' dependence on so-called 'sense experiences' impossible to achieve without photographic or radiographic mediation. For twentieth-century science, the audible was, above all, what *machines* could hear, not the human ear – as all the discussion around the 'Big Bang' and 'cosmic hum' made clear, let alone the spectral cracks and hisses on the short-band radio.

3. *The heard makes no sense*: the exponential increase in the noise of what Heidegger called the 'prattle' of *das Man*, thanks to the democratisation of the public sphere, and the spread of the mass media.[5]

4. *The curvature of social space portends a bang*: more speculatively here, we can point to the 'noise' of an event horizon implicit in capitalist social space; which is to say, the revolutionary 'bang' that is not heard (yet) but which resides in the void, or the gap between social representation and presentation in capitalist modernity.[6]

In all these various senses, the burgeoning literary interest in a sound that cannot or should not be heard is a fascination that pertains to what Badiou calls the 'Century', the twentieth century and its all-consuming 'passion for the real'.[7] For what I am saying here is no more than that the desire to make 'the music that is hidden away from me' stand forth and declare itself is a symptom of that passion for the real – be it the Real of sound waves themselves, or of technological audition and the cosmic hum, or of what resists the babble of opinion, or of an immanent revolutionary rupture.[8] As terrifying as they are irresistible, the 'soundless sounds' circulated by modernist literary praxis figure as signatures of the Real in its alterity to what can be shown or written; only, by some stubborn Beckettian logic, of course it must be written, and shown.

In his Seminar XI, Lacan, thinking about the Real, suggests that 'il n'y a de cause que de ce qui cloche', usually translated as 'there is a cause only in something that doesn't work'.[9] The French pun, *qui cloche*, gets closer to the heart of the matter: the cause in the Real both 'doesn't work' and 'rings' like a bell. The Real is a lapse within symbolic or imaginary space, but that lapse is itself heard as a peal or audible tear in the fabric of sense. For the modernists, from Dickinson to Duncan himself, this conviction (that the Real is a pealing noise stemming from a crisis of representation) is a constant and critical concern, with the added stipulation that, in many of the more illustrious cases in point, it must or should not be listened to, or cannot be heard.

How did modern literature respond to this causal, though purposeless, ringing noise of the Real in the given conditions of its present? This is the initial question, and we can simplify dramatically by, again, reducing the answer to four points:

1. sonic description (representation)
2. onomatopoeia (mimesis)
3. deposition of 'silence' (rhetorical modesty before the Real)
4. suggestion of sound that cannot be described, but which is Real (sublime).

The first two traditional procedures for recording sound in print, representation and mimesis, are time-honoured elements of literature's relationship to sound: on the one hand, an arsenal of richly elaborated linguistic tools – adjectival, adverbial, substantive, verbal, and so on – for the symbolic registration of acoustic phenomena; on the other, when that arsenal fails, the direct deployment of the alphabet's intrinsic sonority. This dialectic between description and mimesis is immanent to literature's storage monopoly, and belongs to an age prior to the one we are considering – prior, indeed, to that driving 'passion for the real' that made literary modernism develop new tactics for the registration of less amenable sonic effects.

First, there emerged what I am calling a rhetorical topos of modesty before the acoustic 'touch', a disavowal of literature's sonic capacity (which, as I am about to argue, has its own precedents). Eliot's 'Looking into the heart of light, the silence',[10] and Rilke's 'Und alles schwieg. Doch selbst in der Verschweigung / ging neuer Anfang'[11] [And all was hushed. Yet even in this silent restraint / a new beginning went forth], are indicative here; but perhaps a brief lyric quatrain by Mandelstam will clinch the point:

> The shy speechless sound
> of a fruit falling from its tree
> and around it the silent music
> of the forest, unbroken . . .
>
> (1908)[12]

That 'shy speechless' sound is only a foil for the poem's real subject, about which it can say only that such profound and primeval silence itself is a form of 'unbroken music'. Modernism discovered that silence had a voice, and sought it out, precisely as its own proper subject, now that all those 'shy speechless sounds' of mere objects were being recorded and mechanically reproduced. For in that voice of silence there gestated an entire new world:

It has not yet been born;
It is both music and word
. . .
Oh let my lips attain
Primordial silence,
Like a crystalline tone,
Pure from birth!

(1910)[13]

But that topos of modesty was not to be sufficient. Although silence certainly plays a large part in the history of modernist engagement with the sonic Real, it cannot really compensate for the radical deficiency now felt in the technical apparatus of literature. For the Real is not silent; it is, insistently, a background hum, an intermittent hiss or crackle, whistle or whimper, not precisely audible, but not inaudible either. The Real *qui cloche* cannot simply be sidestepped via the rhetoric or alibi of silence. A fourth option suggested itself.

It was an option with its own complex genealogy, which I will illustrate only by way of four examples.

1. The parable of Odysseus, the oarsmen, and the Sirens is of course one of the standard reference points for discussions of modernist sound; the wax in the oarsmen's ears allows Odysseus, the nobleman, to hear the Real of sexual seduction: a division of labour that turns on a split between audition and inaudition. From Adorno and Horkheimer to Michael Bull there is an eloquent and sizeable archive on just this subject.[14]
2. Book II of Milton's *Paradise Lost* provides us with a second genealogical reference point. Who can forget the moment when Satan, setting out for Earth from his captivity in Hell, finds that he must traverse the dread realm of Chaos, which the poet can best configure sonically?

> At length a universal hubbub wild
> Of stunning sounds and voices all confused
> Born through the hollow dark assaults his ear
> With loudest vehemence: thither he plies,
> Undaunted to meet there whatever power
> Or spirit of the nethermost abyss
> Might in that noise reside . . .
> And Tumult and Confusion all embroiled,
> And Discord with a thousand various mouths.[15]

Milton's cacophonic depiction of the cradle of the known Universe casts a long shadow over modernism. The middle realm between heaven and hell, our world, is positioned like a speck of cosmic dust on the lip of an immense vortex of chaotic, life-shattering sound. Satan hears it for us, just as Odysseus does for the oarsmen.

3. Our third precedent is Kleist's tale, 'St. Cecelia, or the Power of Music' (1810), which involves the strange denouement of an abortive Protestant raid on a convent at the height of the Reformation. Four brothers, leading a rabble of Lutherans into the chapel where Mass is about to be sung, suddenly find themselves unable to act. The 'performance of an extremely old Italian setting of the Mass by an unknown master' raises 'their souls as if on wings through all the heavens of harmony': with the result that 'it was as if the entire assembly in the church had been struck dead'.[16] The raid is over before it started; but the fate of the brothers is stranger still. For they are taken to a lunatic asylum, where they maintain total silence every day until midnight, when

> they [begin], in voices that filled us with horror and dread, to intone the *Gloria in excelsis*. It was a sound something like that of leopards and wolves howling at the sky in icy winter; I assure you, the pillars of the house trembled, and the windows, smitten by the visible breath of their lungs, rattled and seemed about to disintegrate. (225)

But that is still not all, for six years later, their distraught mother finally locates them, and visits the Abbess in her chambers, where she finds a music-desk.

> She gazed at the unknown magical signs, with which some terrible spirit seemed to be marking out its mysterious sphere; and the earth seemed to give way beneath her when she noticed that the score happened to be standing open at the *Gloria in excelsis*. She felt as if the whole dreadful power of the art of sound, which had destroyed her sons, were raging over her head; she thought the mere sight of the notes would make her fall senseless . . . (228)

4. Finally, very briefly and obviously, there is of course Keats's 'Ode on a Grecian Urn', that 'unravished bride of quietness' which exhorts from the poet his well-known ejaculation:

> What mad pursuit? What struggle to escape?
>   What pipes and timbrels? What wild ecstasy?
>
> Heard melodies are sweet, but those unheard
>   Are sweeter; therefore, ye soft pipes, play on;
> Not to the sensual ear, but, more endear'd,
>   Pipe to the spirit ditties of no tone[17]

Of this I will say only that, in various ways, Keats is using this apostrophe as an occasion to reflect allegorically on the status of poetry in an age of print, and of a now hegemonic silent reading. This is an age whose primary relationship to the written word, even the poem, is not aural but visual. And, to my mind, he is making a virtue of necessity by appealing to the greater power of the non-sensuous audition that a regime of silent reading entails. It is just that, given what we have been saying and reading, Keats's affirmative accents are not the only ones available, nor even the most conspicuous. The injunction to the poem to 'pipe to the spirit ditties of no tone' may rather conjure up 'unheard' sounds of a truly monstrous and inadmissible nature – the 'wild ecstasy' become unmanageable, chaotic, terrible, instead of sweet and endearing.

Which brings us to Franz Kafka. If there is another author for whom sound was felt at a comparable level of affective extremity, I have yet to read him or her. We know from Max Brod that Kafka was uniquely sensitive to sound, and sought perfect silence during composition; and that one of his earliest published pieces was called simply 'Great Noise' (1912).[18] But his literary relationship to sonic phenomena comes to a head in two late, unfinished stories.

What is great about Kafka is not only the logicality of his narrative forms, but the way in which he arranges for the rigorous semiotic structures he sets up to be transformed at the critical point in his story. Some event invariably alters the frame of sense, and makes for a shifting of semiological gears so precise as to 'present' something that has no actual presence in the text. In these late stories, that eventual something takes the form of a sound that we cannot possibly hear – that, like so much in Kafka, is for the protagonist only – but which modifies the character's world to such an extent that it effectively functions as the signature, the transformative touch, of the Real itself.

In 'Investigations of a Dog' (1922), the transfigurative sonic event is abruptly announced, far ahead of the narrator's capacity to make sense of it. The first part of the story concerns what will be seen to have been the narrator's *inability* to be faithful to this event; his attempts to measure its consequences down paths that are irrelevant; particularly, the science of nourishment. And that initial frame, which I will call the 'social frame', assumes a remarkably logical form. Against the governing status quo of canine silence, the narrator discovers an insatiable subjective urge to make noise in the form of incessant questioning. This inaugural dialectic between social quiescence and subjective noise is clearly enough a version of the dialectic between society and individual. What is interesting is where this questioning goes: fatally, it seems to inscribe itself in the meaningless and empty 'chatter' of canine science, knowledge and opinion, which is scarcely better than the silence it breaks. Forgotten is the very cause – *qui cloche* – of the questioning itself, an event so shocking as to prevent reflection on its implications: an encounter with a company of seven singing dogs. Kafka's language is precise:

> They did not speak, they did not sing, they remained, all of them, silent, almost determinedly silent; but from the empty air they conjured music. Everything was music, the lifting and setting down of their feet, certain turns of the head, their running and their standing still, the positions they took up in relation to one another . . .[19]

This uncanny omnipresence of the sound associates it with sublime Miltonic cacophony as well as Kleist's 'power of music':

> the music insensibly got the upper hand, literally knocked the breath out of me and swept me far away from those actual little dogs, and quite against my will, while I howled as if some pain were being inflicted upon me, my mind could attend to nothing but this blast of music which seemed to come from all sides, from the heights, from the deeps, from everywhere, seizing the listener by the middle, overwhelming him, crushing him, and over his swooning body still blowing fanfares so near that they seemed far away and almost inaudible. (77)

The music is entirely unarticulated; it has no internal differentiation – no notes, no rhythm, no melody or form – it is a perfectly unrepresentable cut in symbolic and imaginary space that suffuses by withdrawing: overwhelmingly loud and 'almost inaudible'; 'so near that [it seems] far away'.

But if this is what lies forgotten at the base of the narrator's febrile questioning on the topic of nourishment and the earth, it inevitably mounts a 'return of the repressed' in the tale's peripeteia – when the dog puts his researches to the test, fasting in the desert to attain the 'real' of the body's dependency on nature. Here, at the limit of his bare life, he once again encounters a musical dog, this time singular and handsome. Before that appearance, the desert space is subjected to its own acoustic analysis. Away from the generalised silence of dog-kind, one hears the rustle and clamour of things as they are: the incessant noise of the world. To this, the narrator opposes a disciplinary monastic silence – finally desisting from his own verbal chattering. But the outcome is paradoxical, since a new noise intrudes, 'the greatest noise of all' in the desert 'came from my own belly' (106). That clears the way for the final advent, the structural repetition of the first musical encounter, this one making a point of its perfect singularity:

the hound was already singing without knowing it, nay, more, ... the melody, separated from him, was floating on the air in accordance with its own laws, and, as though he had no part in it, was moving towards me, towards me alone. (109)

Now the point becomes clear: in ritual retreat from the tribulations of the social dialectic, the dog is radically exposed to the opposition between Being and Becoming. The Real addresses itself to him alone, as a song. Recall Duncan's expression: the music of Being is mostly 'hidden away from me'; but when I finally hear it, it seems explicitly written for me, and asks of me that I transform myself:

> It grew stronger and stronger; its waxing power seemed to have no limits, and already almost burst my eardrums. But the worst was that it seemed to exist solely for my sake, this voice before whose sublimity the woods fell silent to exist solely for my sake; who was I, that I could dare to remain here, lying brazenly before it in my pool of blood and filth. (110)

So, the music of the handsome dog, so sublime as to come from all quarters of the universe at once, exists 'solely for my sake'. It works the same way the 'shy speechless' noise works in Mandelstam's poem, to adduce the musical silence of the woods, and its purpose is radically subjective: 'Du mußt dein Leben ändern' [You must change your life].[20] The consequence is that the dog returns to society, pursuing with new vigour his researches into dog music; for he senses that the singular address of the handsome dog's music pertains, not just to a schism or wound in Being, but to some act of Becoming lodged inside the social antagonism itself. The music has taught him, finally, 'to prize freedom higher than anything else. Freedom!' (111). The exclamation is Kafka's. The dog's researches into dog music – his quest for nothing less than a science of music – is a quest for the very science of liberty.

Consider another of Kafka's late stories, the unfinished 'The Burrow', which also turns on a narrative peripeteia. In Part I, we read of the burrowing creature's satisfaction in having completed his life's work: a vast underground burrow which perhaps resembles a cyclopean magnification of another tunnel system: the human ear. The story's opening section ironically celebrates an aesthetic act of completion, whose signal achievement is to have cancelled out the noise of the world itself, which in his trips outside the burrow is referred to by the narrator in terms of limitless 'traffic' and 'rushing'.[21] The burrow is where that noise stops:

> ... the most beautiful thing about my burrow is the stillness. Of course, that is deceptive. At any moment it may be shattered and then all will be over. For the time being, however, the silence is still with me. For hours I can stroll

through my passages and hear nothing except the rustling of some little creature, which I immediately reduce to silence between my jaws. (117)

Here a third, minor acoustic element is introduced, the 'rustling of the
small fry', a kind of residual and intermittent intrusion that is nevertheless psychologically manageable, and can be converted into nourishment. But the semiotic rectangle can only be completed when, outside
the burrow and back among the traffic, the creature suddenly hears an
altogether distinct order of sound: 'Someone, whose invitation I shall
not be able to withstand, will, so to speak, summon me to him' (124).
Such is the distributed acoustic space of Part I.

Part II begins with the discovery of a new species of sound, which
gradually, but inevitably, shifts the entire ground of the fable. For now is
heard, for the first time, that 'almost inaudible whistling noise' that will
have such devastating effects on the narrator, his burrow, and the world
(133). Here again is the outline of an event that does not immediately
declare itself as such, with which the narrator will play a desperate game
of catch-up in his increasingly serious efforts to name it. As his relentlessly logical and increasingly paranoid deduction of a cause *qui cloche*
takes place slowly in the foreground of the narrative, in the background,
the various other acoustic categories fall into place. In his efforts to track
and defend against the new sound, the narrator undertakes a prodigious
amount of work, which interrupts his precious silence constantly with the
sound of his own labours. As the final cause of the whistling sound comes
fatally into definition, it assumes for itself a separate sonic category – the
beast can be said to produce noises of such prodigious volume that their
implications are literally earth-shattering; the narrator speculates that he
merely hears the distant trace echo of those monstrous sounds.

It is the whistling itself that is most insidious. Most of all, 'it is, so to
speak, audible only to the ear of the householder' (134). Like the music
of the handsome dog, this noise that 'goes on always on the same thin
note, with regular pauses, now a sort of whistling, but again like a kind
of piping' seems peculiarly addressed to the narrating instance (134). It
is destined for one ear alone, to wreak its havoc. It is always 'exactly the
same noise wherever I may hear it'; nor is it growing louder or softer;
indeed, 'it is this very uniformity of the noise everywhere that disturbs
me most' (136). Thanks to this indeterminate background noise, and it
alone, there is 'something that I cannot hear now at all: the murmurous
silence of the Castle Keep' (137). So it seems that there has been a whole-
sale reversal of the original situation: the Castle Keep, far from being the
splendid sanctuary from the world's noise, 'has been plunged into the
bustle of the world and all its perils' (143).

Again, I want to dwell on the social dimension of this singular, acousmatic noise. Though no source is visible, the noise brings with it all the density and threat of that social traffic against which the burrow was conceived as a muffle. It is as if, in his perfect solitude, the creature has opened himself up to that very cut in Being that is also a social antagonism. What intrudes doesn't work, doesn't make sense, but it sounds. And increasingly, it assumes a face, an intention, a will: it is the Enemy. The narrator's asymptotic approach to silence has reversed upon itself and unleashed the noise of an all-consuming battle to the death, a battle whose complex social configuration is allegorised by a reduction to the Two.

Perhaps some further light can be shed on this remarkable complex by turning to that related tale, 'Josephine the Mouse Singer', where we read that the singer's otherwise unremarkable 'piping' has the following characteristic: 'the whistling that arises, when all others are enjoined to silence, comes almost as a message from our people to the individual'.[22] This names, precisely, the very truth of Kafka's 'great noise' – which is not the Real in a neutrally ontological sense, but which has been fertilised by a social situation. In Kafka, the ontological Real itself is not true; the truth of the whistling or piping, or the overwhelming music of the dogs, is the truth of a gap between social representation and presentation. Thanks to a transfiguration of the semiotic coordinates, between ontological and social frames, his narrators ultimately construe this sonic gap as 'freedom', or as the struggle against foreign occupation, or as 'a message from the whole people to each individual', separately and not en masse.

Now we must transfer from the sublime to the vernacular, and Kafka's idiot savant twin sibling, H. P. Lovecraft. What is astonishing about Lovecraft is how far he pushes the conceit of a noise that should not be listened to, or which can only be heard at great cost to subjective consistency – much farther, indeed, than any other writer, but without any trace of Kafka's will-to-truth. Lovecraft's is an art of the Real without any recourse to 'the whole people' or 'freedom', or any truth procedure whatsoever. And this, too, is determined at the level of sound, in the acoustic domain where so many of his prototypical effects occur.

His most complete treatment of the theme, which resonates throughout his work, is to be found in one of his very worst stories, 'The Dreams in the Witch-House' (1932), an unhappy narrative fusion of his Cthulhu mythos with the Salem witch trials and Satan worship. We need only briefly indicate the nature of the acoustic architecture here. Walter Gilman goes to stay in an old boarding house where the inspired Salem witch Keziah Mason once saw her awful visions, and finds that his hearing becomes painfully acute, sensitive to every last scurry of the rats in the walls. But what is truly frightening is the depth of noise behind these sounds: 'The darkness always teemed with unexplained sound – and yet he sometimes shook with fear lest the noises he heard should subside and allow him to hear certain other fainter noises which he suspected were lurking behind them.'[23] The tale turns on this stereophonic apperception: of run-of-the-mill haunted house sonic paraphernalia in the foreground, and, just out of audition, the intimation of some far more sinister, 'fainter noises' behind them. That intimation is eventually forced into perception, with catastrophic consequences.

The fainter noises are dialled up to eleven in his dreams. They are consonant with the Miltonic sublime in Satan's traversal of Chaos:

> The shrieking, roaring confusion of sound which permeated the abysses was past all analysis as to pitch, timbre or rhythm; but seemed to be synchronous with vague visual changes in all the indefinite objects, organic and inorganic alike. Gilman had a constant state of dread that it might rise to some unbearable degree of intensity during one or another of its obscure, relentlessly inevitable fluctuations. (242)

Stunning sounds 'past all analysis', but threatening to rise to a shattering crescendo: Chaos has a new orchestra. Pressing ever deeper into the regions of lawless night, 'Eventually there had been a hint of vast, leaping shadows, of a monstrous, half-acoustic pulsing, and of the thin, monotonous piping of an unseen flute' (259). Lovecraft asserts his schlock credentials by doing precisely what Kafka had forborne from doing out of acute aesthetic discretion: he gives us a vision of the sonic enemy itself – Azathoth, the Crawling Chaos, conductor of a cacophony in whose

> cosmic timbre [is] concentrated all the primal, ultimate space-time seethings which lie behind the massed spheres of matter and sometimes break forth in measured reverberations that penetrate faintly to every layer of entity and give hideous significance throughout the worlds to certain dreaded periods. (271)

Broken by his nocturnal auditions, Walter Gilman first falls stone-deaf, his ear drums 'ruptured, as if by the impact of some stupendous sound intense beyond all human conception of endurance', and then, like all the best Lovecraft protagonists, dies mad and alone (275).

This vernacular variation on the exquisitely controlled semiotic economy of Kafka's acoustic order of things has the virtue of giving away everything and nothing. It raises to an hysterical pitch the horror of a sound emanating from beyond the torn curtain of our world, a truly universal noise, impossible to resist or describe without purple, oxymoronic overdrive, and impossible to attend, a 'faintly overheard pulsing which no earthly ear could endure in its unveiled spatial fullness' (273). But he falsely forces the presentation of the source of this 'low, monstrous shaking' as a pseudo-Miltonic figure out of allegory, lapsing into a pre-modern form just where the material was leading him else-where. Lovecraft teaches us, negatively, what Kafka teaches us in truth: namely that the 'hitherto-veiled cosmic pulsing' that becomes audible as a token of the Real's irruption into alphabetic space, must also have an obscure intersubjective, or social logic, in order to assume its full sym-bolic power (273). In Kafka, a studious discretion keeps the source from being forced into the open, the better to distribute its acoustic uncanni-ness in the cryptic form of a communitarian reflux within the subject.

But at last, as a finale, we must turn to the final resting place of this whole dynamic, which is in Beckett's masterly *Texts for Nothing*, written between 1950–2. By this point, for Beckett, literature had begun to hear and depose itself as so much inadmissible noise, so much babble and prattle in the face of silence, that consummation devoutly to be wished. But nor could the world itself be spared this harsh judgement of being too noisy: it too rustles and pulses, albeit with a disgusting Real, rather than Symbolic, excess. All of this falls into a predictable pattern of semiotic relations, adroitly clarified in Text 1, which tells us that 'All is noise, unending suck of black sopping peat, surge of giant ferns, heathery gulfs of quiet where the wind drowns', in contrast to which the narrator offers 'what I'm doing, all-important, breathing in and out and saying, with words like smoke'.[24] But this all-important uttering is haunted by the trace memory of all those other narrative noises that make this one possible in the first place: 'always muttering, the same old mutterings, the same old stories, the same old questions and answers' (298). Against which, the final solution of silence appears, at last, in the form of Beckett's indissoluble image of the late years: 'we walked together [my father and I, who are the same one], hand in hand, silent, sunk in our worlds, each in his worlds, the hands forgot-ten in each other' (298). That these are, of course, words, is the form of the contradiction that the *Texts for Nothing* obsessively rehearse. Each subsequent Text presses further into this painful and paradoxical terri-tory, but without any narrative transformation. The technique here is, rather, to concentrate the very energies of contradiction into a singular, unstable literary pulsar.

Text 3 proposes the task of getting 'something to happen here, someone to be here, then put an end to it, have silence, get into silence' (305); a task perplexed by the incessant babble of those other voices which, 'wherever they come from, have no life in them' (305). In Texts

4 and 5, learning to be speechless entails 'Spells of silence ... when I listen, and hear the local sounds, the world sounds, see what an effort I make, to be reasonable' (307): the realist impulse, to 'say it as I hear it', is again undone, however, by 'all these voices, like a rattling of chains in my head, rattling to me that I have a head' and so calling him back to his own acoustic schism (311). For he is both an immanent dictating swarm of voices, and a binary pulse between silence and words.

Text 6, set amongst 'wretched acoustics ... the merest scraps, literally', reduces the literary situation to this simple binary alternation (313): 'this thing has no end, this thing, this thing, this farrago of silence and words, of silence that is not silence and barely murmured words ... this pell-mell babel of silence and words' (315). The dictating voices have been subtracted, leaving only the binary intermittence of words and the silence they both interrupt and extend (because they are not Voice).

Text 8 knows that:

> Only the words break the silence, all other sounds have ceased. If I were silent I'd hear nothing. But if I were silent the other sounds would start again, those to which the words have made me deaf, or which have really ceased. But I am silent ... (320)

Saying means breaking the silence; but only saying can fashion such silence in the first place, block out 'the other sounds' that obscure the very cause *qui cloche*. Literature's precious silence is, alas, also only rhetoric, a saying that 'this is silence'.

The evident solution is to say it all over and over, only ever 'more softly' and 'more slowly', breaking down the units of sense into a perforated surface of sheer language as such – to attain silence asymptotically by way of a murmur, to become a meaningless purr or buzz: 'forever the same murmur, flowing unbroken, like a single endless word and therefore meaningless, for it's the end gives the meaning to words' (320). To end by never ending, which in the great final Text, number thirteen, attains the most radical form of all – a prose murmur made out of antinomies drawn ever more perilously together, the semiotic rectangle collapsing on itself like a black dwarf:

> It's not true, yes, it's true, it's true and it's not true, there is silence and there is not silence, there is no one and there is someone, nothing prevents anything. And were the voice to cease quite at last, the old ceasing voice, it would not be true, as it is not true that it speaks, it can't speak, it can't cease. And were there one day to be here, where there are no days, which is no place, born of the impossible voice the unmakeable being, and a gleam of light, still all would be silent and empty and dark, as now, as soon now, when all will be ended, all said, it says, it murmurs. (339)

Here again, in the end, the roseate image suggests itself, just barely, a mere flicker of light, cast upon an unmakeable being, borne out of this impossible murmur of antinomial terms. Beckett reduces narrative language to a pulse between zero and one, silence and not silence, a dim and distant repetitive signal from the unrepresentable cause *qui cloche* at the heart of things, the Real, not unlike a monotonous piping or a faint whistling itself, in order finally to recuperate some unmentionable, minimal figure, wandering the no place in no time for no reason other than to say that literature, here and now, is this minimal image conjured out of monotonous droning, or it is nothing. And most likely, it is nothing. Don't listen to it, listen to it, don't listen to it. And it will become an Image that fades faster than you can say: '*Ia! Shub-Niggurath! The Goat with a Thousand Young . . .*'[25]

Notes

1. Duncan, 'Four Pictures of the Real Universe', p. 34.
2. Schwartz, *Making Noise*, p. 823.
3. Duncan, p. 16.
4. Kittler, *Gramophone, Film, Typewriter*, pp. 16–17.
5. Heidegger, *Being and Time*, pp. 107–22.
6. T. S. Eliot's depiction of the existential disappointment inherent in a world ending '*Not with a bang but a whimper*' might be said to have resonated, in 1925, with a series of structural tensions in the West's relations with Soviet Russia – the sense of having always already missed the event, similarly echoed in the famous opening lines of T. W. Adorno's *Negative Dialectics*: 'Philosophy, which once seemed outmoded, remains alive because the moment of its realization was missed.' Interesting to us is the poet's decision to project this condition into the aural dimension. See T. S. Eliot, *Collected Poems*, p. 92. And Dennis Redmond's translation of *Negative Dialektik*, published online in 2001: <http://members.efn.org/~dredmond/ndintro.PDF> (last accessed 30 May 2016).
7. Badiou, *The Century*.
8. Duncan, p. 35.
9. Lacan, *Four Fundamental Concepts of Psychoanalysis*, p. 22.
10. Eliot, p. 64.
11. Rilke, 'Die Sonette an Orpheus', available at: <http://gutenberg.spiegel.de/buch/rainer-maria-rilke-sonette-5562/1> (last accessed 30 May 2016).
12. Mandelstam, *Selected Poems*, p. 3.
13. Mandelstam, *Modernist Archaist*, p. 39.
14. Adorno and Horkheimer, *Dialectic of Enlightenment*, pp. 33–62; Bull, 'Thinking about Sound, Proximity, and Distance in Western Experience', pp. 173–90.
15. Milton, *Complete Poetry and Essential Prose*, pp. 354–5.
16. Kleist, *The Marquise of O*, p. 220.

17. Keats, *The Complete Poems*, p. 344.
18. Kafka, *Metamorphosis and Other Stories* (2007), p. 296.
19. Kafka, *Metamorphosis and Other Stories* (2012), p. 76.
20. Rilke, 'Die Sonette an Orpheus', Sonett 1.
21. Kafka, *Metamorphosis and Other Stories* (2012), p. 139.
22. Kafka, *Metamorphoses and Other Stories* (2007), p. 272.
23. Lovecraft, *The Call of Cthulhu*, p. 235.
24. Beckett, 'Texts for Nothing', pp. 296, 297.
25. Lovecraft, *Call of Cthulhu*, p. 219.

Chapter 3

Advocating Auricularisation: Virginia Woolf's 'In The Orchard'

Tom Vandevelde

Referring in part to the technological advancements in acoustic media around the turn of the century (the invention and popularisation of the telephone, gramophone, radio and sound film), Melba Cuddy-Keane has insisted that there was a 'new focus, in the modernist period [on] the act of auditory perception'. 'In narrative', she says, 'this perceptual "turn" can be traced in both a consciousness of expanded sounds and a heightened sense of sound as something perceived.'[1] Though focusing more on the impact of the First World War, rather than on acoustic media, Sara Haslam has similarly suggested that 'we need to refocus attention on the ways that the experience of war, and therefore the development of modernism, were mediated through sound'.[2] Angela Frattarola adds yet another voice to the growing group of modernist scholars occupied with calling attention to the auditory dimension of modernist texts:

> Modernists wanted their novels to sound out, to be listened to, and they achieved this by including the sounds of everyday life formally in their works and paying particular attention to how their characters are shaped by those sounds. In context, the formal experiments for which modernists are so well know [*sic*] – stream of consciousness, fragmented and nonlinear narratives, poetic prose – all hinge on a shift in sensibilities from the eye to the ear.[3]

As the ranks of modernist scholars interested in unearthing the intricacies of the soundscapes of modernist literature grow, the need for terminology as well as an adequate framework for the study of these sounds becomes ever more pressing.

The absence of a theoretical framework for the study of 'narrative sound' is a common lament. Cuddy-Keane calls for 'the development of a critical methodology and a vocabulary for analysing narrative representations of sound'[4] and even in the broader field of sound studies (where some take to literary texts to learn about the period's actual soundscape), scholars feel the need for 'more and better conceptual building blocks to help us understand what we uncover'.[5] The first place to look for a basis for such a framework, one would guess, is narratology. After all, what better way to study sounds represented in a narrative text than by analysing the way in which they are narrated and perceived? Narrative perspective, then, is key to gaining a better understanding of the auditory dimension of narrative texts. Unfortunately, however, narrative theory's existing framework and vocabulary fall woefully short in this regard.

The Routledge Encyclopaedia of Narrative Theory (2005) contains a substantial entry on 'visual narrativity', half of which considers the problem of 'what is a written image, hence, how can it be read?'[6] In this entry, Mieke Bal argues that narrative texts visualise through a variety of means, including 'metaphor', 'visual images' and 'the representation of viewing positions'. While similar statements can certainly be made with regard to what we might by analogy call 'narrative sounds' or, more generally, 'aural' or perhaps 'sonic' narrativity, a search of the same *Encyclopaedia* for any of these terms, or even for 'sound' in general, comes up empty-handed. This perceived bias towards the visual, it turns out, has roots that go back to the early days of narrative theory, and first needs to be remedied if we want to come up with a framework that will help us understand the intricacies of the auditory dimension of narrative texts, both modernist and other.

The current chapter aims to carve out a space for the study of sound in narrative within existing theories of narrative perspective. In order to do so, it first lays bare the visual bias that has crept into much of the traditional terminology, before proposing a more inclusive model of focalisation based on both existing, mainstream narratology and lesser known, still underutilised narrative theories of auditory perception. Naming each of the sensorial aspects of focalisation and giving each of them its separate space beneath the larger umbrella of focalisation should improve possibilities of comparing different aspects of sensory perception in narrative. Thus, this chapter aims to provide further stepping stones towards a sustained model for the study of narrative sound. The second part of the chapter showcases the proposed model, juxtaposing visual and aural perspective within Virginia Woolf's short story 'In the Orchard' (1923).

On the visual bias in theories of narrative perspective

From the very beginning, critics have discussed issues pertaining to narrative perspective in decidedly visual terms. In his famous essay on 'Point of View in Fiction: The Development of a Critical Concept' (1955), Norman Friedman provides an overview of the study of narrative perspective up until that point. Like most scholars, Friedman attributes the emergence of thinking about 'point of view' (in itself an explicitly visual image) mainly to the reflections of Henry James. The prefaces to his novels became 'the source and fount of critical theory in this matter', in part because of Joseph Warren Beach and Percy Lubbock's book-length interpretations of them.[7] James's description of 'the house of fiction', with its million 'windows', each of which offers a different perspective, remains a potent metaphor to this day, and exemplifies the visual imagery and vocabulary that dominated the theory of narrative perspective from the very start.[8] Friedman himself discerned no less than eight different possible perspectives in narrative fiction. One of these, 'The Camera' (1178), is a good example of how this type of ocularcentric terminology did not necessarily imply an exclusively visual concept. 'Camera' perspective, within Friedman's theory, aims 'to transmit without apparent selection or arrangement a "slice of life" as it passes before the recording medium' (1179). Seen in context, it becomes clear how the visually inclined terminology stands for a much broader idea: Friedman talks of the 'recording medium', not just as something that registers vision, but a broader 'slice of life'. So while the word he uses is decidedly ocularcentric, the concept is not.

A similar visual focus is apparent in the work of French structuralist Gérard Genette, the originator of what is probably still the most well-known theory of narrative perspective: focalisation. In 'Discours du Récit' (1972; later translated as *Narrative Discourse*, 1980) Genette makes the important distinction between what he calls *mode* and *voix* (mood and voice), stating that most works dealing with narrative perspective had confused the two up until that point.[9] While Genette's initial comments with regards to mood refer to perspective in general (although here too, 'point of view' is used), he then simplifies the distinction to two questions still being taught in every narratology class today: 'who speaks?' and 'who sees?'. Although Genette in the same work explicitly states that he does not like 'the too specifically visual connotations of the terms *vision, field* and *point of view*',[10] instead preferring the more neutral term 'focalisation',[11] the simple elegance of these two questions proved powerful, and they quickly became a focal point within the theory of narrative perspective. Eleven years later, in *Nouveau Discours du Récit* (1983, translated as *Narrative Discourse Revisited*, 1990), Genette confides that his 'only regret is that [he] used a purely visual, and hence overly narrow, formulation'.[12] '*Who sees?*', he says, should be replaced 'with the broader question of *who perceives?*' (64) Despite

Genette's efforts to reverse this process of visualisation, focalisation never quite sheds the visual connotation it had gained. This is especially unfortunate considering Genette introduced the term to differentiate his concept from Jean Pouillon's tripartite division between 'vision with' ('la vision "avec"'), 'vision from behind' ('la vision "par derrière"'), and 'vision from without' ('la vision du "dehors"').[13]

More recent accounts of narrative perspective continue to struggle with similar symptoms. Like Genette, most modern narratologists acknowledge that focalisation/perspective is not just about vision but about the entire spectrum of represented experience, including all forms of sensory perception, as well as thoughts, emotions, mental states, and so on.[14] Despite this, narrative theory still seems to look to spatio-visual metaphors to support its theories. Think of James Phelan's distinction between 'vision' and 'voice', or Manfred Jahn and David Herman's more recent cognitive theories that make use of the 'window' already present in James's writings.[15] In her piece on 'visual narrativity' in the *Routledge Encyclopaedia of Narrative Theory*, Mieke Bal, one of the major contributors to the discussion about focalisation, implies that even she tends to blur perspective with the purely visual from time to time. Bal's responses to Genette's theory of focalisation introduce the terms 'focaliser' and 'focalised', in an attempt to localise the concept of focalisation, which, in Genette's mind, defined the relative knowledge of the narrator versus the characters and, thus, could not be attributed to a single entity in the text.[16] Talking about visual narratives, and especially the representation of spectatorship, Bal posits that 'in novels, narrators describe what they see or what they saw when they were younger, and this gives a particular importance to the subject of the gaze, which narratologists refer to as the focaliser'.[17] Her equation of focalisation with 'what narrators see or saw' is just one more example of the visual bias that has haunted theories of narrative perspective from the very beginning.

To this day, visually inclined terminology abounds in narrative theory, thus carrying the obvious risk of unwillingly reducing focalisation to an oversimplified, purely visual concept, and disempowering attempts to garner more attention for other sensorial aspects of narrative perspective. If the auditory aspect of modernist literature is to receive the attention it warrants, a more balanced terminology is a prerequisite.

Towards a more inclusive model of narrative perspective

Douglas Kahn, in the introduction to *Wireless Imagination* (1992), asks: 'How . . . can listening be explained when the subject in recent theory has been situated . . . in the web of the gaze, mirroring, reflection, the spectacle and other ocular tropes?'[18] In an attempt to remedy this persistent issue, a number of scholars have sought to overcome the visual bias in theories of narrative perspective and level the playing field by explicitly defining the non-visual aspects of focalisation. The first to do this was French film scholar François Jost. In his book *L'Oeil-Caméra* (1987), Jost discusses point of view in both literature and film, suggesting three pillars for narrative perspective: 'focalisation', or the 'knowledge' of a character ('ce que *sait* un personnage'[19]), directly derived from Genette's writings, as well as 'ocularisation', or the relationship between what the camera shows and what the character sees ('la relation entre ce que la caméra montre et ce que le héros est censé voir' (18)) and 'auricularisation', ocularisation's aural equivalent, an auditory 'point of view' ('A ce "point de vue" sonore, je donne le nom d'*auricularisation*' (19)). Both new concepts are distinguishable from focalisation, yet related, and both can be either internal or external (or 'spectatorial'). While Jost acknowledges that literature does not entail the actual sounds and images that are contained in film, he argues that the terms might work for literature as well, and comes up with several examples. Focalisation, ocularisation and auricularisation can either work together, or work against each other to create certain effects.[20]

Jost's idea of splitting up focalisation into different components, each of which might hold its own typicalities, has sparked the attention of several other scholars. Sabine Schlickers, for instance, adopts Jost's main concepts of focalisation, ocularisation and auricularisation, while making small changes to his further subdivisions.[21] Her excursions into the realm of literature are brief, but that she picks up on Jost's ideas can be considered an endorsement of their usefulness. A more fruitful exploration is contained in the work of William Nelles, a literary critic who discusses Jost's concepts in a chapter of his book *Frameworks* (1997) and takes the idea one step further: 'by extension . . . we could coin the parallel terms "gustativisation", "olfactivisation", and "tactilivisation" to cover cases centring on details of a character's ability to taste, smell, or touch'.[22] Nelles adds that 'it is difficult to imagine texts that call for such tools', although he suggests that 'Proust's episode of the madeleine might constitute an exception' (96). Recent work on taste and smell in literary history proves that Nelles might be underestimating the presence of what are often considered the lesser senses, however, so including these new terms into a more inclusive framework for narrative perspective can only help prepare the way for current as well as future research that seeks to re-evaluate the underrepresentation of the non-visual senses in narrative theory.[23]

Finally, in an independent attempt to provide structural support for the study of sound in narrative, Melba Cuddy-Keane has at several turns insisted on a separate term for the perception of sound in narrative. She proposes 'auscultation', 'auscultise', and 'auscultator', mirroring the existing concepts of 'focalisation', 'focalise', and 'focaliser' (which seem to refer to Mieke Bal's more personified take on focalisation rather than Genette's more global one).[24] Although Cuddy-Keane's intention to 'signal the way a specialised terminology can help us to discriminate the sense-specific elements in the text' is one that complies entirely with the goals of the current chapter, the terms she proposes seem less attractive than Jost's and Nelles's, for a number of reasons.[25] First of all, 'ocularisation', 'auricularisation' and their peers have already been picked up by more scholars, and have even found their way into Jahn's entry on 'Focalisation' in the *Routledge Encyclopaedia of Narrative Theory*, where Nelles's proposition to '[conjugate] focalisation through the five modes of perception' is briefly mentioned.[26] As such, the terms, though admittedly 'unwieldy', already have some currency within narrative theory, and it might be best to build on this foundation.[27] Secondly, Cuddy-Keane opposes auscultation to focalisation, like 'hearing' to 'seeing'.[28] This is an unfortunate reduction of the concept of focalisation to the purely visual, which is something the current chapter aims to avoid. A model in which focalisation retains its original, broad meaning, and where terms like 'auricularisation' and 'ocularisation' denote the specific sensorial aspects of focalisation, arguably holds more potential.

In order to provide a counterweight to the longstanding visual vocabulary that has traditionally dominated theories of narrative perspective, while at the same time staying strongly embedded in the existing models, the model (Fig. 3.1) should provide a good starting point.

In this model, focalisation serves as the umbrella term, retaining its original meaning, namely the difference between what the narrator knows/experiences and what the character(s) know/experience. This knowledge/experience is then subdivided into its many different aspects, such as emotions, mental states, thoughts, memories, as well as sensory perceptions, all of which are inevitably interwoven. Thus, sensory perceptions might evoke thoughts or memories, which might evoke emotions (one need not look further than the famous madeleine scene in Proust), and so on. Sensory perception itself is in turn subdivided into the five different elements of the sensorium, named after the terms proposed by Jost and Nelles: 'auricularisation', 'olfactivisation', 'tactilivisation', 'ocularisation' and 'gustativisation'. Like the elements on the level above, the five senses regularly intertwine, for example when synaesthesia occurs. The proposed model balances out some of the inequalities

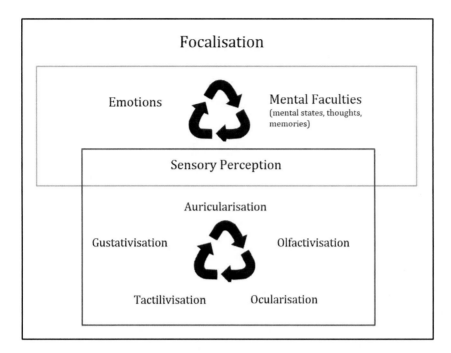

Figure 3.1   Focalisation

that have crept into the existing theories of narrative perception, and the possibility to identify and name each sensorial aspect of focalisation should help lay bare some of the more intricate workings of modernist texts.

What follows gives some indication of what a more detailed look at these different sensorial aspects of focalisation may yield. As I show, dissecting focalisation into ocularisation and auricularisation in the context of one of Virginia Woolf's lesser-known short stories, 'In the Orchard' (1923), provides a means of debunking previously held beliefs that this piece is nothing more than an experiment in visual writing, in the fashion of either a cubist collage or a post-impressionist painting.[29]

'In the Orchard'

It is common knowledge that Virginia Woolf used her short stories in order to experiment with new ways of writing, which she would then go on to explore more fully in her novels. 'An Unwritten Novel' (1920), 'Monday or Tuesday' (1921), and 'Blue and Green' (1921) have all become canonical examples in this respect, each for their own reasons. Focusing on Woolf's experiments with narrative perspective, 'The Mark on the Wall' (1917) and 'Kew Gardens' (1919) have perhaps garnered most of the scholarly attention, although Dean Baldwin also lists 'Moments of Being: Slater's Pins Have No Points' (1928), and 'The Lady in the Looking Glass' (1929) among her notable experiments with point of view.[30]

Several others, however, are equally deserving of a place in that particular spotlight, but have remained under the radar nonetheless. One of these is 'In the Orchard', a three-page piece published in 1923, which, for a long time, was not even considered part of Woolf's short fiction, but instead an exercise in perspective – a sketch rather than a bona fide story. Baldwin lists it alongside the more experimental duo of 'Monday or Tuesday' and 'Blue and Green' as 'meditative sketches with even less narrative than "Kew Gardens"' (24). They are, he says, 'the most poetic of Woolf's prose writings, making no pretence at telling a story or even making a point, at least in the conventional senses. They are perhaps best regarded as experiments in the lyric possibilities of prose' (24).

'In the Orchard' is made up of three parts, each of which offers up the same scene, but from a different perspective. In the first part, a nondescript, heterodiegetic and, at first glance, omniscient narrator sets the scene: a girl, Miranda, is lying in a long chair beneath the apple trees, presumably sleeping. Her book has fallen to the grass, her finger pointing at the sentence she had been reading. A short description of the orchard, showered in colours, is next, followed by an extensive catalogue of the different sounds to be heard above as perspective continually moves upward: the shrill sound of schoolchildren declaiming multiplication tables in unison and the teacher scolding them; a sad solitary cry escaping the lips of drunken Old Parsley; the chiming church organ and its thudding bells; the squeaking feather of the church tower; and, finally, the rushing wind that makes it move. Below, Miranda starts and cries 'Oh, I shall be late for tea!'[31]

The second part of the story provides another take on the same scene. Although the narrating voice starts off with the exact same sentence – 'Miranda slept in the orchard' – it immediately doubles back to reveal doubt: 'or perhaps she was not asleep' (150). Contrary to the first account, her lips seem to be moving this time, as if she were inwardly repeating the words of the sentence she is pointing at. Focalisation then shifts from an external to an internal perspective as 'she smiled and let her body sink all its weight on to the enormous earth which rises, she thought, to carry me on its back as if I were a leaf, or a queen' (150). As she hears the sounds described earlier, her mind races, turning each into an imagined experience or fantasy nothing like the actual source. Finally, as before, the wind changes, the church tower's golden feather squeaks and Miranda jumps up, crying that she will be late for tea.

The third and final part of the story is also the shortest. In this concluding paragraph, the narrator refrains from settling whether or not Miranda is asleep, stating both options – 'Miranda slept in the orchard, or was she asleep or was she not asleep?' – before painting a number of very precise and strictly visual pictures. We learn that there are exactly twenty-four apple trees in the orchard, some growing straight up, some slanting a little bit. They move in the wind as a wagtail flies across the landscape, a thrush hops around among the branches and a sparrow flutters over the grass. Colours are described vividly and the visual images are exceedingly precise and captivating in their description, from the sky exactly fitting the leaves (as seen from below), to the apples blotting out two cows in the meadow (as seen from a bird's-eye view). The sounds, and the objects and people producing them, are suddenly absent from the narrative – even the mandatory '"Oh, I shall be late for tea!" cried Miranda' is put between brackets, as if not to disturb the visual peace (151).

In terms of critical treatment, 'In the Orchard' does not measure up favourably with some of Woolf's more popular short stories, but in what little has been written on it, its threefold structure has inevitably been the main concern. This triple perspective has been interpreted in a variety of ways, albeit again almost exclusively in visual terms. Traditionally, these readings are then related to the post-impressionist movement in painting, which had a major influence on Woolf, in part through the work of her close friend, the art critic Roger Fry. Nena Skrbic, for instance, discerns the 'commonalities with the post-impressionist movement in the visual arts' and goes on to liken the 'quasi-synthetic arrangement of fragments' to 'a cubist collage'.[32] In 'In the Orchard', Skrbic proclaims, 'Woolf moves away from the traditional short-story model as a logical, chronological development of events to a method of storytelling that is told in an economical language of repetitive images' (26). Michelle Levy, meanwhile, compares 'In the Orchard' to 'Kew Gardens'. Both, she says, '[decentre] the human subject in [Woolf's] fiction by shifting narratological perspectives'. 'Varying *visual* perspectives', to be precise.[33] Concentrating on the upward perspectival movement in the first sequence of the story, Levy argues that Woolf works towards an aerial view, 'bringing about a fuller appreciation of life on the earth' (147). 'Woolf is following her own advice', she says, 'from "The Narrow Bridge of Art" (1927), where she enjoins writers to "[stand] back from life, because in that way a larger view is to be obtained of some important features of it"' (147). As Levy explains, then, Woolf 'expresses a vision of life in which the human presence no longer dominates but is simply part of a larger whole' (146).

In an article-length study on 'In the Orchard', Rossana Bonadei goes even further, interpreting the third part of the triptych as a 'still-life', an attempt at a final step in a sequence moving away from storytelling and towards the purely pictorial.[34] The opening pages of the essay at first seem to indicate otherwise, as Bonadei first describes 'In the Orchard' as an example of 'eyeless writing' and a 'deliberate exercise of perception and form, not a story but a narrative experiment (a "try")' (1). Taking Miranda to be the double of Woolf herself, Bonadei argues that 'the writer dislocated into the writing, is herself boldly questioning the conventional tools at hand, the *eye* and the *I* allowed by tradition' (2). Questioning the 'eye', however, apparently does not imply replacing it with one of the other senses, but rather calls into question a Victorian descriptive style and replaces it with more immediate methods of representation, a strategy that is indeed universally associated with Woolf's work, and of course the post-impressionist movement, which aspired to speak directly to and through the senses. Essentially, Bonadei attributes 'In the Orchard' with a different kind of visuality, but visuality nonetheless. She suggests that around the 1920s, 'Woolf was learning how to see the world through painters' eyes' and that this 'fascination with visual techniques and post-impressionist methods of representation is evident in all her writings' (8). Although there are clearly a number of valid arguments in favour of treating 'In the Orchard' as a primarily visual experiment akin to post-impressionist or even cubist painting, Woolf here tinkers with auditory perspective just as much – perhaps even more so.

Eyeless

The story's first sequence's upward moving perspective received much of the attention in both Levy and Bonadei's studies. Levy proclaims its aerial vision to be Woolf's main aim, allowing for a more inclusive image of the landscape, while Bonadei discerns a dual perspective, constructed by Miranda on the one hand, and the roaming wind on the other. 'The scene', she says, 'is the effect of an aggregate, multiperspective point of view, which holds together – in the same scene – Miranda and another gaze' (10). The 'gaze' here almost certainly implies ocularisation. A 'nameless, formless' entity presides over the scene (10). At first, it stays very close to Miranda, lying in her long chair beneath the apple trees.

Then, it puts more distance between itself and Miranda, moving freely, 'master of the view', as Bonadei puts it (10). According to Bonadei, this perceiving instance, 'the mysterious presence to which a point of view is attached and through which we have access to the world, from above', is the wind:

> IT is the active agent, which moves the clouds and the trees, which carries sounds and cries, which touches the world and gently touches Miranda who 'miles below, in a space as big as the eye of a needle' is abandoned to her sleep. (10)

Having come to this conclusion, a problem arises:

> But she is down, in the orchard, lying on the grass: and yet, the gaze-system that constructs the sequence, before the wind reveals itself and establishes the effect of a 'panoramic point of view', implies a view from below. That might be – we understand – Miranda's point of view: from below, Miranda dances imaginatively with the wind, sees the world through that eyeless character; only, it is from the bottom and not from above. (10)

The solution to Bonadei's problem with the apparently contrasting perspectives – that of Miranda on the one hand, and that of (supposedly) the wind on the other – is this: while both Levy and Bonadei heavily stress the visual inclinations of this sequence, clearly considering it an instance of ocularisation, its perspective is in fact much more aural in nature than it is visual. Consider this: Miranda is supposedly asleep, and although there is something to be said for Bonadei's elegant interpretation that the wind itself is the perceiving entity, the wind is in fact described from the outside, not from within. Furthermore, as Bonadei herself already mentions, it is 'eyeless' and 'brainless':

> The wind changed. Above everything else it droned, above the woods, the meadows, the hills, miles above Miranda lying in the orchard asleep. It swept on, eyeless, brainless, meeting nothing that could stand against it, until, wheeling the other way, it turned south again.[35]

Neither Miranda nor the wind, then, is capable of functioning as the visual filter through which the scene is portrayed. In fact, even Old Parsley, we are told, is 'blind drunk'. Rather, ocularisation here is undisclosed and external, roaming the scene without coinciding with one of its inhabitants. After the initial, vividly visual, description of Miranda sleeping – the opal on her finger flushing in all kinds of colours, a white butterfly floating over her – visual references come to a halt and auditory perception (or auricularisation) takes over just as the upward movement of the filter starts off. Each of the sounds described is acousmatic at first (meaning that its source is unknown). Take the following example.

The narrator first describes 'a shrill clamour', comparable to 'gongs of cracked brass beaten violently, irregularly, and brutally' (149). The narrator thus discloses the sound through sonic description alone, and, if only for a brief moment, these sounds seem frightening or dangerous. Only then is the actual source revealed: 'It was only the school-children, saying the multiplication table in unison, stopped by the teacher, scolded, and beginning to say the multiplication table over again' (149). Neither the schoolchildren, nor the teacher are described in explicitly visual terms. The sound's source is known, its general characteristics, but nothing more, true 'visualisation' remains absent. Throughout the ascent towards the church's feather and the wind above, the narrator uses a similar approach. A 'solitary cry – sad, human, brutal' turns out to be nothing more than an old drunkard (149). Next, a 'pensive and lugubrious note', the church organ 'playing one of the Hymns Ancient and Modern' (149). All the way up to the 'sharp squeak' originating from 'the golden feather of the church tower' turning from south to east, it is the sounds that are tracked upwards, each introduced in turn, as if climbing the steps of a ladder (149). Thus auricularised, sounds, rather than sights, bring in the environment, enlarging the scope of the story. This technique is remarkably similar to cinema, and may very well be one of the typical characteristics of the relationship between auricularisation and ocularisation. As Rick Altman argues, cinema often works in such a way that the sound asks 'where?' and the image answers 'here!'[36] Woolf here employs a similar strategy. Notice also how the sounds are described through the effect they evoke ('sad', 'brutal', 'violently', and so on). This, in combination with their initially acousmatic nature, is what coaxes the narrative into these continuously misleading representations of the sounds.

The aerial view Levy discerns thus in fact originates in the sum of auditory perceptions. It is caused by auricularisation, more than by ocularisation. The few references to the leaves of the trees and birds flying past, short instances of ocularisation which interlace with the auricularisation, are very often neutral, hardly tangible. They serve as nothing more than a relative measurement of altitude to go with the narrator's spatial descriptions. As was the case with the sound sources, none of them are presented in visual detail, especially in comparison with the initial colourful description of Miranda's attire and the orchard surrounding her. The focus in this sequence then, and especially in its remarkable perspective, is predominantly on the ear, not the eye.

The second part of the story likewise focuses more on the aural than on the visual. Here, focalisation shifts from the undisclosed, extradiegetic instance that might be situated on the level of the narrator, to Miranda herself; from zero focalisation to internal focalisation. 'The whole world lives through her sensuous body', says Bonadei, 'Miranda is the mastering gaze now'.[37] The image of the gaze is again perhaps too visual for what goes on in this section (yet another instance of the visual bias that has engrained itself into our language), considering that everything revolves once more around auditory impulses. Lying in her chair, (day)dreaming, Miranda lets her imagination run wild, ascribing different experiences to each of the sounds. Hearing the children's voices, she feels as if she is 'lying on the top of a cliff with the gulls screaming above'.[38] The drunk man shouting becomes 'life itself crying out from a rough tongue in a scarlet mouth' and when the organ plays, Miranda imagines getting married (150). The thud of the church bells suggests 'the very earth [shaking] with the hoofs of the horse that was galloping towards her', a horse presumably carrying her knight in shining armour (150). Her fantasy continues as the sullen, intermittent rhythm of the church bells synchs up with the beat of her own heart:

> Mary is chopping the wood, she thought; Pearman is herding the cows; the carts are coming up from the meadows; the rider – and she traced out the lines that the men, the carts, the birds, and the rider made over the countryside until they all seemed driven out, round, and across by the beat of her own heart. (150)

The church tower's golden feather heralds an end to her fantasy as it squeaks and she is reminded that she will be late for tea. Although the imagery that makes up the story in this second part is considerably more visual than it was in the first sequence, these visions originate in the aural triggers that stimulate Miranda's mind. As such, auricularisation once more proves invaluable to the development of the piece. Without sound, very little would occur.

The final section of the story makes this abundantly clear, as the sounds are erased completely, leaving us with nothing but a mute picture. Even the wind, which 'droned' in the first section, is hushed (149). What we get here is indeed a sketch, a painting: 'reality is processed as if on a painted canvas devoid of thymic or pathemic shades'.[39] This time, the scene is undeniably visual in nature. Focalisation is reduced to ocularisation almost entirely, with precise lines and contours – 'The sky exactly fitted the leaves' – and vivid colours – 'across the corner of the orchard the blue-green was slit by a purple streak'.[40] The sounds so vital to the previous two parts are nowhere to be heard. The effect is curious. Whereas the previous two perspectives, though both different, contain something that could be interpreted as a sort of story (namely first the recognition and then the interpretation of a number of 'off-screen' sounds) this one falls well short of that, being nothing but an objective rendition of the scenery. As Bonadei puts it, the observer 'refrains from any move that may betray even a fragment of pathos, the observed object is reduced to a grotesque geometry of apples'.[41] She concludes that 'an implicit author has made a painting out of the story: the orchard is a space in a frame and the scene is constructed like a painting' (11).

Bonadei admits then, that the story is to be found in the first two parts of the triptych, the ones where the emphasis is on the ear, not – as in the last one – on the eye. To state that 'the only story really told is that of the relationship between a subject and the space around it, and of the way a gaze can organise that space into a tale' does not, therefore, do justice to the essential role of auricularisation in this piece (11). Intent listening, even more so than the piercing gaze, is at the heart of this short fiction's storytelling process. In fact, the way in which the sounds guide the events and organise space is reminiscent of the role of a number of visual instruments in a later story of Woolf's, named 'The Searchlight' (1939). The earliest draft of this story, then still entitled 'What The Telescope Discovered', dates back to 1929, at a time when 'Woolf was experimenting with the device of the camera-narrator in her looking-glass stories'.[42] In it, a party standing on a balcony is watching a wheeling searchlight being used in an air force drill. As it moves, patches of darkness light up. These in turn elicit a story by the hostess, Mrs Ivimey, about her great-grandfather, who would spy people through his telescope, the obvious double of the searchlight. The moving gaze of the searchlight and the telescope become the structuring principle behind the events (if we can call them that) narrated in the story, 'identifying and selecting' the key moments, significant figures, and vivid gestures in the drama' (166). As Skrbic notes, 'the telescope's functional role in the storymaking process (its attempts to build up a picture, to locate a chronology, context, and some semblance of a continuous reality) addresses the notion of writing as a way of experimenting with reality' (166). She further argues that 'these experiments with an anti-authorial perspective', which 'reach their culmination in the unexpected and dramatic angles of "The Symbol" [1941]', were first practised in 'The Searchlight', and in a series of short 'portraits', including 'Waiting for Déjeuner' and 'The Frenchwoman in the Train' (166).[43]

While Skrbic could very well be correct about such experiments as far as the visual is concerned, the aural perspective of 'In the Orchard' (published over a decade earlier) displays remarkably similar techniques. Instead of using the gaze or any sort of visual instrument to pick out and order the events of the narrative (through ocularisation), however, it relies on intent listening, or auricularisation. In the same way that 'the chance happenings that the searchlight and the telescope reveal organise the storyteller's view' in 'The Searchlight', the different filters of auditory perception arrange the events of 'In the Orchard', not only creating the upward movement through the succession of initially acoustic sounds discussed earlier, but also introducing previously extraneous events into the scene, thus expanding its scope and sculpting its story.[44] The story thus constructed is repeated in parts two and three, where it is expanded first through Miranda's interpretations of the sounds, next by their complete absence, which in turn creates contrast. In this way, the story's soundscape is not only of quintessential importance to the construction of perspective, but also to the structuring of the story matter. This importance is underlined by the final, muted sequence, in which the reader is confronted with a word-based painting instead of a story.

Advocating auricularisation

Juxtaposing ocularisation and auricularisation in 'In the Orchard' instead of defaulting to a visual interpretation has lead to a number of interesting conclusions. Not only does it provide solutions to passages other analyses have had trouble interpreting, revealing how auricularisation and ocularisation can work together to great effect (building tension, creating misinformation in order to keep the reader guessing and creating what one might call a dual perspective, with ocularisation and auricularisation vying the scene from different positions), it also reveals how auricularisation can be just as important to the structure of the narrative as ocularisation. This proves, once more, why it is essential that we pay attention to the auditory dimension of modernist texts as well as to their visual aspects.

Notes

1. Cuddy-Keane, 'Modernist Soundscapes and the Intelligent Ear', p. 382.
2. Haslam, 'Modernism and the First World War', p. 50.
3. Frattarola, 'Developing an Ear for the Modernist Novel', pp. 147–8.
4. Cuddy-Keane, p. 382.
5. Smith, 'Introduction', p. x.
6. Bal, 'Visual Narrativity', p. 629.
7. Friedman, 'Point of View in Fiction', p. 1163. These two famous interpretations of James's theoretical reflections are Joseph Warren Beach's *The Method of Henry James* and Percy Lubbock's *The Craft of Fiction*.
8. James, 'The House of Fiction', p. 58.

9. Genette, *Figures III*, p. 203.
10. Genette, *Narrative Discourse*, p. 189.
11. See Genette, *Figures III*, p. 206.
12. Genette, *Narrative Discourse Revisited*, p. 64.
13. Pouillon, *Temps et Roman*, pp. 74, 85, 102.
14. For one example, see Chatman, 'Characters and Narrators', p. 192.
15. Phelan, 'Why Narrators Can Be Focalisers', pp. 51–64; Jahn, 'Windows of Focalisation', p. 241.
16. See Bal, *Narratology: Introduction to the Theory of Narrative* (1985), p. 104.
17. Bal, 'Visual Narrativity', p. 629.
18. Kahn, 'Introduction: Histories of Sound Once Removed', p. 4.
19. Jost, *L'Oeil-caméra: Entre film et roman*, p. 18.
20. See Jost, pp. 114–36.
21. See Schlickers, *Verfilmtes Erzählen*, pp. 153–67, as well as Schlickers, 'Focalisation, Ocularisation and Auricularisation', pp. 243–58.
22. Nelles, *Frameworks: Narrative Levels and Embedded Narrative*, p. 96.
23. Pioneering this movement are Denise Gigante, whose *Taste: A Literary History* (2005) aims to draw attention to the importance of taste in literature throughout history, and Mark M. Smith, who recently followed up his *Hearing History* (2004) with a work on *The Smell of Battle, The Taste of Siege: A Sensory History of the Civil War* (2014).
24. Cuddy-Keane, 'Woolf, Sound Technologies, and the New Aurality', p. 71.
25. Cuddy-Keane, 'Modernist Soundscapes', p. 385.
26. Jahn, 'Focalisation', pp. 173–7.
27. Nelles, p. 95.
28. Cuddy-Keane, 'Woolf, Sound Technologies, and the New Aurality', p. 71.
29. Nena Skrbic, for instance, finds elements of the 'post-impressionist movement in the visual arts' and compares the piece to 'a cubist collage'. See Skrbic, *Wild Outbursts of Freedom*, pp. 26, 11. In 'Glimpses into a System', Rossana Bonadei likens the final part of the story to 'a Cezanne painting' and a 'mock-Cubist vision' (10).
30. Baldwin, *Virginia Woolf: A Study of the Short Fiction*, p. xiii.
31. Woolf, 'In the Orchard', p. 150.
32. Skrbic, *Wild Outbursts of Freedom*, pp. 26, 11.
33. Levy, 'Virginia Woolf's Shorter Fictional Explorations', p. 146, emphasis added.
34. Bonadei, 'Glimpses into a System', available at: <http://www00.unibg.it/dati/corsi/3009/14840-glimpses%20into%20a%20system.pdf> (last accessed 15 June 2016), p. 10.
35. Woolf, 'In the Orchard', pp. 149–50.
36. See Connor, 'The Modern Auditory I', p. 213.
37. Bonadei, p. 10.
38. Woolf, 'In the Orchard', p. 150.
39. Bonadei, p. 11.
40. Woolf, 'In the Orchard', p. 151.
41. Bonadei, p. 11.
42. Skrbic, p. 166.
43. The latter two stories were probably written in collaboration with Vanessa

Bell, likely around 1937. While compiling *The Complete Shorter Fiction of Virginia Woolf,* Susan Dick placed 'Waiting for Déjeuner' and 'The Frenchwoman in the Train' (in addition to 'Portrait 3') under the broader title 'Portraits'. See Woolf, *The Complete Shorter Fiction of Virginia Woolf,* pp. 242–6, 307–8.

44. Skrbic, p. 166.

Part Two

Mediated Voices

Chapter 4

Bottled Bands: Automatic Music and American Media Publics

Lisa Gitelman

Beginning around 1890 nickel-in-the-slot machines were used to vend a range of goods and services in metropolitan areas across the United States.[1] It started with gum machines, apparently, and spread from there. *Scientific American* magazine called it a 'craze' and the Commissioner of Patents called it a 'flood'.[2] 'It begins to look as if the drummer and the saleslady [will] be superseded by this speechless monster', he offered, 'and [soon] every mortal want [will] come to be supplied through the slot' (223). As speechless monsters or so-called silent salesmen, vending machines were defined partly according to the sounds of exchange they replaced: the patter and pressure of sales talk, drumming, near relations of hawking, barking, street cries, and the palaver of auctioneers. Yet none of these machines, it must be admitted, was technically silent. Not only did the new vending machines come with a peculiar repertoire of mechanical noises – gears grinding, clicks and whirs – the most popular among them for a time were the automatic phonographs that played a minute or two of pre-recorded sound for every nickel.

The nickel-in-the-slot phonograph and its contemporary, the multi-user exhibition phonograph (for which nickels were collected by hand), both enjoyed relatively brief popularity before fading from view amid the popular success of home phonographs, gramophones and mass-produced musical records during the first decade of the twentieth century. Automatic phonographs are a footnote in the history of Las Vegas slot machines, then, a fossil amid the genealogy of the jukebox. But they are important to a history of aural cultures in the US on a number of counts. Most notably, as Jonathan Sterne has argued, the 'audile technique' of listening through hearing tubes helped to 'construct an individuated, localized sound space' for consumers, an acoustic space that was 'modeled on the form of private property'.[3] So at the same time that nickel-in-the-slot phonographs helped to suggest that musical play-back (rather than office dictation, say) was what phonographs might be *for* in the next century, nickel-in-the-slot phonographs also helped newly to commodify sound and audible performance, modelling private property coincident with – that is, as – a specific audile interiority.

The nickel-in-the-slot phonographs were a telling symptom of acoustic modernity, then, and in what follows I extend Sterne's argument in order to enrich our account of aural cultures in the US. The nickel-in-the-slot machines were typically clustered in train stations and special purpose amusement parlours or saloons in city centres, public spaces that served what Walter Benjamin (writing of arcades, exhibition halls and railway stations) called 'transitory purposes'.[4] The contemporary exhibition phonographs were meanwhile plied for trade at fairs, summer resorts and similar venues. In this the phonographs of 1890 differed from the emergent medium of telephony, which worked to connect a network of subscribers located in private homes, businesses or other nodal sites identified for their proximity to homes, such as boarding houses or corner stores. The subjects of telephony were interior, private subjects connecting outward to other private subjects, even if conducting business of some kind. Meanwhile the users of nickel-in-the-slot phonographs were always out – away from home if not out of doors – and the audile interiority they relied upon remained crucially embedded in the public arena.

Nickel-in-the-slot phonographs possessed at least three salient design attributes: first, those stethoscope-like ear tubes, which one business leader suggested washing 'every few days';[5] second, the return device, which reset the machine after each use; and third, the cabinet housing the machinery, which included a window or glass dome at the top. Each of these design elements hints at a cultural politics, at the structured conditions of the use and usability of the machines. The windowed housing of the machinery meant that the performance of the phonographs remained a public spectacle while the electrical and financial power behind their performance was private and mystified in a bit of oak cabinetwork. (You couldn't see a pile of nickels and you couldn't see the battery, but you could watch the machine's 'reproducer' – as it was called – scan slowly across a spinning record.) Meanwhile, the return device meant that repetition was built into the machinery. Each patron's deposit of a coin formed a single transaction among an implied infinitude of transactions that were exactly and *automatically* the same. And of course the ear tubes meant that users paid for private, even intimate encounters with public machines. 'So distinct are the sounds', one account put it, 'that you imagine that every one within a radius of fifty feet must hear them', but all they hear is 'a faint mum, mum, mum. They can see . . . through the glass . . . but' nothing is heard by anyone but the person wearing the ear tubes.[6] Audile interiority involved the specific condition of visibly listening to something that observers couldn't hear.

What this suggests is that the design of nickel-in-the-slot machines helped to create immensely intricate experiences of public and private, experiences variously animated by distinctions between performance and power, seeing and hearing, self and other. These were repeated, repeatable experiences that suggestively tended to standardise, automate and depersonalise exchange, to aggregate and yet atomise consumption, and thus effectively to essentialise the marketplace. Repeated play was conditioned by repeated payment, while both the performing recording artist and the proffering phonograph company remained effectively – one might say virtually – offstage. At the same time that vending machines of all sorts helped to characterise and thereby contain retail exchange in acoustic terms (to wit, the silent salesmen), the automatic phonographs helped to commodify sound itself as well as to reify the money economy. Novelist Frank Norris realised as much, when amid the clutter and the clamour of the Imperial barroom – first in student theme papers from 1895 and later in the novel *Vandover and the Brute* (1914) – Norris drops 'two nickel-in-the-slot machines' into a corner across from the bar, where 'at every instant the cash-register clucked and rang its bell'.[7]

Those self-acting sounds of commerce are striking: the cash register rings up business on its own. With its dis- or misplaced agency, Norris's automatic till recalls the patent commissioner's prediction that someday soon 'every mortal want will be supplied through the slot'.[8] Of course, no 'wants' came through the slot itself. The 'greedy slot', elsewhere the 'all-devouring slot', was the mouth where the coins went in, not a mouth where the purchases – sonic or otherwise – came out (869). Consumer capitalism must kindle our desires partly in the mystification of the means of their potential fulfilment, while the mysteries of recorded sound seem to have entailed a proliferation of machine orifices. It is a little as if one said, 'every mortal want will soon be supplied through the Internet'. The Internet doesn't bring us our wants, the Post Office or Parcel Service truck does, except – if you want to be picky about it – when we download music or other digital files. Downloading further attenuates the distinction between output (speakers or headphones, playing or streaming device) and input (keyboard or touchscreen) in partial mystification of the interface with its empty box – that little graphical slot – where maybe you type your credit card number.

I digress, but I think there is a problem here. I want to argue from the design of the machines themselves, yet I also want to reject a normative psychoacoustics whereby the apparatus fully produces its subject.

There's more to it than that. Because they flickered briefly as a conjunction of publics and markets, automatic phonographs provide a way to read out some of the conflicts attending the money economy during the 1890s; not those broader, framing debates about a gold standard, bimetallism, or the intrinsicality of monetary value, but rather the related psychic tax incumbent within what Norris's contemporary, Georg Simmel, described as 'the modern form of life'.[9] Indeed, one of Simmel's most provocative analogies posits exchange (exchangeability) in auditory terms. 'As a visible object', he writes, 'money is the substance that embodies abstract economic value, in a similar fashion to the sound of words which is an acoustic-physiological occurrence but has significance for us only through the representation that it bears or symbolizes' (120). Money is to value as sound is to meaning. Visible forms convey the *value* that is 'constituted by [the] mutual relationship of exchangeability' (120). Correspondingly, audible forms convey the *meaning* that is constituted by the mutual relationship of linguistic communication.[10] Meaning is sound at once spendable and spent.

What meanings might the psychoacoustic occurrences of nickel-in-the-slot phonographs have conveyed to customers in the early 1890s? There are a number of ways to pursue this question. One of the most obvious is to consider repertoire. We know it varied widely, although newspaper accounts suggest that consumers broadly associated 'the slot' with 'the band' (often within quotation marks just like that, to indicate a commonplace). The earliest surviving record catalogues help to suggest why. The Columbia Phonograph Company in Washington, DC, was an early leader in the field, placing 140 nickel-in-the-slot machines in its territory by the end of 1891.[11] Relying on its presence in the nation's capital, Columbia took advantage of local talent while also capitalising on its transcendent localism. Newspapers reported that the United States Marine Band was 'render[ing] itself immortal by having its most harmonious strains bottled in large quantities'. Band members played to an empty 'room on E Street' but 'for the entertainment of people in all parts of the United States'.[12] By 1892 the Edison Phonograph Works in Orange, NJ, was offering 143 different records, still heavily weighted toward band selections by the US Marine Band and others, along with other things like 'artistic whistling' and racist 'darkey songs' [sic].[13]

Band music formed part of the experience of public and local spaces in America. There were an estimated 10,000 bands in the United States in 1889, among them perhaps 150,000 bandsmen.[14] The bands were in some sense the successors to an earlier parade tradition. If their personnel suggest a voluntarist, male citizenry performing acts of public representation, the sounds of their play must have powerfully articulated a

local community, a literalised commonplace.[15] Like Old World village
bells, American bands produced auditory markers dense with inarticulate messages about identity, tied in this instance to residual leisure practices and norms of civic ceremony.[16] Though cities of course had plenty
of bands, band music tended to connote the auditory landscape of more
rural life. John Philip Sousa lived and worked in Washington, DC, but
one of his many tirades disparaging the new 'canned music' waxes eloquent about 'the village band' and 'the country band, with its energetic
renditions, its loyal support by local merchants, its benefit concerts,
band wagon, gay uniforms, state tournaments, and attendant pride and
gayety'.[17] 'The band', it would seem, was party to an American pastoral
imaginary, a wistful sense-memory or compensatory surmise directed
toward some prelapsarian, pre-industrial existence.

The nickel-in-the-slot phonograph brought this outdoor, public music
inside, 'canned' or 'bottled' it, and saved it under glass for every person's
public tender and private audience. Patrons each heard their own band
for the first time: they together had individual, individually purchased
experiences of common, communal sounds. Those sounds were specifically sounds of public life, sounds for the first time dislodged from the
inter-subjectivities of live performance and installed within the emergent
techno-social logic of recording and playback. Like the eighteenth-
century print artefacts Michael Warner has described, in other words,
these brassy strains were themselves 'metonyms for an abstract public',
newly 'embodied' in cylinders of wax.[18] Of course the coherence of the
public sphere is a powerful fiction that belies exclusion and oppression.
To the generalised cultural imaginary of 'the band' in these years must
be added the persistent popularity of the blackface minstrel tradition in
the United States, evident in a host of performance and musical genres
as well as in the adaptive uptake and popularity of new media, both
recorded sound and motion pictures. Band records might metonymically embody the public sphere, but the racial violence of its structuring
exclusions are evident in the minstrel songs, dialect humour, and 'lynching records' of the same era. In his important account of phonographic
modernity, Gustavus Stadler argues that a small number of records
which re-enacted public spectacles of racial violence for public consumption worked in this context to displace pressing questions of racial
justice in favour of more anodyne concerns about the decency of recordings and the meanings of the new recording medium.[19]

No matter how embodied, then, these sonic metonyms did not cir-
culate freely or perform transparently. They were part of the ongoing
self-organisation of the public sphere stuck under glass. And they were
bracketed by two additional sonic layers in addition to repertoire, a

heteroglossia which helped to render them as products as well as public. First, there was 'a slight buzzing sound', or a whirring, which one author compared to the frying sound 'emitted by a defective telephone'.[20] Second, there was a recorded announcement giving the title of the recorded selection, the identity of its corporate sponsor and the name of its performer(s). So after you dropped your nickel in the slot, you heard a little electric motor and the turning of the phonograph mandrel, and then you heard that 'This recording was made by [such and such an artist and] for [such and such a] company.' Yet if the recordings were made by and for someone, the recorded announcements themselves – and that inarticulate whirring of the motor – were neither by nor for anyone in particular. They sounded with an inexplicit, abstract or anonymous authority, early gestures in a form of indeterminate public address that still characterises network administration: 'Stay tuned for scenes from next week', 'All circuits are busy', 'Mind the gap', and 'File not found'. Using this mode of address, networks hail or interpellate their corporate(-ised) subjects by modelling them as an abstract public. No wonder, then, that 'the slot', with 'the band', became such an active character in the popular discourse surrounding automatic phonographs.

Newspaper accounts confirm that 'the slot' became briefly and powerfully cathected with the bountiful novelties of the era and the concomitant desires and anxieties that attend a market economy. Indeed, when coin-operated telephones were introduced in Chicago boarding houses and apartment buildings starting in 1894, they were commonly called 'nickel-in-the-slot', even though they cost a dime.[21] It would seem, then, that the implied subject of the automatic phonograph and its slot was only apparently 'the band'. Instead these machines and recordings hailed what one journalist called 'blasé men about town'.[22] 'The band' was conjured out of and in opposition to a species of urban *flânerie*, while the slot and the roving blasé made perfect sense together. The blasé attitude arises, as Simmel proposed, from an economy 'where more and more objects are encompassed', able to be acquired in the same 'mechanical and indifferent way', so that 'their value differences are actually reduced', and their 'charms fade away'.[23] The result of such an economy was an insidious 'craving today for excitement', Simmel noted, or 'the search for mere stimuli in themselves' (257).

This starts to sound like a fairly typical criticism of public amusements and the emergent culture industry, the kinetoscopes, vitascopes, amusement parks and arcades that flourished during this period in keeping with wage labour and a modest increase in disposable incomes. But nickel-in-the-slot phonographs actually proved a little more amusing than their promoters intended. Press notices almost universally include accounts of 'beating' the machines.[24] An arms race of sorts developed, and reporters lovingly detail the ingenuity of inventors as they countered the ingenuity of unscrupulous patrons – inventors themselves – who used broom straws to start the mechanism, or pulled their nickel back out of the slot on a string, or dropped in slugs, washers, orange peels or bits of ice. This is what is so interesting about these devices. Just as they helped to standardise and depersonalise exchange they seem also to have allowed patrons to make a standardised currency into a momentary joke. Alongside 'the slot' and 'the band', one sees – maybe a little differently – the blasé and his 'nickel'. (A standardised currency and nickels were relatively recent developments in the US.) Just as the design of these machines divided auditors from one another, they offered 'beating the machine' as a new form of male sociability. It was fun, but it wasn't a form of market critique. 'Beating' these machines did not deny the emergent commodification of sound as much as it affirmed it, subverting one transaction and thereby granting the exchange relationship. What 'beating' did do was turn from the consumption of audible representations back to the fact of psychoacoustic occurrence as such. In this as in Stadler's account of the lynching records, the new medium of recorded sound remained briefly its own subject, bumping aside questions of more pressing concern about the inequities, uncertainties and psychic costs of modern life.

Notes

1. This chapter extends Gitelman, *Always Already New*, pp. 48–50, upon which it is based.
2. *Scientific American*, p. 105; Croffut, *Current Literature*, p. 223.
3. Sterne, *The Audible Past*, pp. 162–3.
4. Benjamin, 'Paris, the Capital of the Nineteenth Century', p. 97.
5. Andem, *A Practical Guide for the Use of the Edison Phonograph*, p. 60.
6. *Thomas A. Edison Papers*, Digital Edition [elsewhere TAED], SC90071B.
7. Norris, *A Novelist in the Making*, pp. 96, 94.
8. Clegg, 'Slot Machinery', p. 869.
9. Simmel, *The Philosophy of Money*, p. 477.
10. Michaels, 'The Gold Standard and the Logic of Naturalism', pp. 128–9.
11. Brooks, 'Columbia Records in the 1890s', pp. 4–35.
12. TAED, SC90045A.
13. TAED, CA025C.
14. See Kreitner, *Discoursing Sweet Music*; and Hazen and Hazen, *The Music Men*.
15. See Ryan, 'The American Parade', pp. 131–53.
16. Corbin, *Village Bells*, ff.
17. Sousa, 'Menace of Mechanical Music', p. 281.

18. Warner, *The Letters of the Republic*, p. 62.
19. Stadler, 'Never Heard Such a Thing', pp. 87–105.
20. TAED, SC90071B.
21. John, *Network Nation*, p. 296.
22. TAED, SC90071B.
23. Simmel, p. 257.
24. Clegg, pp. 869–70.

Chapter 5

How to Listen to Joyce: Gramophones, Voice and the Limits of Mediation

Helen Groth

In 1932 Christina Stead, living in Paris and struggling to finish her first novel *Seven Poor Men of Sydney* (1934), purchased a gramophone recording of James Joyce reading from the 'Anna Livia Plurabelle' section of *Finnegans Wake*. Prompted by the publication of Joyce's *Work in Progress* in Eugene Jolas's avant-garde little magazine *transition*, Stead's account in a letter to a friend of her frustration with her costly purchase reveals both the powerful allure of Joyce, the celebrity and cachet associated with his signature style and voice, as well as the disappointing reality of early gramophone recordings. Stead writes excitedly, 'a gramophone record of James Joyce the English litterateur, reading from his own works, a rare thing costing 200 francs'.[1] Given Stead's description of Joyce as English, her alienated response to the recording in which Joyce assumes various Dublin accents is hardly surprising. Indeed one of the many pleasures of listening to Joyce's 'beautiful' performance of 'Anna Livia', as Sylvia Beach effused in *Shakespeare and Company*, was Joyce's amusing 'rendering of an Irish washerwoman's brogue!'[2] Distracted by the logistics of acquiring the recording, Stead fails to hear, or at least to note, these nuances of accent and place in her letter. She tells her friend that not only does the recording, which was made at the Cambridge Orthological Institute by the renowned linguist C. K. Ogden, cost 200 francs, you have to pay the full amount before listening 'on the pretense that it wears the record (and I suppose once you have had the experience you are not so likely to buy it)'.[3]

Compounding this disappointment is the confusion and uncertainty that hearing Joyce's performance of his characters' distinctively Irish voices prompts in Stead. Rather than enhancing her understanding of the complexities of Joyce's linguistic experimentation, which she admiringly describes in the same letter, Stead finds her hopes of a more revelatory form of communication dashed: 'I have had to telegraph and telephone and visit to get this record and now I am not sure of it' (51).

She accordingly reverts to the comforting materiality of a more traditional authorial trace, the writer's autograph:

> I hope to get it signed by the writer himself, as he lives in Paris, and I know his friend Sylvia Beach, the one that published his great book *Ulysses*. James Joyce is the new Euphues: the melting pot of the language and of present literary idiom and banality: ... no living writer in English there is who is not indebted to his methods and his vocabulary: he has been translated in all tongues, despite the enormous difficulty of the translation. (51)

Stead's positive characterisation of Joyce as the new Euphues implicitly contradicts her admiring account of the accessible translation of Joyce's work into 'all tongues' and her avowal of the universal debt of all writers to his unique method and lexicon. Both Euphues and Joyce prioritise the sound and the rhythmic sequencing of words over meaning; a parallel that suggests Stead was ultimately more drawn to the untranslatable formal aspects of Joyce's work, rather than its universal mediation in 'all tongues'. In this sense Stead's letter points to a tension that this chapter will explore. As an Australian writer living in Paris in the 1930s Stead was keenly aware of the distance between herself and the central figures of the modernist avant-garde. Her desire to leave the parochial constraints of her life in Sydney compelled her identification with both the didactic strand of international modernism that generated Ogden's recording of *Finnegans Wake* and the cosmopolitan bravura of Jolas's *transition*. And yet, when Stead hears Joyce's voice for the first time, her desire for communication and connection is confronted with an irreconcilable difference. Rather than opening up the text by transforming it into a universally accessible audible translation, the sonic specificity of the recorded voice, including accent and pace of delivery, reinforced the *Wake*'s systematic dismantling of the grounds of language and the conventions of meaning making.

Joyce's August 1929 recording of 'Anna Livia Plurabelle' at Ogden's Orthological Institute was, from the beginning, an experiment with sounding out the semantic limits of modernist style. Joyce described this section of the *Wake*, which he began writing in 1924 and intensively revised before its publication in 1928, as an experiment with subordinating words to the rhythmic undulations of the Liffey.[4] The local precision of Joyce's account of writing this section as a rhythmic capturing of the particular sound and flow of the river seems at odds with Ogden's stress on universal translation and basic expression.[5] Yet Joyce clearly did not see any contradiction, as Aaron Jaffe and many others have noted, given that he authorised C. K. Ogden to translate a substantial section of 'Anna Livia Plurabelle' into Basic English in the same year that the recording was made. While there is clearly a parallel between the commercial popularising agenda underlying Ogden's gramophone recordings of well-known literary voices and the didactic *techne* of Ogden and I. A. Richards's invention of a new 'International Language of 850 words in which everything may be said', Ogden and T. S. Eliot's selection of Joyce performing 'Anna Livia Plurabelle' as the inaugural recording in a proposed series of famous modernists reading from their work remains a perplexing chapter in the history of the Basic English programme and its various offshoots.[6]

Taking Stead's frustrated response to the sound of Joyce reading a text that was, in turn, deeply invested in the sound of words and the acoustic dimensions of reading as a starting point, this chapter will explore the tensions between elitism and universal access that the recording and its reception materialised. The first section examines the context for the recording, including Ogden's translation of 'Anna Livia Plurabelle' which appeared in both *Psyche* and then in *transition* in 1932 as part of a 'Homage to James Joyce'. Reading *Ulysses* and following Joyce's 'Work in Progress' in *transition* during her time in Paris confronted Stead with the limits of her competency as a reader of the modernist avant-garde and, more generally, with the limits of human communication itself. In this sense Stead's reading experience aligns with Derrida's famous contention that 'if *Finnegans Wake* is the sublime babelization of a *penman* and *postman*, the motif of postal difference, of remote control and telecommunication, is already powerfully at work in *Ulysses*'.[7] Stead was immersed in the modern babel of telecommunication Derrida describes. She longs for the proximity that the new media of the telephone and gramophone promised and resists the irresolvable absence both simultaneously generate. The second section of the chapter analyses the recording's intensification of the sonic aspects of *Finnegans Wake* and concentration on the texture of Joyce's voice. One way of understanding Stead's alienated reaction to Joyce's voice as indicative of the recording's uneven reception is to think about it through Mladen Dolar's account of the obfuscation of meaning that takes place when the ear turns the voice into an object of aesthetic pleasure, 'an object of veneration and worship, the bearer of a meaning beyond ordinary meanings'.[8] This is particularly true of Stead listening to Joyce's recorded voice while struggling to understand and connect with its alienated human source; an unnervingly mechanical affect which nevertheless produces an uncannily intimate presence sounding in her ear in the privacy of her small Parisian apartment.

Ogden's recording of 'Anna Livia Plurabelle' was not the first attempt to record Joyce. In 1924 Sylvia Beach approached the Paris office of His

Master's Voice to see if they would record Joyce reading from *Ulysses*. They agreed as long as Beach paid all expenses and the record did not appear in their music catalogue or bear their label. Piero Coppola, who was in charge of musical records, advised Beach that there was no demand for literary recordings, a commercial reality that Beach ignored, choosing instead to take inspiration from the fact that writers had been recorded in France and England since 1913. Buoyed by this precedent she agreed to fund thirty copies much to the delight of Joyce, who chose the passage from the Aeolus episode of *Ulysses*, where Professor MacHugh re-enacts a speech given to the college historical society by the notable Irish nationalist and barrister John F. Taylor for the entertainment of the men at the *Freeman* newspaper offices. Joyce made this selection, according to Beach, not because its declamatory style made it more suited to recital, but because 'it expressed something he wanted said and preserved in his own voice. As it rings out – "he lifted his voice above it boldly" – it is more, one feels than mere oratory'.[9] Leaving aside the question of the 'something he wanted said' for the moment, Beach's stress on preservation is notable. In her mind at least the recording was of aesthetic and archival rather than commercial value. She describes listening to it as a moving beautiful experience, in contrast to Ogden who recoiled at the poor quality of the recording, the indistinct vocal performance, the distracting snaps and crackles. If 'the something' Joyce wanted said related to the content of Professor MacHugh's speech, which linked the Irish nationalist struggle and necessary survival of the Irish language to the plight of the Hebrews in Egypt, the message was lost on Ogden. All he registered was the potential to produce a better recording.

Yet, as Adrian Curtin observes in his insightful reading of the Aeolus recording as audiotext, Ogden's response fails to appreciate 'how successful and multilayered Joyce's recitation is, despite the technological distortion'.[10] What is striking about the sound of Joyce's voice, as Curtin notes, is its confident theatricality and precise diction amplified by emotion and complexly textured by his own idiosyncratic version of Hiberno-English (273). On the latter point, Curtin diverges from Sebastian D. G. Knowles's earlier response to this recording, which emphasises Joyce's 'relish' for speaking 'an outlaw language' and participating in the creation of 'a new Irish literature'.[11] In contrast to this stress on national tradition, Joyce's relish for a more international translation of the Irish language is more consistent with his engagement with Ogden's Basic English translation and his investment in the potential of the gramophone to be something more than an uncanny medium of the voices of the dead. Bloom notably imagines the future gramophone in exactly this way in the Hades section of *Ulysses*. In a graveyard of recording devices the bereaved will be able to hear the voices of their departed loved ones:

> Besides how could you remember everybody? Eye, walk, voice. Well, the voice, yes: gramophone. Have a gramophone in every grave or keep it in the house. After dinner on a Sunday. Put on poor old greatgrandfather Kraahraark! Hellohellohello amawfullyglad kraark amawfullygladaseeragain hellohello amarawf Kopthsth. Remind you of the voice like the photograph reminds you of the face after fifteen years, say.[12]

Metonymic vocal traces of once familiar friends or relatives reanimated by mechanical reproduction had become commonplace by 1922 and it is this sentiment that informs Beach's investment in preserving Joyce's voice in the Aeolus recording. But Ogden and T. S. Eliot's interest in recording Joyce was driven by very different imperatives, primarily didacticism, mediation and communication.

While she was dismissive of Ogden's objections and described *The Meaning of Meaning*, which he co-wrote with I. A. Richards, as well as the Basic English books as a 'strait jacket for the English Language', Beach still claims to have facilitated Joyce going to Cambridge to record 'Anna Livia Plurabelle' in the 'state of the art' recording studio of the Orthological Society.[13] Her account of their subsequent collaboration also nicely captures its inherently contradictory nature:

> So I brought these two together, the man who was liberating and expanding the English language and the one who was condensing it to a vocabulary of five hundred words. Their experiments went in opposite directions, but that didn't prevent them from finding each other's ideas interesting. Joyce would have starved on five or six hundred words, but he was quite amused by the Basic English version of 'Anna Livia Plurabelle' that Ogden published in the review *Psyche*. (176)

Despite their differences, Joyce, Ogden and Richards shared an interest in the workings of the English language and the fundamental ways in which meaning gets made. In contrast to Beach who 'thought Ogden's translation deprived the work of all its beauty', Joyce was clearly engaged by both aspects of the experiment – the parallel translation of 'Anna Livia Plurabelle' into Basic English and recorded sound (176). Nor was he alone in his support for Ogden's Basic programme: G. B. Shaw, William Empson, George Orwell and Ezra Pound actively engaged with its precepts. In his typically acerbic fashion, Pound even distilled Basic's three key virtues in *The New English Weekly* in 1935:

I.   As a training and exercise, especially for excitable yeasty youngsters who want so eagerly to mean something that they can't take out time to thin: What?

II.   As a sieve. As a magnificent system for measuring extant works. As a
      jolly old means of weeding out bluffs, for weeding out fancy trimmings
      . . . If a novelist can survive translation into basic, there is something
      solid under his language . . .
III. The advantage of BASIC vocabulary limited to 850 words and their
      variants . . . for the diffusion of ideas is, or should be, obvious to any
      man of intelligence.[14]

Pound's support for Basic English is consistent with his railing against
superfluity and prolix ornament. Additionally, and this is vital for thinking through Joyce's interest in Ogden's translation, Pound accords Basic
with the power to strip away all ornamental excess to reveal the essence
of a novelist's language. To quote Jaffe on the application of this particular virtue to Joyce:

> If 'Anna Livia Plurabelle' remains Joycean in Basic form, then original words
> are proved to be more than prolix ornaments . . . What else is Pound's *solid*
> referent *under language* besides Joyce the authentic remainder, the remainder
> for the sake of which an author is admitted into the active register of *extant*
> names, the list of survivors for which literary value had been thus secured.[15]

What remains, the residuum, is the authentic product of genius and of
inestimable literary value.[16] To survive the Basic process is to simultaneously join an elite and become legible to a broader audience.

   The same conflicting impulses to be both elite and accessible drove
the production of the recording of 'Anna Livia Plurabelle', according
to T. S. Eliot's account of the process in a letter to the American author
and journalist Herbert Gorman. Expressing his frustration with Ogden's
delays in producing the record, Eliot informs Gorman that he intends to
take over the process and propose to the board of Faber & Faber that
the recording should be deposited with them, rather than in Cambridge.
Eliot planned to use the press's American and European mailing lists to
promote sales of the recording and establish a list of fifty or more well-
heeled subscribers able to pay seven or eight guineas annually to receive
up to four recordings a year by well-known authors, such as Joyce,
Yeats and Woolf. Eliot also speculates about the possibility of assembling a suitably prestigious editorial board to preside over the selection
of authors, texts and recording lists.[17] Two weeks later, Eliot wrote to
Joyce to clarify what was happening. He assured Joyce that the recording scheme was still in train and described the potential subscription list
as a society of at least twenty-five to ensure indefinite production of new
records, which he felt would be infinitely superior and more appealing
than limited signed editions. Eliot also suggested Joyce make further
recordings from *Ulysses* and *Haveth Childers*, based on the success of

Faber's edition of *Anna Livia* which had sold 4,600 copies by October 1930.[18] A year later Eliot wrote to Joyce again praising the recording as 'magnificent' and the 'perfect' sound of his voice. Eliot also felt that the recording would help those readers, like Stead, who found *Anna Livia* difficult: 'It ought to have more publicity, as it should be a great help to people who found A. L. P difficult – as well as for the sake of its own beauty.'[19] True to his word, Eliot would continue to promote the recording as a reading aid throughout the 1940s. In *Introducing James Joyce* Eliot wrote:

> Most readers of that massive work would agree to the choice of the passage which was published separately, before the completion of the whole work, as *Anna Livia Plurabelle*. This fantasy of the course of the river Liffey is the best-known part of *Finnegans Wake*, and is the best introduction to it. It was recorded by the author: I have found that the gramophone record of the author's voice reciting it revealed at once a beauty which is disclosed only gradually by the printed page.[20]

He reiterated this advice a year later in an essay guiding readers on ways to approach *Finnegans Wake*:

> Joyce's last book has to be read aloud, preferably by an Irish voice; and, as the gramophone record which he made attests, no other voice could read it, not even another Irish voice, as well as Joyce could read it himself.[21]

Yet despite Eliot's vigorous promotion, Joyce told Sylvia Beach in a letter dated 18 May 1931 that the record had only sold between eight to ten copies and expressed some uncertainty about Ogden's suggestion that he do another recording.[22] Aside from the recording's price, the fact that Christina Stead was one of only ten purchasers, if this figure is correct, would seem to be a further indication of the intensity of her desire to hear and understand Joyce's work. Unsurprisingly, given the low sales, no further recordings were made, although copies of Ogden's recording were available for listening prior to purchase from Alfred Imhof's on Oxford Street, London so it is hard to measure the true number of contemporary listeners.[23] Indeed Imhof's actively encouraged London-based readers to come to 'Alfred Imhof's salons . . . to hear every new record in comfort and privacy' in one of twenty-six sound-proof 'listening rooms'.[24]

The recording of Joyce reading from *Anna Livia* was made a year before the publication of Eliot's pamphlet edition of the text and was promoted by Ogden in his own journal *Psyche* as the first 'portion' of Joyce's 'Work in Progress' and then subsequently as an essential supplement to Eliot's pamphlet.[25] As Eleni Loukopoulou notes in her detailed account of the recording's production, Ogden took great pride in 'the ultra-modern equipment in his studio'.[26] He claimed that he could produce a superior listening experience than the American electric Victrolas, the dominant product on the English market at that time, and was at great pains to achieve a quality recording of *Anna Livia*. He also provided translations and notes in 'Basic English' to assist readers in a series of issues of *Psyche* beginning in July 1929. Ogden described these translations in a later issue as offering 'a general setting for the neologistic effects which Mr Joyce is trying to achieve' for those 'who have possessed themselves of the book and the disc, but still fail to make sense of the combined testimony of eye and ear'.[27] In the same note Ogden provides an optimistic account of the recording's growing celebrity and understandable commercial appeal to Faber 'without which it is safe to say that 95% of its readers will fail to extract more than 5% of its significance' (95). He also adds further explication and translations of the lexicon of *Anna Livia* instructing the reader that Joyce has 'superposed' his interest in the divergence of Greek and Roman churches and the cyclical theory of history '*loup, teems of times*' on his memories of Dublin and 'the aesthetics of river surfaces' (95). Consequently any 'word-form, not otherwise transparent', he continues, 'is liable to conceal the name and character of one or more of the world's waterways (*Kennet, Cher, Wharnow, Ussa, Ulla* etc.). Anna of course, is the Liffey, the mother, Dublin, the city, the father' (95).

This is followed by an outline of the basic plot of the sequence – the speaker sees her reflection as an inverted tree, which augurs her transformation into a tree at the conclusion of the episode. The two washerwomen initially bump into one another and exchange gossip across the river. But as the episode continues the river gradually widens until the women find themselves too far away to hear one another. After this helpful distillation Ogden adds a few more useful translations – '*Waterhouse's clogh*' = '*the Big Ben of Dublin*', '*Poolbeg flasher*' = lighthouse, '*pharos*' = far away, '*Who was then the spouse?*' refers to the incestuous origin of society – before concluding with the speculation that

> one day, no doubt, some pious commentator will do for this 'Work in progress' what Mr Stuart Gilbert has so successfully undertaken for its predecessor (*Ulysses*, a study; Faber 22/- post fee). Till then, and perhaps more especially thereafter, for all who think it worth while to occupy themselves with Mr Joyce's Meaning, the aforesaid disc should provide the first step to its discovery. (96)

Gilbert aptly began this critical process in his introductory contribution to the 'Homage to James Joyce' published in *transition* in 1932.

Gilbert's dual stress in that article on the fundamental untranslatability of *Work in Progress* on the one hand and its 'universality' on the other, aligns with the tension between the elitism and universal access in Stead's letter to her friend, which is hardly surprising given both emanate from the same moment of Parisian-based optimistic cosmopolitanism and that Stead followed Joyce's work in *transition* which vigorously promoted the international appeal of modernism. Gilbert, like Stead, writes of the 'imprint' of Joyce on a global literature of the future, and of the misleading initial impression 'the synthetic language' of *Work in Progress* conveys of reproducibility: 'given a certain verbal adroitness and a smattering of foreign tongues, many a writer may seem to recompose the Joycean technique', but, he warns, all imitations will inevitably fail.[28] The universal appeal of Joyce's work lies, according to Gilbert, in its uniqueness:

> That power of discovering symmetry and coherence in all phenomena, of whatever species and place and epoch, of assimilating the present with the past, passion with intellect and (on the technical side) the utmost verbal freedom with strict precision in the handling of vocabulary, is a power beyond the scope of any but the greatest. (247)

In the next essay in the same issue of *transition*, Eugene Jolas echoes Gilbert's stress on Joyce's exceptional writing and the parochial banality of the banning of *Ulysses* in America and England as 'an everlasting disgrace to both countries'.[29] He then goes on to celebrate Harold Nicholson's radio broadcast on Joyce, which included Ogden's recording of *Anna Livia* as a triumphant struggle against the BBC's edict that banned books were not allowed to be mentioned in broadcast lectures (251).

Jolas also revels in the multiple ways in which new media were integrated into the writing and publication of Joyce's *Work in Progress* in the sixth number of *transition*. He speaks nostalgically of a last minute addition of four pages being announced by telephone after the review copies had been stitched, and still further 'telegraphic corrections' arriving after the second clean set of proofs had been delivered to the printer (252). This was matched by *transition* readers, like Stead, who pragmatically enlisted the telegraph and the telephone to acquire Ogden's recording and through it an enhanced virtual connection with Joyce. These parallel multi-medial processes also resonate with David Trotter's recent observation that the *Wake* is itself 'just about as close to connectivity as literature was ever to get in the first media age'.[30] Knowingly inter-medial, Joyce's prose moves fluidly between the novel analogue technologies of his day. A suggestive instance of this occurs in the last of the published sections of *Work in Progress* when the Light Brigade charges across the 'bairdboard bombardment screen' in the inn where Humphrey Chimpden Earwicker presides:

> In the heliotropical noughttime following a fade of transformed Tuff and, pending its viseversion, a metenergic reglow of beaming Batt, the bairboard bombardment screen, if tastefully taut guranium satin, tends to teleframe and step up the charge of a light barricade.[31]

These lines typify Joyce's enduring interest in what he dubs in the *Wake* as 'verbicovisual' communication (341). In the timeless 'noughttime' of the inn, Tuff's radio broadcast fades out only to be replaced by the intrusive bombardment of screen and sound. Word fragments are elided in sonically driven sequences – most notably the insistent alliterative b's – that the eye scans and the ear fleetingly registers. Onomatopoeic resonances, as well as complex networks of literary and cinematic allusions, dismantle alphabetic sense and linear chronology here, freeing the reader to summon images and sounds from within and beyond the frame of the text, including the Charge of the Light Brigade at Balaclava – one of the iconic failures of English imperial hubris.

To return to 'Homage to James Joyce', Jolas's stress on international connectivity and communication in his praise of Nicholson's broadcast on Joyce also serves as a fitting prelude to the reproduction of Ogden's Basic English translation of *Anna Livia* which follows. This reprint of the original in *transition*, which had first appeared in *Psyche*, includes a brief prefatory statement by Ogden that again stresses the link with 'the simple sense of the Gramophone Record made by Mr. Joyce'.[32] Ogden also contends that the Basic English translation, like the recording, retains the 'same rhythms' insisting that priority was given throughout to sound patterns rather than literal translation into Basic words (259). Notably, as Ogden himself stresses, Joyce perceived the two forms of the text as written in different languages, and this can also be said of the comparison with the recording. Yet despite Ogden's claims, the Basic translation diverges significantly from the rhythms of the *Wake* from the first line substitution of 'conscious' for 'know' in the original, which breaks the alliterative flow of the women's exchange, followed by an equally disruptive substitution of 'telling' and 'taling' with story and ending. To quote Joyce followed by Ogden's translation:

> Well you know or don't you kennet or haven't I told you every telling has a taling and that the he and she of it. (213)
>   Well are you conscious, or haven't you knowledge, or haven't I said it, that every story has an ending and that's the he and the she of it. (259)

As Levin notes in his influential early study of Joyce, Ogden reduces the 'suggestiveness of the original' to direct statement, ignoring 'harmonies and conceits', ruling out ambiguities and leaving nothing but a literal residuum.[33] Like Beach, Levin praised 'Joyce's captivating phonograph record' (149) and resists the juxtaposition of 'Mr Ogden's language of strict denotation and Joyce's language of extreme connotation' (164). Yet, as John Nash observes of Joyce's notorious approach to James Stephens to complete 'Work in Progress', 'auratic humanism and technological reproduction' were entwined in all aspects of the design and mediation of the *Wake*.[34] Rather than diminishing the 'auratic illusion' of Joyce's originating genius, Ogden's parallel forms of reproduction – the Basic English translation and the recording – only amplified the powerful affect of listening to Joyce reading from the original. Joyce actively encouraged this effect by accelerating the rhythms of his reading, which is incantatory in its rapid delivery, a technique that Nash astutely notes is symptomatic of both a technically mechanistic and a ritualistic understanding of language and of reception (127). This in turn translates, according to Nash, into Joyce's divided sense of the potential audience for the *Wake*, which never quite elides the distinction between expert and general readers. The former with the time, erudition and ear for the subtle rhythms of the text, and the general reader without the time or knowledge to make sense of the sound patterns created by Joyce's carefully orchestrated prosodic design.

To return to Joyce's original lines as cited above, which mark the two washerwomen's transition from the to and fro rhythms of conversation to storytelling – 'every telling has a taling' – the alliterative metre works on multiple levels, moving associatively, for the erudite reader well versed in the history of the evolution of English poetry at least, between potentially registered echoes of the old English metrics of *Beowulf*, as William Martin has noted, as well as nodding to 'the regular alternation between stressed and unstressed syllables to create a trochaic hexameter that mimics' Homeric style.[35] To demonstrate this point Martin breaks Joyce's prose into poetic lines to emphasise the movement into poetic language that he argues occurs at this moment in the *Anna Livia* section:

> <Well you know or don't you kennet or haven't I told you
> every telling has a taling and that's the he and she of it.> (194)

This translation into poetic lines reinforces the divergence between those who listen and those who understand the *Wake* and aligns with a deeper tension between the desire to be heard by many and closely read by a parochial few – Joyce himself estimated the few to number around twenty-five of the 'world's 1,500 million' in a letter to his patron

Harriet Weaver.[36] Ogden's account of the translation process in his preface to his basic version of *Anna Livia* in *transition* maintains this division between the 'greater audience' and the 'complex ideas' of men of letters.[37] He even summons a parallel reading scene in which future readers could compare 'the two languages' – Joyce's text and Basic English: 'In this way the simplest and the most complex language of man are placed side by side' (259). As this suggests, the translation for Ogden functions like the gramophone recording, as a simplification of complex ideas into accessible prosaic sounds. But Joyce's accelerated rhythmic delivery had the opposite effect on listeners like Stead. For Stead the mechanical reproduction of Joyce's voice fails to answer her search for something more in Joyce's language, for a connection that exceeds 'language and meaning' to return to Dolar's theory of the voice as object.[38]

Stead's account of her frustrations with listening to Joyce also exemplifies the specific relationship voice, in contrast to other acoustic phenomena, has with meaning, to further adapt Dolar. Unlike other sounds to which we ascribe meaning, the voice is intimately connected with the intention to mean or make sense of something. The voice functions as a conduit or medium for meaning without ever contributing to making meaning – 'it makes the utterance possible, but disappears in it, goes up in smoke in the meaning being produced' (15). In this sense, Stead listening to Joyce's voice in order to find a revelatory opening into his complex densely associative prose only intensifies the gulf between sound and sense that is intrinsic to the very nature of the voice itself as Dolar defines it: 'It is the material element recalcitrant to meaning, and if we speak in order to say something, then the voice is precisely that which cannot be said' (15). The voice is untranslatable, yet material, an uncanny presence that sounds an irrevocable and intransigent absence. Echoing Dolar's observations, William Martin, in the midst of his careful metrical and etymological analysis of the text of *Anna Livia* concedes that all of the 'graphic dimension of the text', its complex networks of puns and allusions, disappear when the 'text of the *Wake* is read aloud'.[39] For Martin, however, the performer can reconcile 'the latent conflict between sound and meaning' by reproducing Joyce's alliterative stresses on meaningful and recurring words (200). While this is true of Joyce's reading to some extent, Joyce's intentionally fast-paced delivery conspires against any easy reconciliation of sound and meaning.

If anything, the alternating rhythms of Joyce's voice reading *Anna Livia*, initially fast then gradually slowing, widens the gulf between sound and meaning and in so doing returns to Joyce's primary interest in the *Wake* liberating 'all sounds from their servile, contemptible role' and attaching 'them to feelers of expressions which grope for definitions of the undefined'.[40] Joyce sounds out individual vowels and consonants with relish, unmooring them from lexical sequences and heightening their affective resonances. The washerwomen's words signify as sound, summoning the ebb and flow of the river, the back and forth of their washing, the circular rhythms of their conversation. As with the alliterative b's that capture the intrusive affects of 'the beaming Batt, the bairboard bombardment screen' (341) in the inn where Humphrey Chimpden Earwicker faces his accusers, 'sound in and of itself' creates 'a potential opening for *significance*', in Barthes's sense of the latter as a phonic residue of the materiality of language, that has nothing to do with communication and everything to do with beauty and pleasure.[41] Joyce's apparent relish in letting his tongue roll over each consonant and vowel amplifies the auditory pleasure of the listener willing to surrender to hearing him sounding them out in turn. Yet it is precisely this carefully constructed lack of reconciliation of sound and meaning that disappoints Stead and, one imagines other like-minded readers whom Eliot and Ogden were speculating might buy into the idea of a globally networked audience for the recorded voices of renowned modernist authors that they hoped would generate a tidy profit. To return to Stead's letter in conclusion, her palpable frustration with the lack of a clear connection between Joyce's performed reading and reading Joyce also signals the gulf between how Stead heard Joyce and the archaeological acoustics that informs how we listen to Joyce's voice. While she may have heard other recorded voices (Stead had a significant collection of gramophone recordings), the experience was still a relatively novel one, which was one of the reasons why Ogden and Eliot were keen to capitalise on its appeal. The recording ensnares Stead in a confusion of contradictory impulses, to understand, but also to simply possess an authentic trace of a world renowned *littérateur* that somehow exceeds the deadening repetition of mechanical reproduction; an unresolvable, yet indicative, modern dilemma that her exile in Paris only intensified, so near and yet so far, as the cliché goes, from the hub of international modernism.

Notes

1. Christina Stead to Gwen Walker Smith, 25 July 1932, in *Selected Letters*, p. 51.
2. Beach, *Shakespeare and Company*, p. 177.
3. Stead, *Selected Letters*, p. 51.
4. Joyce describes his style in these terms in a letter to a friend cited in Ellmann, *James Joyce*, p. 564.
5. Jaffe, *Modernism and the Culture of Celebrity*, p. 63.

6. Ogden, 'James Joyce's Anna Livia Plurabelle', p. 259.
7. Derrida, 'Ulysses Gramophone', p. 30.
8. Dolar, *A Voice and Nothing More*, p. 4.
9. Beach, p. 176.
10. Curtin, 'Hearing Joyce Speak', p. 271.
11. Knowles, 'Death by Gramophone', p. 4. I owe this reference to Adrian Curtin.
12. Joyce, *Ulysses* (1961), p. 114.
13. Beach, p. 176.
14. Pound, 'Debabelization and Ogden', p. 411.
15. Jaffe, p. 65.
16. Although, as Jaffe notes, Pound's private correspondence with Ogden implies that he did not think Joyce had survived the test (213).
17. T. S. Eliot to Herbert Gorman, 14 October 1930, *Letters of T. S. Eliot*, vol. 5, p. 343.
18. T. S. Eliot to James Joyce, 29 October 1930, *Letters of T. S. Eliot*, vol. 5, p. 362. *Anna Livia Plurabelle* was published in pamphlet form in Eliot's *Criterion Miscellany* in 1930.
19. T. S. Eliot to James Joyce, 30 June 1931, *Letters of T. S. Eliot*, vol. 5, p. 602.
20. T. S. Eliot, introductory note, *Introducing James Joyce*, pp. 6–7.
21. T. S. Eliot, 'The Approach to James Joyce', pp. 446–7.
22. James Joyce to Sylvia Beach, 18 May 1931, *Joyce's Letters to Sylvia Beach*, p. 170.
23. Eleni Loukopoulou traces Joyce's connections with London literary and musical networks that included Imhof's shop in two related articles 'Upon Hearing James Joyce', pp. 118–27 and 'Joyce's Progress Through London', pp. 683–710.
24. Cited in Loukopoulou 'Joyce's Progress Through London', p. 693.
25. Ogden, 'Orthological Institute, International Orthophonic Archives', p. 111.
26. Loukopoulou, p. 693.
27. Ogden, 'The Orthological Institute', p. 95.
28. Gilbert, 'Homage to James Joyce', p. 247. Gilbert also contributed to a further piece in this issue – 'The Veritable James Joyce, according to Stuart Gilbert and Oliver St John Gogarty' (pp. 273–82), which had initially appeared in the Berlin journal 'International Forum'.
29. Jolas, 'Homage to James Joyce', p. 250.
30. Trotter, *Literature in the First Media Age*, p. 13.
31. Joyce, *Finnegans Wake* (2012), p. 349. All further quotes are from this edition.
32. Ogden, 'James Joyce's Anna Livia Plurabelle. In Basic English', p. 259.
33. Levin, *Joyce: A Critical Introduction*, p. 164.
34. Nash, *Joyce and the Act of Reception*, p. 126.
35. Martin, *Joyce and the Science of Rhythm*, pp. 194–5.
36. James Joyce to Harriet Weaver, 4 November 1927, cited in Nash, p. 127.
37. Ogden, 'James Joyce's Anna Livia Plurabelle', p. 259.
38. Dolar, p. 11.
39. Martin, p. 200.
40. Joyce cited in Petr Skrabanek, 'Night Joyce of a Thousand Tiers', p. 231.
41. Barthes, *A Lover's Discourse*, p. 279.

Chapter 6

Sounding Region, Writing Accent: A. G. Street and the BBC

Debra Rae Cohen

Midway through his brilliant cultural history of ventriloquism, Steven Connor quotes part of a poem by Thomas Hood, about the 'polyphonist' Mr Love, who, reputedly, could move like lightning between 'the voices of persons of all ages, grades and professions' while deriving his power and value (his cultural capital) from the 'very invisibility of the objects, entities, and actions' he invoked:[1]

> His Landlord of the Nag's Head is
> By scores admired most
> Indeed, in this he couldn't fail
> Who's in himself a HOST.
> Nine perfect voices he commands,
> And quickly changes each:
> He's quite a walking grammar –
> For he boasts nine parts of speech! (312)

Later, in the interwar period, that hyperbolically delineated role was occupied by the BBC, which equally drew on its ability to remake space with invisible vocalities, which equally controlled the power to voice all shades, ranges and regions – and yet, so often failed in a sense to be, like Mr Love, a good 'host'. Indeed, in its inclusion of regional and working-class accent (or even that of the landlord of the Nag's Head), whether ghettoised into variety performance, framed and offset by the 'official' BBC vocality of received pronunciation, or quite literally ventriloquised, performed by actors, the Corporation generally reproduced what Connor refers to as the 'ludicrousness of ventriloquism as spectacle' (313) – here, the spectacle of difference.

The positioning of regional broadcasting under the BBC Regional Scheme put into place beginning in 1929 was in this respect doubly vexed. Although the seven administrative regions were able to feature on their own regional wavelengths, and often across the regional network, local speakers, dialects and productions – serving as both alternative and corrective to the BBC monoculture – they were expected to contribute only twenty or so original hours a week, and to draw extensively on 'diagonalised' programming from the national service. Their budgets were allocated and programme planning overseen by London, which operated on the principle that 'no Region should embark on an activity which could be better done elsewhere' – especially in London.[2] At least up until the late 1930s, this meant that regions were often rebuffed from attempting serious talks, features or drama of other than regional import – limiting them, in other words, to those very areas considered 'typically' regional by the metropole. And in fact, 'typical' is a word one often finds in BBC internal memoranda from London to the regions, used as a term of approbation for high-quality productions.

It is worth noting in this connection that the initial BBC rationale for the Regional Scheme was to provide at least the illusion of choice, defined as 'contrast' – with the clear implication that the choice would always be between the serious and the not-so-serious, between 'items which demand concentrated listening and those which repay more casual listening'.[3] That cultural regionality per se was not the Corporation's initial goal, but rather economic and technological efficiencies, was implicit in the very design of the 'Regions', which lumped together divergent local cultures and dialects with imperial arbitrariness: the Northern region covered a full third of England; the Western region comprised both Wessex and Wales.[4] Not only was regional accent, therefore, still marked as secondary, in terms of both status and seriousness, but the regional directors were themselves forced to engage in a kind of ventriloquism in order to do justice to the varied local accents within their territory.[5]

In fact, throughout the 1930s, the Regional Scheme did little to disturb the perception of BBC monovocality. Early in the novel *South Riding*, published posthumously in 1936, the Yorkshire-born novelist Winifred Holtby describes the code-switching practices that more than a decade of broadcasting had helped bring about: 'like most of her generation and locality', she writes of a young working-class woman, 'Elsie was trilingual. She talked BBC English to her employer, Cinema American to her companions, and Yorkshire dialect to old milkmen'.[6] Note the lack of any reference in this formulation to Regionality, the implied opposition between the monovocal BBC and creeping Americanism (a perception shared by the BBC hierarchy), and the emphasis on separation between distinct 'languages'. An intermittent Talks broadcaster, a regular writer for the *Radio Times* and a dedicated listener-in, Holtby regularly explored the implications of broadcasting in her work – particularly

its potential for control, homogenisation and the stifling of local variation. Her 1929 satirical piece 'The Ruin of Mr Hilary' depicts a village
man tapped to do local sports commentary for the BBC who is driven
mad by his efforts to speak 'the BBC way' – a training Elsie's generation, by 1935, had absorbed from childhood on. In one of Holtby's last
pieces, commissioned by *Nash*'s magazine during the 1935 Ullswater
Committee hearings on the BBC's charter review, she slammed the
monopoly as both politically dangerous and 'intellectually enervating'.
Holtby urged that under the new charter, 'each regional division' should
be 'a completely independent public corporation'. 'Then', she continued, tongue-in-cheek, 'if Daventry is Tory, Anglican and Carnivorous,
Manchester may be Atheist, Communist, and Free Love, and Edinburgh
Vegetarian, Liberal, and Ethical. At least we should abolish monopoly,
achieve variety, and rob respectability of its sting.'[7]

Holtby's snarky recommendations acknowledge BBC language standards and the Regional Scheme as complementary mechanisms for the
suppression of diversity. Formal language standards were a feature of
the BBC almost from its inception: 'almost' because it was the proliferation of local practices between 1922 and 1925, whether defined
as personalisation, informality or accent, that the flurry of head office
regulation in the years before incorporation was designed to control and
standardise. The Advisory Committee on Spoken English – later to generate a series of pronunciation guides even more controversial in their
conception than their specifics – was established quite early, in 1926.
At first headed, at least on paper, by the elderly Poet Laureate Robert
Bridges – who, judging from the correspondence in the BBC Written
Archives Centre (much of it written by his wife), was often too unwell to
attend meetings, the committee was guided by its secretary, phonetician
Arthur Lloyd James, who became a close advisor to Director-General
John Reith. Though its initial charge was the recommendation to BBC
announcers of the 'proper' or 'preferred' way to pronounce words and
place names that presented difficulty, in fact even this limited mandate
could not help but be political: who 'owns' the pronunciation of a town
name, for instance, if even those who live there disagree?

Too, such phonetic 'advice' – without getting into current name-
calling over who should and should not be termed a 'prescriptivist'
– necessarily took on the character of official pronouncement when
promulgated and reproduced both by and beyond the BBC. Though
Lloyd James stressed in his book *The Broadcast Word* (itself adapted
from a series of broadcasts that were reproduced in the BBC's middle-
brow weekly, the *Listener*) 'a language is never in a state of fixation',
even his means of explicating this idea is tellingly disingenuous:

> Remember that a language is never in a state of fixation, but always changing; you are not looking at a lantern slide, but at a moving picture. And remember also that we are not all looking at the same portion of the film at the same time. The part that is on show, as it were, in London this week, may not reach Glasgow until 1984, and the part on show at Eton may never reach the Council schools of Bethnal Green. But wireless does give you all a chance of seeing, in some way, what is going on in other parts, and it is not surprising that if it does not fit in with your local show, as it were, you get angry and complain! But do not blame the BBC for it. No great harm will be done if we all see the same reel at the same time. But the BBC does not make the film – it only shows it.[8]

Thus while often claiming that he thought the nation attached too much social significance to local accent,[9] Lloyd James also served as the standard-bearer for a standardisation he saw as progressive, inevitable and inevitably based on the metropole, a standardisation that the BBC could make 'available' to listeners, especially children. This prescription only became more explicit over the course of the 1930s; despite the increasing mockery surrounding the 'etiolated' voice of the standard BBC announcer,[10] and the negative press that met each new edition of the pronunciation guide, Lloyd James continued to identify 'educated southern English' as that variety of the language 'thought to be most desirable for the general purposes of broadcasting'.[11]

Yet it was important to the BBC that its policy of standardisation, as obvious as it was, not be too overtly articulated. Within its own publications, then – especially during the introduction of the Regional Scheme – editorials naturalised the institutional valorisation of 'Southern English' as necessary 'to avoid confusion' and made claims for the Corporation's position as a 'friend to healthy diversity'.[12]

But the very means by which the Corporation made this case in its publications, especially the *Listener*, often undermined it, in part because of the fraught relations in the journal between the relative claims of ear and eye. As I've discussed elsewhere, the *Listener* was structurally in the paradoxical position of making extraordinary claims for the trans-formative power of radio, claims that were nevertheless required to be validated by print publication.[13] Its often confused response to accent and dialect partook of this difficulty. Discussing a May 1931 broadcast debate, 'Should Dialect Survive?', for instance, a *Listener* editorial came firmly down on both sides, arguing that 'dialect' – by which they apparently here mean accent – can be 'undeniably attractive' when manifested as 'a characteristic intonation', a 'burr or a brogue', but loathsome when it means 'pages disfigured by diaereses and full of uncouth words which can only be elucidated with a glossary' (758). Yet this does not simply register the preference for spoken over written 'dialect': the editorial backs up its defence of the 'characteristic intonation' with reference to the novels of Thomas Hardy and Mary Webb. It goes on to reassure the *reading* public that dialect will never challenge 'the normal form of English' exactly because of the primacy of print: 'though a word may be pronounced differently in Edinburgh and Exeter, the fact that both places spell it the same puts a limit to its possible deviations' (758). And the editorial, though it reproves all 'slovenly and inefficient speech', winds up condescendingly approving 'deviations from the normal' as benign so long as they do not 'hinder the fundamental unity of print or meaning', and akin to the pleasures of tourism: 'it is local variations in food and drink that give half the zest to a country holiday' (758). The inter-medial negotiation between radio and print, in other words, here reinforces the primacy of the metropolitan audience, while leaving vague the BBC's own role and methodology in arranging that 'country holiday'.

In fact, the ventriloquistic nature of the BBC's treatment of region was both reinforced and made more pointed by remediation into the *Listener*'s pages. Because only 'dialect' rather than mere 'accent' could be orthographically marked – since, no matter how anxious the Talks Department might have been to reproduce scripts 'as broadcast', rather than journalistically reshaped,[14] such reproduction would never take note of 'a burr or a brogue' – markers of regional aurality were always indicative of those 'extreme' pronunciations against which Lloyd James warned.[15] And because these markers were rarely presented as representing the 'accent' of the author him or herself, let alone the 'accent' of the publication, their divergence from the norm of received pronunciation was underscored.

Take for example the mid-1930s talks on the National Programme by Wiltshire farmer-author A. G. Street, whose successful 1932 memoir *Farmer's Glory* launched him into broadcasting at exactly the same time as Lloyd James was giving the talks that became *The Broadcast Word*. Street was a tough-minded critic of interwar farming policy and practices, having suffered the decline and near-bankruptcy of his family's large and formerly prosperous tenant farm in the late 1920s (indeed, he took up writing for extra income). Alun Howkins has detailed the paradoxical cultural shift after the First World War whereby the perceived 'decline' of agriculture and rural traditions itself became the spur to a new touristic and suburbanised 'ruralism';[16] Street's own career, founded as it was on the success of his elegiac memoir *Farmer's Glory*, sits athwart these trends, demonstrating, as Jed Esty observes of Orwell, the inter-implication of the romantic and realistic aspects of an inward turn in 1930s national culture composed of 'domestic romance, pastoral idealism, and Anglocentric preservation'.[17] While Street's columns for *Farmers Weekly*[18] often focused on issues such as the depredations wrought by the national overemphasis on wheat farming, and the lack of commitment to the land itself among those who saw the countryside as a 'free playground', he was well aware that his address to broader audiences relied on 'readily saleable rural charm', on an appeal to precisely those whose touristic nostalgia he decried.[19]

In his broadcasts Street often recurs to the appeal of yearly cycles, traditional practices and vanishing traditions, centrally those of speech:

> one effect of modern conditions which I regret is the passing of the old Wiltshire dialect. The speech of the older labourer is pure joy. They find the right word always, and never need to use a dictionary. I heard a man say one summer that his damson tree 'wur fair diggled wi' 'em'. Is there any other word in our language which describes that happy state of things quite so well?[20]

Street's broadcasts were larded with references to and choice quotations from 'the [generic, and often anonymous] Wiltshire labourer' to whom he looks, he says, as 'guide, philosopher and friend' (33).[21]

In both the scripts prepared for broadcast and in the pages of the *Listener* these quotations are rendered in written dialect, standing out from the smooth expanse of Street's standard English prose:

> The rickmaker requires different treatment. He is by way of being an artist, and has developed a temperament. He needs to be consulted. 'Jim', I said to him, 'I've got to be away to-day, and I oughtn't to go. What about it?'
> 'That's all right, zur', he said. We kin manage. Thee goo up Lunnon, and show they wun, and we'll show 'ee wun yer, when you gits back. You got no call fur to worrit'.
> His last remark is quite correct. I have no cause to worrit, for the agricultural labourer is a better man than a good many people imagine.[22]

> During our talk the old man delivered himself of one proverb of his own making. 'Tidn' no use bein' cunnin' unless you be cunnin' enough', and he proceeded to illustrate the truth of this with a story concerning a shepherd of bygone days, whom he called Wold Tommy.
> 'Wold Tommy wur lazy, an' zo 'ee 'ad to be cunnin' wie it, but 'ee werpen cunnin' enough, an' 'ee come to grief proper. An' as fer bein' a shepherd. Pah!' And the old man spat his disgust viciously.
> 'One time 'ee turned 'is maister's sheep into a bait 'o rape, an' went 'ome'. (Perhaps I should explain what he meant by 'a bait 'o rape'. A bait is the local term for the square piece of a root field which is hurdled off for each day's feeding.) 'Niver bid there to zee as they wur all right, an' niver went back atterwards. Went to pub, I 'low, lazy twoad. Next mornin' there wur zix ov 'em dead, blowed wie too much vittles.

'Wold Tommy, artvul zod, 'ee drawed 'em into the vurrers on thur backs, an' tells 'is maister, when 'ee come up to the vold, as 'ow they died droo gettin' on their backs in the vurrer . . .'[23]

In each of these cases Street's interaction with the dialect form – deliberately repeating within his 'own' speech the word 'worrit', stepping out of the anecdote in order to gloss 'a bait of rape',[24] leads to speculation about the original circumstances of broadcast, to the fact that that Street himself 'does' all the voices (as the surviving scripts of these Talks indicate), dropping in and out of a broad Wiltshire dialect that was never really his own.[25] Yet the orthography of the rendered speech in the *Listener* presents it as an authentic 'artifact', a nugget of regionality served up for appreciation. The justification of the Regional scheme as 'contrast' is reproduced as orthography; dialect is always both relational and other, its atypical 'typicality' literally marked by liberal use of apostrophes.

Given the resistance of *Listener* editor Richard Lambert to running broadcast talks from the regions themselves (something about which Regional Directors repeatedly complained throughout the 1930s), such typifying and nostalgic versions of dialect – a version of what Elizabeth Outka has termed the 'commodified authentic' – effectively displaced 'real' regional voice in the journal's pages; and indeed the *Listener* was generally far more likely (despite its national circulation) to feature broadcast pieces on regions from the National Programme, like Street's, that either deliberately underscored the 'country holiday' relationship or were framed in such a manner as to do so.[26] Perhaps even more troublingly, the journal's practice with regard to dialect tended to cement the association of accent and ruralism during a period of economic crisis for the industrial North; and indeed a 1932 editorial almost casually declares that 'not all dialects are beautiful, and if the progress of standard English does away with some of those which are best known in our big industrial towns, the world would not be the poorer'.[27] In 1931 the *Listener* began running a compendium of various Talks 'on gardening, farming, allotment culture and the countryside topics generally' remediated and grouped together under the rubric 'Out of Doors'; Street's 1932 talks ran under as part of this section.[28] Although the introduction to this section gave as the rationale for such a feature 'our present national needs for growing our own food and developing the resources of our land' – tying it explicitly to the depression – much of what actually ran was, again, 'country holiday' material, nature and travel writing that depicted the regions in terms of metropolitan leisure: 'Where to Fish Sea-Trout'.[29]

Yet it was within this series that the journal ran, as well, an anomalous piece called 'A Yorkshire Spade Club' – anomalous, because it is the one example of dialect I have identified in the journal during this period that purports to be spontaneous and unventriloquised, in the form of a first-person statement. It appeared on 27 January 1932, beneath another 'Out of Doors' item, this one an anecdotal nature piece on 'Foxes, Geese and Ducks' by the biologist and essayist E. L. Grant Watson. Watson's piece retains, in written form, many of the conversational indicators of the 'intimate' mode of address developed for the BBC by Talks Director Hilda Matheson;[30] it also, incidentally, includes one moment of remediated oral marking; the author describes asking a farmer if he has been able to trap a fox, and the farmer replies 'Oh, I got 'un alright. . . . I just stroked 'un with a stick.'[31] The casual use of regional accent here, with the apostrophe as its indicator, corresponds, as with Street, to a ventriloquistic moment in the broadcast talk; its inclusion works to lend Watson's own anecdotes the imprimatur of 'authenticity'. So much is standard. But the juxtaposition of this piece with 'A Yorkshire Spade Club' highlights the latter's unsettling inter-medial peculiarities.

Whereas Watson, like Street, serves as the custodian of the 'authentic' dialect and derives legitimacy from its inclusion, 'A Yorkshire Spade Club' is presented both anonymously and officially, with the only identifying information the editorial gloss: 'The personal experiences of one of the unemployed, given in his native dialect.'[32] But this gloss inevitably begs the question of just what, and how, is being 'given'. Why does this piece appear in 'dialect'? Clearly this is not the written output of the broadcast speaker himself, who would have no reason to mark his own 'authentic' speech in this manner. If this represents the actual scripted redaction of the words of the 'authentic' speaker – a process that was par for the course for most 'man-on-the-street' talk programmes – why would it be necessary to mark the Yorkshire accent for a speaker whose natural accent it was? If script, it casts doubt on the very authenticity of this anonymous speaker; if a post-broadcast 'translation', it only underscores the stakes involved in the official processes of ventriloquism. This single Yorkshire voice, serving as a synecdoche for a regionful of unemployed, must, in the *Listener*, retain its claim to authenticity through the written markers of dialect for the BBC to derive the benefit from 'giving' it. The 'personal experiences' of this anonymous representative, simply by their remediation, serve as a written claim of good faith, an indicator that the BBC is operating as a 'friend to healthy diversity' of both region and class.[33] And yet the circumstances of that remediation reproduce exactly the casual marginalisation the Corporation is trying to refute; the anonymised Yorkshireman is 'unemployed' but that status and his 'typical' Northerness are his sole identifiers. With his trade effaced, he is presented as pastless; he is ruralised both literally – in his 'personal experiences' of allotment work – and also structurally, through the placement of the piece within the journal. The un-beautiful dialect of the industrial worker blurs into that of Street's homely philosophers.

Indeed, the remediation in the *Listener* of Street's dialect set pieces subtly reconfigures and reconstitutes the relationship between him and the rural workers to whom he both literally and figuratively gives a voice. All of Street's 1930s work – novels, articles, broadcasts – appeals at its core to the rhetoric of rural stewardship, in which 'the practice of agriculture becomes an essential part of the cultural construction of England'.[34] Within this discourse he aligns himself, sometimes quite overtly, with the position of the worker who, like himself, a tenant farmer, does not 'own' the land so much as devote himself to it: 'I am not a free agent – I am a farmer, and therefore the servant of my farm. The land is the farmer's mistress and all else must take second place.'[35] Despite the language of landscape idyll into which Street often slips, he presents the labourer and the farmer as both, and in concert, coping and interacting with the onrush of an inevitable and in not all ways undesirable modernity:[36]

> Have you ever thought how wonderfully efficient the average farm labourer has become with all sorts of complicated machinery? That man with the slow ploughman's plod wandering between the exhibits is to the average towns-man just one more rather vacant looking yokel. But watch him. See him with his head and maybe his beard dangerously close to the moving bowels of the tractor. Listen to him asking pertinent questions of the smart salesman. Hear his criticisms or his approval of a new power-driver motor. 'I tell 'ee, guvner, that you do want to make thic part a deal stronger. 'Er do bust in a heavy cut of grass'. The salesman pooh-poohs this until he is brought up short by, 'Tidn' no manner o' use fer thee to talk, guvner. Tha's a good tool, thic mower. Gits awver the ground amazin', but I've cut aighty acres wi' one o' they this year, an' I've busted thic part dree times'. . . . It always pleases me to hear the Wessex dialect used in connection with modern machinery. 'Why dussent put this magneto where a feller kin get at un?' A very pertinent question that . . . But somehow I don't think that the inventor of the magneto or even the men who make them today have ever realized that the product of their ingenuity and craftsmanship is referred to as 'Thic magneto'. When you hear a man say, 'Thic magneto, zno', you are listening to the best type of Wessex farm hand in this year of grace 1934.[37]

Here Street serves as custodian and authenticator not of a linguistic survival, but of a new kind of linguistic fusion, 'Wessex as she is spoke',[38] a fusion that, on the air, of course, he performs vocally. Sonya Rose's analysis of Street's use of dialect in a 1942 broadcast thus both overestimates the extent to which he represents such dialect as part of an unchanging rural England, and misses the irony of its ventriloquistic presentation:

> His use of dialect reinforces the distinctiveness of rural people, emphasizing their imperviousness to change in their 'country' mode of speaking in spite of nearly seventy years of publication, and the influence of BBC English daily brought into many rural dwellers' homes on the wireless.[39]

In fact, where Holtby, like Rose, saw opposition between linguistic practices, or at least a discrete separation – trilingualism – Street recognises slippage and change, a change that is not always rendered as decay.[40]

The complexities of such linguistic positioning – and the nuances of 'speaking for' the labourer – were often rendered moot in the *Listener*'s pages. Street's broadcasts deploy three basic modes of framing dialect – as a chronicler of rural life (in which the farmer-speaker, in the course of quotidian events or reverie, encounters a dialect speaker), as mediator (in which the farmer-speaker oversees a dialogue between town and country speakers), and as auditor (in which the farmer-speaker 'yields' the microphone for the bulk of the broadcast to a ventriloquised dialect speaker) – and each of these modes of framing was affected by the journal's editorial decision-making and the processes of remediation. To begin with, the move into the *Listener* eliminated the double oral framing of these broadcast anecdotes. The absence of the authorising BBC announcer introducing the broadcast Talk removes in the *Listener* the distinction between Street's own Wiltshire inflections and the benchmark of received pronunciation; it establishes Street as the 'standard' English speaker indistinguishable in this regard from the surrounding articles and editorials, and thus emphasises the difference between dialect and 'norm'. Second, the *Listener*'s self-definition as journal rather than a '*Hansard* for Talks'[41] usually resulted in the blue-pencilling of the 'conversationally' rambling scripted introductions and final thoughts that Street would use to establish connection with his broadcast audience, what Paddy Scannell calls the occasion of 'sociability'.[42]

In general these alterations work to make dialect leap more obtrusively from the page, emphasising the journal's role in proffering it as artefact. Street's observations about 'thic magneto, zno' *as broadcast* made up only a small part of his journey to and observations of a county fair, mined by *Listener* editors for a quotable selection to include in a 'Microphone Miscellany', turning perambulatory chronicle into rural souvenir.[43] Similarly, *Listener* versions of those broadcasts in which Street represented himself primarily as auditor were often edited so as to eliminate all or part of the framing in which he establishes the condition of audition, thus making them function even more as dialect set pieces;[44] in almost all cases Lambert and his staff truncated the pieces to leave as the last line a pithy bit of orthographically marked dialect: 'I bain't a wold man eet. I be but seventy-dree, an' thee's know, I be vairish. I low I shall zee it come agen all right'; 'Most volk in trains do zit up mum, zno, as though if they did speak they'd be giving zummat precious away. But you've spoke I vair all the way along, an' you've telled I a lot. Good-day to 'ee.'[45] In each of these examples the truncation removes Street's encomium on the speaker from whom he has just parted – removing both the diagetic and the extradiagetic occasion of sociability. In the case of 'The Art of Conversation' it also – in the service of highlighting the difference of the speaker – allows to stand the irony of his statement that Street has 'telled [him] a lot', when he has in fact done all the talking. On the air, Street's movement into his own voice to tell his audience that 'the boot was decidedly on the other foot' would have instead both re-established his intimate connection with his audience, and mitigated to some extent the appropriative nature of his dialect turn.

The decision to truncate similarly pieces where Street serves as mediator – such as 'Thatching and Thatchers', in which he negotiates between a 'townsman' friend determined to purchase rural charm and a busy artisan – is perhaps even more key. Here the editorial decision to eliminate Street's own closing paragraph and end with the thatcher's judgement of the townsman ("Ee got a main bit to learn, but 'ee'll rest more contented like atter 'ee've bin in these parts a bit longer')[46] in fact enacts the same desire for the 'commodified authentic' that drives the townsman.

That Street restored his original scripts when they were collected as part of volumes like *Hedge-Trimmings* (1932), *Country Days* (1932) and *Thinking Aloud* (1934) does not simply attest to the author's vanity. In fact, Street was quite conscious of the particularised orality of the scripts he chose to reproduce, and apologised, in a preface to *Hedge-Trimmings* 'if the reader should find their conversational form a trifle irritating' (9); later, in *Wessex Wins*, he described in detail his training in how to write for broadcast, going so far as to 'translate' a paragraph of his own writing into conversational style (77). Over the course of the 1930s, in fact, his work shows an increased focus on the processes of mediation, processes that the *Listener* often, for its own purposes, effaced or removed. A comparison of versions shows how often the *Listener* removed Street's references to his own bilocation, to the ironies of 'mediating' rural life from inside a London broadcast booth.[47] Broadcasting on 'Haymaking' for example, Street opened with the admission that:

> Quite honestly, I ought not to be at Broadcasting House at all this evening, for we are making hay this afternoon, and if a farmer doesn't stay home for things like hay making and harvest, well, he ought to know better.[48]

A consciousness of his own position between cultures and his role in mediating accent came increasingly to mark Street's writings of the mid- and later 1930s. Accent becomes marked not just orthographically but narratively in his novels of the period, and serves as a key plot point in *A Crook in the Furrow*. In a peculiarly discomfiting scene early in the novel, the head of the group of fences, a Harley Street physician explains to the protagonist, Frank, why a farm will make the perfect cover for his criminal activities:

> The doctor chuckled.
> 'As American slang has it, my dear Frank, "You said it, big boy." In other words, to quote the scriptures in contrast, "Thy speech bewrayeth thee."'
> 'Why? I don't get it, sir?'
> 'You wouldn't, my son, but most people would. For instance, Peggy does.'
> Frank turned to his wife, who nodded assent.
> 'You see', triumphed the doctor. 'Peggy, ah, gets it, "it" in this instance being the faint flavour of Wessex dialect, of which neither a public school, your aunt, Leytonstone, nor the Great War could rob you. My dear boy, when you so charmingly address me as "Sir", a courtesy which I have always appreciated tremendously, you articulate the word as "Zur". The Wessex Z for S clings to you like a burr. A few years farming in Wilts and you will be substituting "thic" for "that", and saying "I 'low" as to the manner born.'[49]

The doctor's mustachio-twirling aside, his villainy is highlighted by his own switching between accents and languages – Wessex, American, biblical. The orthographic portrayal of S and Z add up to a performance of ventriloquism, the aping of Frank's own (unmarked) Wiltshire accent that presages his exploitation of the rural. It is difficult not to connect this scene to Street's own mediatory position, coming as the novel does directly before the publication of his second memoir, *Wessex Wins*, which picks up after *Farmer's Glory* ends, and covers Street's initiation into writing and broadcasting as well as his increasing sense of internal conflict. If *A Crook in the Furrow* is a conversion narrative in which stewardship triumphs, and 'Wiltshire straightens all crooks . . . Never to plough crooked again' (316), *Wessex Wins* is a Bunyanesque chronicle of self-division and self-criticism that traces a 'full circle from farming to town and back again', and comes round to the triumphant reaffirma-tion of the title.[50] In it, Street berates himself for his own temporary lapse from good stewardship, tempted by the 'insidious attraction' of his media work into the 'barren desert of town cleverness' (356). Given that Street went on to write and broadcast (including a stint on *The*

Brains Trust and at least one appearance on *Desert Island Discs*) until his death, his rededication to the rural verities and the 'precious metal of simplicity' (175) is perhaps less salient than how the preceding conflict is staged as linguistic self-division.

Kristin Bluemel has convincingly argued for *Farmer's Glory* as 'an ideal site of rural modernity', with Street himself its perfect 'spokesperson':[51]

> He is not only a man of the land, and thus received by readers and critics as authentically rural, but also a master of the forms and processes of modern metropolitan literary life and a Faber and Faber author earning commissioned wood engraved 'decorations' by the already famous Gwen Raverat; glowing reviews in major papers and on radio; and multiple reprints attesting to successful sales. (247)

Yet this characterisation reads back onto *Farmer's Glory* itself a sophistication that Street acquired only as a result of its success. *Wessex Wins*, though perhaps it protests too much, emphasises the haphazard and amateur journey of *Farmer's Glory* to print – its origin in response to the importunings of Edith Olivier, a local novelist; its composition in a set of old account books, its fortuitous arrival at Faber through Olivier's connections. The book seems designed in part to reclaim from the 'forms and processes of modern metropolitan literary life' a pre-literary language that, of course, cannot be its dominant narrative voice. The negotiation between region and metropole, which in Street's short pieces such as 'Thatch' often casts him as mediator between urban and rural sensibilities expressed as dialectical modes, is here effected as a mediation between his own 'oral' and written discourses. The framing of accent and dialect that his broadcasts perform here renders his earlier self the 'authentic' rural speaker, whose dialogue is staged in contradistinction to Edith Olivier and her ilk. Thus he orthographically marks his own dis-ease with literary language at the outset of his writing processes:

> 'No', I said aloud to my golden retriever, Trinket, who thumped her tail in agreement. 'Books ain't like milk. You can't measure 'em up in pints and quarts and gallons. Books ain't just a matter of quantity, it's quality that matters. Golly, at that rate mine'll be as blue as watered milk. Probably get prosecuted for offering such stuff for sale'.[52]

That it is Street's oral voicings at the BBC that most distinctly link him to the metropole in the narrative that ensues, a narrative rendered in an orthographically unmarked standard English, only serves to emphasise the sensitivity to mediation that by 1941 permeated his work.

Street's case points to a hitherto underexplored dimension of the 'inward turn' of the 1930s, and its popular genre of the rural novel. What Phyllis Bentley, writing in 1941, famously termed the 'regional renaissance' necessarily partook of the heightened consciousness of accent fomented by the BBC.[53] One can read the genre parody of *Cold Comfort Farm*, for instance, as engaging with the wireless ventrilo-quism of regional dialect as much as it does regional novels themselves. The written reproduction of 'dialect' for the national readership – the 'Boots Library public' Queenie Leavis sneered at in her 1936 takedown of 'Regional novels' in *Scrutiny*[54] – structurally remediates the tensions between region and metropole, highlighting and subtly undermining the doubly artificial positionings of aural dialect as both ventriloquistic token and 'authentic' corrective.

Notes

1. Connor, *Dumbstruck*, pp. 214, 296.
2. Quoted in Briggs, *The Golden Age of Wireless*, p. 329.
3. *BBC Handbook 1929*, p. 57.
4. For a useful overview of the Regional Scheme see Hajkowksi, *The BBC and National Identity in Britain*.
5. According to the personnel file of the broadcaster Wilfred Pickles at the BBC Written Archives Centre, one reason he was so desirable as a per-former and then a member of staff at Manchester was that he was 'fluent' in both Yorkshire and Lancashire dialects, as well as the relatively 'unmarked' standard English expected of announcers.
6. Holtby, *South Riding*, p. 8. It's hard not to read this as a deliberate updat-ing of Thomas Hardy's description of Tess Durbeyfield: 'Mrs Durbeyfield habitually spoke the dialect; her daughter, who had passed the Sixth Standard in the National School under a London-trained mistress, spoke two languages: the dialect at home, more or less; ordinary English abroad and to persons of quality', Hardy, *Tess of the D'Urbervilles*, p. 26.
7. Holtby and Tallents, 'Two Resounding Arguments', pp. 13, 14.
8. Lloyd James, 'Is There a Standard Pronunciation?', p. 867.
9. See for example Lloyd James, 'Speech Today and Tomorrow', p. 16.
10. Postgate, 'A Listener's Commentary', p. 284.
11. BBC WAC R13/283/1. Postgate, the first 'official Listener for the *Listener*' – far in advance of Grace Wyndham Goldie, often credited as the first radio critic (*Listener*, 15 June 1930, p. 119; Briggs, *Golden Age*, p. 291) – was quickly purged from its pages after his socialist sympathies became too evident, and became one of the BBC's toughest critics of the 1930s. See especially his *What to Do with the BBC*.
12. 'Should Dialect Survive?', p. 758.
13. Cohen, 'Intermediality and the Problem of the *Listener*'.
14. The ongoing conflict on this score between the demands of Hilda Matheson and her successors as head of Talks on the one hand and Richard Lambert and his successors as editor on the other helped shape the *Listener* and determine its often paradoxical intermedial form. See Cohen, esp. pp. 575–8.

15. Lloyd James, 'Extremes of Pronunciation', *Listener* (22 June 1932), p. 901.
16. See Howkins, *The Death of Rural England*, esp. Ch. 6; Howkins observes of *Farmer's Glory* that 'the personal and emotional tone of Street's work obscured his often rather hard-nosed analysis to produce a popular and generalised sense of agricultural decay' (Howkins, 'Death and Rebirth?', pp. 11–12).
17. Esty, *A Shrinking Island*, p. 43.
18. Street wrote a weekly column for *Farmers Weekly* (founded 1934) until his death in 1966. See the tribute to him posted to commemorate the journal's 75th anniversary: http://www.fwi.co.uk/farm-life/fw-75-the-enduring-appeal-of-ag-street.htm (last accessed 26 September 2016).
19. Street, 'The Countryman's View', p. 125; *Wessex Wins*, p. 25. In reference to his broadcasts, Street writes: 'I think the task set for me in these talks is to try to tell some of these stories [of rural life] in such a form that the listener, especially the town listener, may obtain from them little pictures of the countryside, in which perhaps he spent his childhood, or at any rate some of his more pleasant holidays'. Street, 'With April's Permission', *Country Days*, p. 18.
20. Street, 'Old Hands', p. 33.
21. Street dedicated his 1936 novel *The Gentleman of the Party* to 'The Agricultural Labourer, The Salt of England's Earth'.
22. Street, 'Haymaking', p. 912.
23. Street, 'A Well-Spent Evening', p. 869.
24. This interpolation is indicated as a handwritten edit on Street's script at the BBC Written Archives Centre; notably, he removed the explanation when he published this piece in the volume *Country Days*, where it is titled 'A Gentleman of the Old School' (pp. 107–18).
25. Street did have a distinctive Wiltshire inflection; he describes in *Wessex Wins* being coached at his first rehearsal by Talks producer Margery Wace to '"let me hear the final syllable". That was trying a Wiltshireman rather highly, for the Wessex habit is to swallow the final syllable whenever possible. I can remember being teased at school because of my inability to articulate the word "Latin". I always referred to that hated subject as "Lat'n"', p. 74.
26. 'Should Dialect Survive?', p. 758.
27. 'Week by Week', p. 657.
28. See also Weiner, *English Culture and the Decline of the Industrial Spirit*, p. 74 for the BBC's 'rural vogue'.
29. Castle, 'Where to Fish Sea-Trout', *Listener* (29 June 1932), pp. 949–50.
30. Matheson, *Broadcasting* (London: Thornton Butterworth, 1933). p. 163.
31. Watson, 'Foxes, Geese and Ducks', p. 144.
32. 'A Yorkshire Spade Club', p. 144.
33. 'Should Dialect Survive?', p. 758.
34. Howkins, 'Land', p. 189. Indeed, one can see this doctrine as the implied 'plot' of all his novels of the period – *Strawberry Roan* (1932) follows a cow from farm to farm to delineate community, and illustrate varied forms of rural stewardship/ownership; *The Endless Furrow* (1934) tells the tale of a young man who desires nothing more than to be a farmer, becomes one, and endures, 'a white-haired servant of England's land' (p. 373), at the end, despite the death of his son; *The Gentleman of the Party* (1936) retells

Farmer's Glory's chronicle of agricultural change largely from the point of view of a worker 'keep[ing] faith with the good earth' (p. 356); *Already Walks To-Morrow* (1938) projects a near future in which a clear-eyed farmer rescues a starving England by setting the nation straight on farm policy and proper stewardship; and, perhaps most bizarrely, *A Crook in the Furrow* (1940), which Street referred to as his 'detective story' (*Wessex Wins*, p. 349), follows the arc towards proper stewardship of a pair of fences and money launderers whose 'cover' as farmers becomes felt reality.

35. Street, 'Weather or No', in *Country Days*, p. 33.
36. See for instance the distinction in his novel *The Gentleman of the Party* between ill-informed and what one might call 'stewardly' use of new farming technologies: on inspecting a new system of milk machinery, an old farmer tells his wife, "Tis right, thic job . . . That feller's makin' money, he'm producin' milk cheaper'n I be, an he'm improvin' his land tremendous. I do hate everythin' about his job. Do mean less labour an' all that. But 'tis right. God! I wish I were a younger man. I'd show they folk at Sutton the right way to use machinery on a farm. Use it to improve land, not to ruin it' (p. 314).
37. Street, 'Machinery and the Farm-hand', p. 201. Note that here the prolific Street is, as often, recycling earlier material – perhaps an example of the 'mass production' he decries in *Wessex Wins* (p. 175); in *Farmer's Glory* he mentions that one might find 'on any farm two or three weather-beaten peasants, to a townsman's eyes just dull, vacant, or suspicious locals, who were rarely at a loss in running a machine as complicated as even a binder or thresher' (p. 68). Kristin Bluemel terms this passage 'inverse pastoral' in 'Rural Modernity and the Wood Engraving Revival', p. 243, and identifies it as an exemplary site of Street's 'rural modernity'.
38. Street, *Wessex Wins*, p. 349.
39. Rose, *Which People's War?*, p. 202. Rose is of course talking about a wartime broadcast, in which the less nuanced image of an unchanging rural England so central to WWI propaganda (see Howkins, 'Discovery', pp. 79–82) was mobilised once again. But although the dialect politics of the BBC were signally reshaped in wartime, with regional programming put on hiatus and the national wavelengths gesturing to more accent inclusion – including the rise of J. B. Priestley, and a brief controversial stint by Wilfred Pickles reading the national news – as a mechanism for building morale, such moves in fact undermined the simple oppositionality Rose reads here. See Nicholas, *The Echo of War*, pp. 239–40.
40. Street described the 'Wessex dialect' of 1940 as 'a mixture of old Wessex, BBC, elementary school, American film, and internal combustion engine' (*Wessex Wins*, p. 349).
41. This phrase occurs often in early memoranda debating the journal's mission.
42. Scannell, *Radio, Television, and Modern Life*, p. 24.
43. See 'Farming on Show', in *Thinking Aloud*, pp. 160–73, for the full version.
44. The full version of 'The Art of Conversation' in *Country Days* (pp. 93–105) does function sufficiently as a dialect set piece to be included in a 1986 regional dialect compendium. See Wakelin, *The Southwest of England*, pp. 185–7 for the phonological annotation of an extended passage.

45. Street, 'A Well-Spent Evening', p. 870; 'The Art of Conversation', p. 832.
46. Street, 'Thatching and Thatchers', *Listener* (10 May 1933), p. 754; reprinted as 'Thatch' in Street, *Country Days*, pp. 67–80.
47. Street stresses in *Wessex Wins* the physical incongruities of his constant transitions, as does his daughter Pamela in her memoir: 'He still got up early and helped with the morning's milking, but at least once a week and sometimes more often, he would hurry home, have breakfast and change, and catch the London train', Pamela Street, *My Father, A. G. Street*, pp. 27–8).
48. Street, 'Haymaking', and *Hedge-Trimmings*, p. 59.
49. Street, *A Crook in the Furrow*, p. 25.
50. Street, *Wessex Wins*, p. 356.
51. Bluemel, p. 243.
52. Street, *Wessex Wins*, p. 37.
53. Bentley, *The English Regional Novel*, p. 13.
54. Leavis, 'Regional Novels', p. 440.

Chapter 7

Partial to Opera: Sounding Willa Cather's Empty Rooms

John Plotz

Overtones

In her 1922 aesthetic manifesto, 'The Novel Démeublé', Cather argues that meaning inheres not in what's put on the page, but what's left out. The novel works by under-specification and by omission.[1]

> Whatever is felt upon the page without being specifically named there – that, one might say, is created. It is the inexplicable presence of the thing not named, of the overtone divined by the ear but not heard by it. How wonderful it would be if we could throw all the furniture out the window; and along with it, all the meaningless reiterations concerning physical sensations, all the tiresome old patters, and leave the room as bare as the stage of a Greek theatre, or as that house into which the glory of the Pentecost descended; leave the scene bare for the play of emotions great and little.[2]

Fiction's spaces, though architectural, are meant to be filled by voices from elsewhere.[3] The novel, for Cather, is a physical substrate on which individual readers can hang, must hang, a wide set of memories, dreams or speculations. In her remarkable not-quite-*kunstlerroman*, *The Song of the Lark* (1915), Willa Cather begins developing an account of the novel's capacity for such empty occupation. She does so by way of an implicit claim that fiction is both a supplement and a superior successor to the experience of listening to music.[4]

In one sense, Cather's early novels are a significant site to explore the ways in which the complex modernist textual experiments of the 1910s are shaped by live opera's afterglow – a European cultural telos Cather both reveres and distrusts. However, the present volume's investigation of the materiality of sound (the column of air in a singer's throat, or in the wiggling passage of a needle along a record's grooves) prompts new attention to the word overtones, and to the implications of Cather's subtle, complex assimilation of some of music's aesthetic powers (overtones as a kind of absent presence), as well as her equally subtle differentiation of her prose from other of music's attributes (the novel's capacity to allow readers to divine meaning distinct from the overt denotative content of words on a page). As scholars begin chronicling the 'history of the *possibility* of sound reproduction' it becomes possible to discern *The Song of the Lark*'s awareness of a new sonic universe in which both live and recorded sound reshapes expectations for aesthetic totality, so that music, whether viva voce or 'in hair lines on metal disks' serves both as type and antitype of the novel's own formal aspirations.[5] Both borrowing from and rejecting the power of live or recorded music to generate experiences of absorption, this novel (often overlooked in a genealogy that moves smoothly from the prairie locodescription of *O Pioneers!* (1913) to the high modernism of *The Professor's House* (1925)) marks a crucial stage in Cather's thinking about fiction's capacity to generate among its readers the experience of semi-detachment.

The Song of the Lark describes what we might call music's overtone-generating power: its capacity to spark in individual characters a variegated set of experiences that are prompted and directed but not specified by the music they are hearing. For example, Thea goes on a picnic early in the novel with the first musician she has ever known, Johnny Tellamantez. When he sings, every listener is affected by the music in a different way:

> Johnny, stretched gracefully on the sand, passed from 'Ultimo Amor' to 'Fluvia de Oro' and then to 'Noches de Algeria,' playing languidly.
>
> Every one was busy with his own thoughts. Mrs Tellamantez was thinking of the square in the little town in which she was born ... Thea, stirred by tales of adventure, of the Grand Canyon and Death Valley, was recalling a great adventure of her own. Early in the summer her father had been invited to conduct a reunion of old frontiersmen, up in Wyoming, near Laramie, and he took Thea along with him to play the organ and sing patriotic songs. There they stayed at the house of an old ranchman who told them about a ridge up in the hills called Laramie Plain, where the wagon-trails of the Forty-Niners and the Mormons were still visible ... the top of the ridge when they reached it, was a great flat plain, strewn with white boulders, with the wind howling over it. There was not one trail as Thea had expected; there were a score; deep furrows, cut in the earth by the heavy wagon wheels, and now grown over with dry, whitish grass ... As Thea ran about among the white stones, her skirts blowing this way and that, the wind brought to her eyes tears that might have come anyway ... For long after, when she was moved by a Fourth-of-July oration, or a band, or a circus parade, she was apt to remember that windy ridge.[6]

The dream is originally about the Wyoming plains, but soon, via the tales of 'an old ranchman', it centres on the people who went there before her, their wagon marks making 'a score' (with its implicit reference to writing or to musical scoring) of furrows.

Johnny's playing topples Thea backward into memories (her own or someone else's) and the crux for Cather is the pleasure of just such juxtaposition: to be moved by a band or a parade is to be moved back towards memories. Memories others can discern only because they too have different memories or recalled feelings of their own: 'Every one was busy with his own thoughts.' What Cather makes available for readers is something that belongs, like that incommunicable past, to an aesthetic realm accessible to each of us. Sociable solitude. The novel's paradoxical strength offers the reader access to what is putatively the most isolated aspect of individual experiences. Not the song itself, but the poignant glimpses of an individual past such songs bring.

Cather, semi-detached

This chapter's account of Cather's relationship to sounding modernism arises from a project attempting to make historical sense of the sort of doubled experience that Cather represents occurring to her characters (under the influence of music, for example) and understands her own prose as producing among her readers. When you half lose yourself in a work of art, what happens to the half left behind? The critical vocabulary to describe that sensation is lacking, but it is a familiar feeling nonetheless. When most carried away, audiences even of compelling artworks remain somewhat aware of their actual situation. Ideas about this kind of semi-detachment play a crucial and generally unrecognised role in shaping a wide range of nineteenth- and twentieth-century fiction. In such works, the crux of an aesthetic experience is imagined, or depicted, or understood as residing neither in complete absorption in an artwork nor in critical detachment from it, but in the odd fact of both states existing simultaneously.

Think of the narrator who in the opening chapter of George Eliot's *The Mill on the Floss* (1860) muses to himself that his arms have grown cold resting on the stone bridge near the Mill – only to realise that they have instead grown cold resting on a chair-arm back in the study where he is actually sitting. Or an occasion at the end of Henry James's *The Ambassadors* (1903) in which a minor character, Marie Gostrey, proposes to Ralph Strether, the novel's focaliser. The second he understands her offer he gets mentally busy thinking about how he will refuse her, and how she will understand his refusal – so busy he fails to notice that she's continuing to talk to him. James wryly brings this cognitive glitch to the reader's attention: 'That indeed might be, but meanwhile she was going on.'[7] The sense of ongoingness a novel can provide is an acme of the late realist novel's art: a seismograph of the divergence between experience and event. Fiction has the capacity to put on view the discrepancy between one's actual position and one's conceptual location – where one's mind is when it wanders.

In recent years, the concept of virtuality has emerged as one important way to think about the interplay between actual and the represented real as made manifest in mimetic artworks.[8] The concept of semi-detachment, though, offers an approach instead to what we might call artisanal questions: it asks what it means for writers (and other artists) to take note of and reflect on the partial nature of such experiences of aesthetic dislocation, as practical problems related to getting their work done. The concept of semi-detachment helps shed light on how writers understood what it meant for readers to experience the world of a book as if it were real, while nonetheless remaining aware of the distance between such invention and one's tangible physical surroundings. It is true that a wide variety of intellectual disciplines have taken up the question of unexpected sorts of cultural or cognitive recombination that take place in a way that fails to fit neatly into a pre-established order of knowledge. The English psychoanalytical theorist Donald Winnicott sketched out a 'third area', a realm of play neither precisely part of the everyday world nor entirely removed from it; Johan Huizinga's *Homo Ludens* anatomises the realm of 'serious play' in which ludic rule-following rehearses the right life; Victor Turner's notion of threshold or 'liminal' moments of cultural transition; Roland Barthes's suggestive category of 'the neutral' also points towards similarly suspended zones.[9] What moments like that reverie-plunge in *The Song of the Lark* suggest, however, is that the social sciences could stand to look sideways to the arts in making sense of 'third areas'.

Over the decades, indeed over the centuries, ideas about semi-detachment have been emerging, developing, waning and waxing in the practice of those who rely on the concept most: novelists, painters, designers and film-makers. Throughout their working lives, these artists were pressed by the constraints and possibilities of their respective media to explore the curious state of aesthetically induced semi-detachment, in ways that are not accounted for in sociological, philosophical and anthropological approaches to the space between absorption and distraction. My interest in Cather – early indebted to, yet later repudiating James's mode of late realism – arises from the sense that the provocative notion of the *novel démeublé* explores just such states of semi-detachment. Accordingly my focus on *The Song of the Lark* is motivated by her explicit attempt in that novel to sketch out a manifesto for fiction that both depends upon and repudiates the cultural cynosure of classical music.

Let people love and hate each other to death

The Song of the Lark looks like a classic *kunstlerroman* with cosmopolitan ambitions: how can it belong to a tradition of semi-detachment? How can a novel about a young American who makes her way slowly east from Colorado to Chicago, then New York, with Bayreuth visible just offstage, be anything but a passport out of the Nebraska that *My Antonia* calls 'nothing but land: not a country at all, but the material out of which countries are made'?[10] Cather's provincial background (*humiliating* provincial background, her peers might have silently added) links her to Ernest Hemingway (born 1899 in Oak Park, Illinois), to T. S. Eliot (1888, St. Louis), to F. Scott Fitzgerald (1896, St. Paul). You can sense the claustrophobia that dogs the small towns of their (broadly defined) Middle West by looking at Edgar Lee Masters's 1915 *Spoon River Anthology* (Masters was born in 1868 in Garnett, Kansas), Sherwood Anderson's 1919 *Winesburg, Ohio* (1879, Camden, Ohio) and Sinclair Lewis's 1920 *Main Street* (1885, Sauk Centre, Minnesota). Despair and confinement are the dominant notes in childhood according to Masters, Anderson and Lewis – mixed with odd, often inexplicable gleams of hope.

In her fiction, though, Cather avoids pegging herself either as an émigré from the Midwest (like Fitzgerald, Hemingway and Eliot) or as a regionalist devoted to chronicling its mores (like Anderson, Masters and Lewis – or like Jewett, who may have been Cather's inspiration but was not exactly her model). That is true even though as a child Cather was perhaps the most tied down of them all. Born in Virginia in 1873, Cather moved out to Red Cloud, Nebraska with her (Episcopal, half-Confederate half-Unionist) family at the age of nine. Her letters paint a remarkable picture of a writer struggling, like Thea in *The Song of the Lark*, to 'make herself born'.[11] Snapshots: Willa successfully begging her mother for a tiny little room of her own; going on call with the town doctors; working in a drugstore as a teenager and taking her pay in George Eliot novels and cheap translations of Tolstoy; hanging around, but learning no music from, an old German music-teacher who drifted in from somewhere; wandering the prairies: 'the grass was the country, as the water is the sea ... there was so much motion in it; the whole country seemed, somehow, to be running'.[12]

The chance to go off to Lincoln for college was Cather's lifeline. Her early published work is plucky, brash and absolutely infatuated with theatre and opera. Her music and theatre reviews praise 'old gods' (Wagner especially) because such geniuses 'create knights and ladies' and are the opposite of 'the moderate and proper and conventional'. Cather praises 'the Wagnerian flashes and tempest of Carlyle' and complains that 'the parlour people have a right to run their parlour world the way they want to, but let them leave the stage world alone'. 'Knights and ladies' should 'love and hate each other to death' on a Wagnerian stage somehow bigger and brighter than the ignoble world that surrounds it.[13] She was successful enough as a student journalist that by the time of her graduation from the University of Nebraska in 1894, she was more or less single-handedly producing a college paper *The Hesperian* – as well as bringing in a dollar a column in the *Nebraska State Journal*.

After a slack year back home in tiny Red Cloud, Cather was delighted to find herself writing for such Pittsburgh papers as *The Home Monthly*, the *Leader* and the *Library* while also keeping up a steady stream of reports back to the *Nebraska State Journal* and the *Lincoln Courier*.[14] In an America where even the tiniest Western towns had bouts of opera-madness, it is unsurprising Cather could place her pieces both in Pennsylvania and back home. Live music made by church choirs and local musicians was popular enough, but the arrival of professionals from the East made for red-letter days. When a visiting opera company performed *Camille* in Bozeman's People's Theatre, it was paid with a 'gold brick valued at $711'.[15] The traces of that world are only faintly visible now: in Central City, Colorado you can still see the now-shuttered Opera House which opened to arias from *Lohengrin* in 1877; but none of the fifty opera houses listed in an 1889 Wisconsin directory remain.

Cather's idea of her own vocation was formed principally by her sense of performers – singers especially. That quasi-identification took different forms. Early in her career, the worship of art sometimes seemed to be the quest for an unsullied realm. In 'A Wagner Matinee' (1904), a young man struggles to describe the transformation he sees coming over his aunt's face when she listens to Wagner after long years trapped on the prairie:

> From the trembling of her face I could well believe that before the last number she had been carried out where the myriad graves are, into the gray, nameless burying grounds of the sea; or into some world of death vaster yet, where, from the beginning of the world, hope has lain down with hope and dream with dream and, renouncing, slept.[16]

Like James Joyce (the memorable final sentences of his story 'The Dead', published a decade later, bear a striking similarity to this passage) Cather is struggling to find a style that approaches music – to write prose as if it were a tone poem. Art is impersonal, deadly and irresistible. Hence the aunt's reluctance to return to the prairie life sketched grimly in the story's final line: 'naked as a tower, the crook-backed ash seedlings where the dishcloths hung to dry; the gaunt, molting turkeys picking up refuse about the kitchen door' (110).

However, Cather is tricky. Such naked revulsion for the material facts of life is rare in her work, even in those early days when the allure of art ran strong in her. True, she glows as she describes the power of music (the 'two cardinal needs of humanity' are 'religious chant and love song') and registers childish awe observing the lives of its performers ('there were two people who lived all their life in a theater. The world outside was only a sort of big hotel to them.')[17] Yet that admiration is always keen-eyed; she fixates in those early pieces on the way that a great singer could step onstage and instantly switch off her vanity and coquetry, turning into 'the artist, controlled, carried beyond herself' (51). Cather is struck by the way that great feeling is always channelled through a poor ordinary mortal who also has to eat, to sit, to move between engagements. Cather wants readers to know how hard this work is. Making your artistic 'irregularities . . . [into a] regular mode of life' is not accomplished simply by running away from mundane duties: at age twenty-two she is already remarking with asperity that 'Bohemia is preeminently the kingdom of failure.'[18]

Cather's artistic breakthrough has been linked to her life-changing friendship with the gifted regionalist writer Sarah Orne Jewett, but early critics were also quick to associate her success with a modest retreat to her home region. In *O Pioneers!* Cather ditched the Henry James worship that had sunk her wispy first novel, *Alexander's Bridge* (1912). With a decade of Pittsburgh reviewing under her belt, however, the cosmopolitan musical world too formed a vital part of what Cather knew. Cather loved, and loved to write about, music and theatre. And the place where those two things came together, in a late-nineteenth century dominated by Wagner and his grand synthetic vision of the apotheosis of *music drama* was unmistakably opera.

Whether in Pittsburgh or New York (where she moved for good just as she was writing *The Song of the Lark*) Cather was a fantastically loyal operagoer. She attended more or less weekly, first with her companion of seventeen years, Isabelle McClung, and then (especially after McClung's marriage in 1916) with Edith Lewis, who was Cather's partner until her death in 1947. Her fascinating triple interview/profile ('Three American

Singers') with the three reigning American divas – Louise Homer, Geraldine Farrar and the Wagnerian soprano Olive Fremstad, a Swedish immigrant who grew up in Minnesota – appeared in *McClure's* in 1913, but Cather had more yet to say about opera. In *The Song of the Lark* by tracing a singer's coming of age alongside her own (Thea Kronborg's tale fuses details from Fremstad's and her own life), Cather is in part asking what connects and what separates the art forms.[19]

Cognitive experts who analyse the power of music nowadays begin by dwelling on the solitary listening experience.[20] Nicholas Cook hears in Beethoven's music an injunction to each listener to attend passionately – and in utter solitude: 'the listeners may be physically in a single room, but each of them is wrapped up in a different, private world. Music has taken them out of the public world of people and things.'[21] The crux of classical music's absorptive power, in Cather's day, was that it gave listeners a way to have, en masse, a sublime experience that went on at once inside one's mind and out in the world of shared sound waves. Rapturous youth (Paul of her story 'Paul's Case', for example) would not have been 'wrapped up in a different, private world' but in the first circle at the opera, head moving along with a thousand others in ecstatic response to the harmony of the orchestra, or the delicate phrasing of an aria. Opera's aficionados found in their art form the deepest well, a repository for dreams as strong in its way as the medieval church. If poetry was spilt religion, opera might have seemed to some old sacred wine carefully decanted into new bottles.

Walter Pater's 1877 maxim about art aspiring to the condition of music took hold as it did because it pointed toward the perfect formal accomplishments of music, its mathematical sublimity, the way that it could wrap the listener inside its folds so deeply that the question *where am I?* would not even occur. Free of voices and of any kind of overt representation, such absolute music refers to nothing beyond itself. (To German Romantic Jean-Paul Richter is attributed one memorable formulation for the idea: 'music is the echo from a transcendent harmonious world; it is the sigh of the angel within us'.) From the 1850s on – as Wagner fever swept through both Europe and America, and as Wagner himself proclaimed that wordless music could never be music's ideal – musical utopia came to be represented by the Wagnerian ideal of the *gesamtkunstwerk*, a compellingly composite art form that, by fusing musical intensity with theatrical enchantment, could cast over audiences a temporary but impregnable spell.[22]

Yet classical music, even opera, meant more than highbrow uplift in Cather's America. As the Great War era began, the one thing audiences seemed to want out of opera was two-minute arias they could play on a home gramophone. Geraldine Farrar's admirers ('Gerry-flappers') notwithstanding, Lisa Gitelman makes the point that popular formats such as 'two-minute opera records had about as much to do with actual operas as the Vitagraph Company's fifteen-minute films had to do with actual plays by Shakespeare'.[23] 'By 1910 recorded sound had become the first nonprint mass medium' and one of the key things buyers were looking for was 'the opera at home' – complete with that familiar Victor dog.[24] Focusing on an aspiring classical singer for her third novel has less to do with putting Cather on the road to Bayreuth than locating her squarely in the popular mainstream.

In a 1915 letter to her editor that accompanied the manuscript, Cather told him that the '"My country, 'tis of thee" feeling that it always gives me' proved to her 'how much of the West this story has in it'.[25] That the song she quotes belongs to Fourth of July celebrations, not the concert hall, is telling. Not visible on the page but palpable behind it (an overtone) is still that Western 'score [of] deep furrows, cut in the earth by the heavy wagon wheels'.[26] Cather picks up on classical music's immanent doubleness – its availability as both a marker of European culture and as an ingredient of a distinctively American provincial yearning. Thus *The Song of the Lark* itself accumulates overtones: it is not so much the story of what it's like to make it big in Germany (never depicted in the novel) as it is the story of what Germany, larger than life, twice as beautiful, imperfectly grasped, means in the ears and minds of those who dream about it from afar.

Hair lines on metal disks

Comparing Cather's account of opera's appeal to that in a comparable Naturalist novel helps reveal what is distinctive about her partial attachment to the aesthetic power she understands to be lodged in music. Frank Norris's 1903 *The Pit*, like *Song of the Lark*, is an opera-preoccupied novel set in Chicago. It actually begins with its heroine waiting outside an opera house, eager to lose herself in opera's grand amnesiac experience: 'Laura shut her eyes. Never had she felt so soothed, so cradled and lulled and languid. Ah, to love like that! To love and be loved. There was no such love as that today.'[27] However, a revealing interruption occurs almost immediately. 'But a discordant element developed . . . she heard, in a hoarse masculine whisper, the words: "The shortage is a million bushels at the very least. Two hundred carloads were to arrive from Milwaukee last night"' (23). As Norris sees it, Laura's despair at being yanked out of her reverie misses the point. Commodity trading is real drama; opera only fake. Its melodrama only comes to real throbbing life in Chicago's other Pit – that is, the Commodity Exchange.

In *The Song of the Lark*, by contrast, opera itself turns into a material realm: singers debate what remedies and what sleep schedule will keep their voices in shape for thousand-dollar performances, and the aspiration to enter into a realm of Wagnerian sublime goes hand-in-glove with cold-blooded calculations about hotel costs and fights over laundry. In Norris there is an unavoidable choice between dream worlds and commodities; in Cather, the overlay persists, so that the artistic realm is both removed from and unavoidably interwoven with mundane materiality.[28] Thea's triumphs are celebrated but their price in other realms is always noted. She decides that she can't come home when her mother is dying, because her career hinges on staying in Germany: 'It was not that she chose to stay; she had to stay, – or lose everything.'[29] Singing both belongs to an evanescent realm and is the product of trained throats straining to wrest the right notes from a trembling column of air.

In Norris's naturalism, opera is mere cultural efflorescence, a balloon easily punctured by the hard cold commercial facts. In Cather, though, the capacity to see symbolic relationships by way of fiction runs right up and down the social spectrum, rather than occupying the ethereal zone occupied by opera. In fact, when Thea enters fully into a triumphant operatic career in *The Song of the Lark*, the novel draws to a close. In Cather's work, the most highly charged symbols emerge from, and return to, the ordinary earth. Even the memorable plough from *My Antonia*, the one that seems 'heroic in size, a picture writing on the sun' has, just after sunset, 'sunk back to its own littleness somewhere on the prairie'.[30] Tom Outland in *The Professor's House* not only simply sees images of the cliff-dweller's mesa when he is reading *The Aeneid*, it lodges itself into his consciousness so comprehensively that 'by closing my eyes I could see it against the dark, like a magic-lantern slide'.[31] Mystery and banality are comprehensively mixed in Cather as she strives to articulate the complex relationship between what is materially present and the experiential dislocation that presence can induce.

It makes sense, then, that *The Song of the Lark* ends with an extended simile that involves neither decomposition nor paradoxical incommunicability. *The Song of the Lark*'s Epilogue focuses not on Thea herself, but on her old aunt Tillie Kronborg, who drifts in a semi-detached way through the little town of Moonstone, sustained in her habitual daydreaming by a gramophone record she has received of Thea singing: 'evidence in hair lines on metal disks'.[32] What can such recordings do for (and to) distant provincial audiences? In one sense quite a lot: Tillie can keep 'bursting out with shrill snatches of song' because newspaper accounts of Thea's overseas triumphs buoy her up (704). But in another sense Tillie's imago back in Moonstone is glimpsed imperfectly, distantly. ('A boy grew up on one of those streets who went to Omaha and built up a great business, and is now very rich. Moonstone people always speak of him and Thea together, as examples of Moonstone enterprise' (704).) Such imperfections and mediations sanctify, rather than undermine, the aesthetic force that Thea embodies.

This sketch of Aunt Tillie undergirds Cather's concluding meditation on what such mementos (and the dream-lives they spawn) mean for those who live vicariously. Cather offers an intriguing aquatic metaphor for news bulletins from the world of fame and fortune, like Tillie's record of Thea:

> The many naked little sandbars which lie between Venice and the mainland, in the seemingly stagnant water of the lagoons, are made habitable and wholesome only because, every night, a foot and a half of tide creeps in from the sea and winds its fresh brine up through all that network of shining waterways. So, into all the little settlements of quiet people, tidings of what their boys and girls are doing in the world bring real refreshment; bring to the old, memories, and to the young, dreams. (706)

The Song of the Lark is akin to other Cather novels in ending with the materialisation of the pathways of thought: into metallic grooves of a record, or into the brine that ebbs and flows around the islands of Venice. Towards the end of her life Cather speaks of aspiring to write books that emulate

> Old . . . Dutch paintings . . . [in which] there was a square window, open, through which one saw the masts of ships, or a stretch of gray sea. The feeling of the sea that one got through those square windows was really remarkable.[33]

Like those sea windows on a canvas, both the record of Thea's voice and the brine are valedictory signatures of an elsewhere, a beyond imagined as beyond even the artist's own handiwork, capable of sustaining farflung provincial lives.

Late of Valhalla

This chapter concludes not in Venice but Pennsylvania. The 17 June 1899 edition of the Lincoln, Nebraska *Courier* reviews a 'most brilliant performance' of Wagner's 1870 *Die Walküre* at the Pittsburgh Opera House. 'Frau Lehmann's stilted posings' are mocked, 'Herr Van Rooy' as Wotan is praised for his 'vitality', and the instant when 'the sword song, glorified, flashes up from the orchestra like the steel itself' is celebrated. However, the article twice leaves off describing the opera itself.

> During the intermission between the first and second acts I left the theatre and was crossing the bridge between the stage entrance of the grand opera house and the Avenue Theatre, when I was arrested by a most marvelous sound. The bridge extends above the dressing rooms of both theatres; in the dressing room just below me the skylight was open, and from it there streamed up a flood of light and a perfect geyser of the most wonderful notes that were quite unmistakable. It was Mme. Brema practicing the 'Hi-yo' song of the Valkyries. The night was murky and starless; only the red lamps of the Hotel Henry and the line of river lights above Mount Washington were visible; on every side rose the tall black buildings that shout out the sounds of the streets. Those free, unfettered notes seemed to cut the blackness and the silence, seemed to pierce the clouds which lay over the city and reach the stars and the blue space of heaven behind.[34]

This fragment of backstage song affects young Willa Cather quite differently from the opera itself. Readers can feel the song reshaping her experience of an ordinary evening, smogged over by the relentless Pittsburgh iron mills. The overpass is readily pictured, and readers doubtless seemed to hear then (as I seem to hear now) that bit of rehearsal song drifting into it, a lyrical overlay on prosaic reality.

After the final curtain, the article slides away for a second time:

> That night, when the singers boarded their special streetcar to take the long run out to the Hotel Schenley, where they were stopping, I got on the same car with several local musicians who were going out to a supper party. When the car was bowling off across the hill tops, I noticed a man in the further end fast asleep. His coat collar was turned up, his linen crumpled, the make-up still discolored his eyes, his face was damp with perspiration, and he looked gray and drawn and tired. It was Herr Anton Van Rooy, late of Walhalla, tired as a laborer from the iron mills. It is hard work apparently, this being a god. (625–6)

Music's 'other world' no longer points the writer up towards the stars. Like any worker at the end of his shift, Van Rooy sleeps off his efforts in our shared, everyday world.

Even as a callow twenty-five year old reluctantly teaching Latin by day and earning a dollar a column by night, Willa Cather knew a good streetcar anecdote when she saw it. Put that story by itself at the end of a column and you show the reader the iron fist of industry beneath the velvet glove of culture. But adding Brema's song curling up from below during an intermission walk does something quite different (as do the interwoven references to Pittsburgh's iron mills in Cather's account of the forging of swords and smelting of steel that goes on within Wagner's opera). As long as Anton Van Rooy performs, operatic glamour applies; but when he closes his eyes on the streetcar, prose is on hand to continue making art. In Norris, prose is what cuts through the operatic enchantment; in Cather, prose continues that enchantment by other means. Cather understands her prose as transfiguring rather than demystifying opera's power (à la Norris): her prose offers a vision of the world of art that retains life's actuality and a vision of life's actuality that retains the power of art.

'Herr Anton Van Rooy, late of Walhalla, tired as a labourer from the iron mills' returns transmogrified as the sleep-deprived Thea Kronborg, similarly glimpsed from afar by Spanish Johnny at the end of *The Song of the Lark* (626). Seen on the street or on a streetcar, Van Rooy and Thea both personify the after-effects of great excitement slowly percolating through an unenthusiastic world. If Norris's naturalism proposes that placing opera in its material context makes a mockery of its power to enchant listeners, Cather's prosaic observation of the singer with his mouth shut, or open to snore rather than to sing, signals that enchantment and disenchantment are both crucial components of her own prosaic aesthetic experience. Cather's novels are machines for generating that feeling, and simultaneously subtle investigations of just what it means that fiction works on its readers in this way.

Cather wants her readers on the bridge, listening to music floating through an open window, and she also wants them in that streetcar watching the singer sleep. Her trick, if trick it is, is to make an ordinary account of that sleeping singer into the kind of music that serves as the soundtrack to her readers' lives. *Turns out that you've been reading prose not listening to opera*, is the demystifying way to explain away Cather's charm. But the converse really constitutes Cather's achievement: turns out that prose, the ordinary prose of the world, has a surprising capacity to push you out of the cut and dried. It is a sign of Cather's maturing talent that *The Song of the Lark* breaks off when Thea actually becomes a successful singer. The novel's representational capacity, in Cather's eyes, is not for onstage moments but for the ordinary interweaving of performance and backstage, of rehearsal as reality. Cather returns to the question this little piece raises repeatedly: what do opera and the prosaic space of pedestrian bridges and streetcars have to do with one another? Streetcars may be humdrum, operas incantatory. Cather wants her own work to partake of both qualities at once. Cather's distinctive form of modernism comes out of her fascination with the dichotomy between the world of aesthetic dreaming and the world of hard facts – and her surprising assertion of fiction's semi-detached capacity to inhabit both simultaneously.

Notes

1. Of Cather Van Ghent writes: 'It was through giving up and blindness that she was able to speak in a way that often reveals to the reader something extraordinarily valuable that seems to have been in his mind always.' Van Ghent, *Willa Cather*, p. 44.
2. Cather, 'The Novel Démeublé', p. 51.
3. The early reviewer who praised Cather for 'sparseness of detail . . . absoluteness of phrase' (cited in O'Connor, *The Contemporary Reviews*, p. 182) was probably responding to this emptying-out.
4. This chapter contains portions adapted from *Semi-Detached* (forthcoming Princeton, 2017) and from 'Overtones and Empty Rooms: Willa Cather's Semi-Detached Modernism' (forthcoming in *Novel*, 2017).
5. Sterne, *The Audible Past*, p. 2; Cather, *The Song of the Lark*, p. 703.
6. Cather, pp. 340–1.
7. James, *The Ambassadors*, pp. 325–6.
8. Peter Otto has argued that it is in the late eighteenth century that 'the virtual first becomes understood as the space of emergence of the new, the unthought, the unrealized' (*Multiplying Worlds*, p. 191). That artworks may preserve their relationship to reality precisely by disavowing any claim to actuality is the underlying claim of work initiated by Deleuze and cogently argued in Pierre Levy's *Becoming Virtual*. Levy's notion is that 'an intellectual activity nearly always exteriorizes, objectifies, virtualizes a cognitive function . . . because it is virtual, writing desynchronizes and delocalizes' (*Becoming Virtual*, pp. 50–1). The book's crucial distinction is between the possible (or potential) and the virtual. By Levy's account, the possible is digitisable, quantifiable, renderable in statistical terms: it may be thought of as belonging to the 'taming of chance' that Ian Hacking (in his book of that name) describes as accompanying the rise of the statistical sciences in the nineteenth century. The virtual, by contrast, exists as a *qualitative* rather than a quantitative experience, not to be expressed as a possible percentage.
9. See Winnicott, *Playing and Reality*, p. 138; Huizinga, *Homo Ludens*, p. 48; Turner, *Forest of Symbols*, pp. 93–111. Barthes, *The Neutral, passim*.
10. Cather, *My Antonia*, p. 723.
11. Cather, *The Song of the Lark*, p. 328.
12. Cather, *My Antonia*, p. 727.
13. Cather, *World and the Parish*, p. 48.
14. See O'Brien, *Cather: The Emerging Voice*; Lee, *Cather: A Life Saved Up*.
15. Dizikes, *Opera in America*, p. 275.
16. Cather, 'A Wagner Matinée', p. 109.
17. Cather, quoted in Lee, *Cather: A Life Saved Up*, p. 50.
18. Cather, *World and the Parish*, vol. 1, p. 294.
19. Cather, *Selected Letters*, p. 199.
20. Daniel Levitin begins *This is Your Brain on Music* with an image familiar from iPod ads: a rapturous youth listening to music alone. 'Headphones forever changed the way I listened . . . music was coming from inside my head, not out there in the world' (pp. 1–2).

21. Cook, *Music: A Very Short Introduction*, p. 21.
22. As the nineteenth century wore on, opera audiences got quieter and quieter, more and more in awe of German music. Enter the so-called *Bayreuth hush*, introduced by Wagner for *Parsifal*'s premiere at his music festival in 1882. Wagner soon became his own victim: when he shouted 'Bravo' at an aria two weeks later he was violently hissed.
23. Gitelman, *Always Already New*, p. 76. In *The Song of the Lark* Thea occasionally spends a poignant evening entertaining a friend with 'Flow Gently Sweet Afton' or Scottish folk songs. That seems related to Gitelman's observation that American 'Opera records' circa 1915 generally featured snippets of arias, or even 'popular songs . . . performed by musicians trained at a conservatory' (p. 76).
24. Gitelman, pp. 59, 80.
25. Cather, *Selected Letters*, p. 199. For further discussion, see Plotz, 'Cather's Remarkable Quotation Marks', p. 21.
26. Cather, *The Song of the Lark*, pp. 340–1.
27. Norris, *The Pit*, p. 22.
28. This is perhaps the one naturalist aspect to *The Song of the Lark* – the implication of even the higher realm of opera itself in a material universe of profit and loss – a point omitted in 'Full-Blooded Writing and Journalistic Fictions', Ahearn's astute article on the topic of Cather's naturalism in this novel.
29. Cather, p. 659.
30. Cather, *My Antonia*, pp. 865–6.
31. Cather, *The Professor's House*, p. 222.
32. Cather, *The Song of the Lark*, p. 703. The epilogue is heavily pruned in Cather's 1937 revision of the novel.
33. Cather, 'On *The Professor's House*', p. 31.
34. Cather, *World and the Parish*, vol. 2, p. 624.

Chapter 8

Elliptical Sound: Audibility and the Space of Reading[1]

Julie Beth Napolin

' . . . . . .' the drummer sang softly.

Ernest Hemingway

Sonifying narrative voice

I begin in a rented cabin room in Georgia in 1923. For a moment, I hang suspended, waiting for the arrival of the imputed final revelation of Jean Toomer's *Cane*. Its last vignette, 'Kabnis', begins as, 'An oil light on a chair . . . burns unsteadily. The cabin room is spaced fantastically about it. Whitewashed hearth and chimney, black with sooty saw-teeth.'[2] Something of the logic of the figure in relation to the surface of the skin brings both the literary world – as a space of appearance – and the body of its narrator and character into being. Light writes on the room, the condition of all vision. The walls of the room, as a surface of reflection, bear the very bodies whose skin has not yet been identified as the content of spatial form. Is it darkness that affords the body its blackness or blackness that affords the darkness its body? Facsimile and simile here share a most fundamental ground.

There is a hiatus in the phenomenal as the presence of substance. This room has been structured in advance by my determinate expectation, now haunted by the sense that a narrator has omitted or is withholding some 'object' from me: blackness in a work that, before this final vignette, had probed the vicissitudes of a black life of song on the cusp of disappearance in 1920s Georgia. The narrator finally sees a someone in the room: 'Brown eyes stare from a lemon face' (111).

The third-person narrator is not a someone I can claim to imagine or imagine that I hear. The narrative voice that reports the colour of Kabnis' face has been divested of subject position, one that might utter, '[I see that] Brown eyes stare from a lemon face.' The anonymous voice of a narrator confers a face on Ralph Kabnis; that much is clear – there has been an elliptical appearance of a character's body. But behind that appearance, as it were (for it is without proper topography or location), there has been a disappearance of the narrator. There is an as-yet unnamed other within (or perhaps as) the room that occupies that site of a more primary ground: the blank space against which things may appear.

'Behind' narrative space and its figures is a motivating voice, irrecuperable, one that brings narrative into being. This force is not itself narrated. Samuel Beckett has dramatised the divine performative of literary appearance: 'A voice comes to one in the dark. Imagine.'[3] There has been a sleight of hand, one internal to the very structure of third-person address. Someone is narrated into existence. That someone doing the narrating evokes, brings into being, but is not itself called forth; it simply manifests.

The elliptical power of this room is testimony to the fact that we have yet to understand audibility and visibility in relation to the production of written narrative. Narrative discourse is, Gérard Genette insists, the only level 'directly available to textual analysis'.[4] To ask after the forces that determine that availability, but also reveal its availability as the realm of the apparent, is to exit the realm of narrative theory as it concerns itself with the realm of the signifier. And yet, as I will describe, pursuing that project to its own logical conclusion, particularly as it concerns a racial signifier of voice, opens up a series of questions regarding a level that does not, and cannot, come under the purview of narrative theory without at the same time becoming an acoustics, rather than, strictly speaking, a poetics or rhetoric.

A number of studies have described the politics of transcribing dialectic and vernacular voice in American modernism.[5] Yet, the phenomenological threshold between the sonic and the literary has yet to be elaborated, given the turn away from the linguistic and semiotic upon which sound studies is so often premised. My interest here is drawn to the ambiguous ground of narrative theory – narrative voice – and with it, the difficulty in retrieving its auditory threshold, a virtual or hypothetical hearing. Modernist literary production bore witness to new forms and spaces of interracial encounter, most palpable in the acoustical spaces in which voices, sounds and bodies touch. This encounter is not to be found solely within the diegetic space of the literary world. It is related to a hiatus in the no less material space of readerly consciousness. The space of reading presents an interracial encounter.

We can return for a moment to Kabnis' room. Its *fiat lux* is not without a certain surplus sound. The wind whispers through the cabin's horizontal cracks that bring shards of darkness (dark writing). Afforded the space is not only a looker, but a listener:

> Night winds in Georgia are vagrant poets, whispering. The warm whiteness of his bed, the lamp-light, do not protect him from the weird chill of their song:
>> White-man's land.
>> Niggers, sing.
>> Burn, bear black children
>> Till poor rivers bring
>> Rest, and sweet glory
>> In Camp Ground.[6]

The wind's message is encrypted in sound, just above the threshold of audition. But before chilling the body, it is wrapped once more in a second, graphic layer of poesies. It is as if the wind sings. Its chill stands in relation to the surface of the body, but also in circular relation to figuration. The song refers back to itself, commanding song and singing of song. It is what Jean-Luc Nancy might call (after Schelling and Coleridge) 'tautegorical', for 'it says nothing other than itself'.[7] Something of (facsimile) in relation to an imputed racial substance is being performed. This performance, we will find, exposes the highly mediated quality of narrative space. Visually, the page suggests the citation of an unnamed singer or group of singers, but also figures a burrowing inward, as if the narrator overhears an interior auditory space. Kabnis might be remembering a song while he lies awake, but whose voice(s) he remembers is perhaps even less articulated or more diffuse than the anonymous narrating voice that communicates the scene of haunting recitation.

While a reader arrives at an interior more historical, further away in time from the moment of audition, the historical content is itself encrypted. The transmissive force that has brought the song here – historicity as such – is lost to representation. The song acts as an elliptical and difficult to interpret preface to the story of the lynching of Mary Turner, referred to in 'Kabnis' as Mame Lamkins. Her story is carried, but also omitted or waylaid, by the sound of the wind. Mary Turner, lynched while eight months pregnant in Georgia in 1918, was nearly expunged from public record to be remembered principally by the unofficial histories of modernism.[8] Throughout the story, Toomer's mode of presentation – a half-presentation – absorbs into itself public memory's mode of silencing.[9] The sound of wind is disarticulated in relation to content. It remains unclear who is hearing it as song or if this song has ever been sung outside of its citation by narrative, one that will refrain throughout the story and never through an attributed singer. It is not even clear that Kabnis hears it as such. It has been internalised as an interpellative voice of social memory. The song is an imaginary auditory object, yet voices something of the reality of racial consciousness. There is very little of this sound that 'is' available to audile presentation.

The threshold of audibility is not simply a matter of loudness, nor is it one of pronunciation or timbre. There are sounds that do not become more or less audible through volume. We cannot make reference to audibility solely in its brute materiality. Sound is, as the *Oxford English Dictionary* suggests, 'that which is and may be heard'.[10] We should hear a curious tautology, an *is* that *is*. I cite this definition as one that opens the recent volume, *Keywords in Sound* (2015), but also because of its passive grammar that masks the subject position and with it, audibility as it is always-already in relation to a listening subject. There is always a spatial configuration of audibility, or a distribution of sounds and points of their reflection in relation to an imputed listening subject. But the space of configuration is precisely that, a figuring of relations between subjects.

I suggest we reopen for inquiry a simple question that Barthes once asked of a sentence from Balzac in 'The Death of the Author': 'who speaks thus?' Barthes begins his famous essay by forcefully resolving this question in tautology:

> As soon as a fact is narrated no longer with a view to acting directly on reality but intransitively, that is to say, finally outside of any function other than that of the very practice of the symbol itself . . . the voice loses its origin, the author enters into his own death, writing begins.[11]

Barthes continues: 'No one, no "person," says it: its source, its voice, is not the true place of writing, which is reading' (147). But what is reading?[12] As if in answer to this also quite simple question, Barthes concludes his essay by invoking a scene of listening. He recalls the ambiguity of Greek tragic utterance, or words woven with 'double meanings' and misunderstandings that lend drama its tragic dimension: 'there is, however, someone who understands each word in its duplicity and who, in addition, hears the very deafness of the characters speaking in front of him – this someone being precisely the reader (or here, the listener)' (148).

Barthes moves from drama to the novel, from listening to dramatic speech to 'listening' to sentences on a page. His parenthetical remark leaves open this gap or transference that is metaphor. Listening appears to be an attribute of reading while also its figure. Perhaps this attribute of reading is necessarily incomplete, requiring a figure to make itself known in its effects. Further, it remains difficult to establish if, in this account, one would merely be listening to oneself. We will have occasion to return to these questions in the case of Ralph Ellison.

The reader-voice is perhaps only a terminological convenience, one that borrows from the long tradition of inner speech. 'I'm aware of it *sounding* in a very thin version of my own tone of voice. I can hear myself in its silent sound, a paradox audible only to me.'[13] It is the immediacy of this experience that Jacques Derrida named auto-affection or 'hearing (understanding)-oneself-speak'.[14] If a reader-voice carries, transmits and transports the words into consciousness, then what is the nature or structure of the 'invisible distance' it traverses?[15] Sound, in this space, is pushed through into an alternate dimension. When I read, there is nothing that, properly speaking, separates written voices from one another: no surface of another body emerges by which to posit their limit. The space of reading is a singular, absolute space.

'There' the threshold of audibility concerns the very 'voice' that might be recognised as the immediate, internal voice of reading. One readily speaks of seeing narrative, or of reading as an ideational space in which characters, settings and scenes appear in acts of what phenomenologist Wolfgang Iser has called 'image-building', a phrase that promises the substantiality of architecture.[16] There are various forms of support for this space that are non-ideational because they produce no images. Reader-response theory and phenomenology of reading are deeply eidetic, unable to ask after the very force of voicing that is the traversal of an invisible distance. There is a rhetorical sliding between listening as metaphor and listening as act, a sliding that must be designated the threshold of audibility. The history of philosophy would indicate that such a threshold is impossible in the case in visibility, so coequal are the image and the idea.

Even Barthes must retain an ideal space (metaphorised as listening) where all levels of articulation are simultaneous and coterminous.[17] There is merely a transfer of power from the voice (of the writer) to the ear (of a reader). But this ear, I will argue, is not without its own stratification, particularly in these scenarios, so difficult to recuperate and narrate. There is an ellipsis, a dot-dot-dot in our own ability to think through reading in relation to listening and its subject.

The narratological category of voice remains instructive, for properly speaking, it is without body and a face. It is merely what Genette calls 'the narrating instance'.[18] Genette describes at length the structure that distinguishes the narrator, the one who reports the scene, from a focaliser, the agent who 'sees and selects' the particularities of world to be given over to representation. We must suspend for a moment the provocative point that Genette makes no distinction in focalising between *seeing* and *hearing*, that is, between an object that has been selected for a character or narrator's audition and an object that has been selected for a character or narrator's vision. Genette's use of 'voice' is not, Stephen Ross summarises in his own monumental study of speech and writing, 'a medium of utterance, but rather a set of relationships among time of narration, implied or actual narrators, and diegetic levels of the fiction's discourse'.[19] Ross continues: 'From this fundamental relationship Genette can derive subtle and elaborate configurations of narrative without pretending to solve the mystery of an author's (or implied author's) assumed presence behind voice and absence from discourse' (7–8).

In this structure, the distinction between first- and third-person is ontologically abridged. I suggest that what matters most in narrative discourse is focalisation, a selection of sensory data. That selection at times coincides with the person narrating and at times does not. Genette, for example, typologised focalisers that are 'internal' and 'external' to the diegesis, but also made an allowance for 'zero focalization' in the case of classical narrative or epic.[20] In any event, what matters – and I say it with all the weight of trying to open for inquiry the focaliser's material reality – is that selecting goes on ontologically and temporally prior to narrating. In among the most enigmatic contributions to narrative theory, Maurice Blanchot writes 'the speech of narrative always *lets us feel* that what is being recounted is not being recounted by anyone: it speaks in the neutral'.[21] Blanchot does not address the question of where it would speak. I suggest that even in this floating, yet purposive dimension of voice, in the zero, there is a focaliser, a focaliser of what Blanchot names 'the neutral space of narrative' (384). The focaliser is an anonymous accompaniment to any literary voicing, available to narrative, though not fully retrievable by it as its condition. Even the most neutral of spaces, that lets me feel as though 'it speaks', is a selected space.

The sensible is never simply or immediately such but rather regulated, censored or organised by laws that are perhaps not fully discoverable as laws for there is no place outside of representation from which to see them. Visibility is the perceptual condition of the object as it might present itself to vision.[22] As we move from the visual to the acoustical register, there is also a passage between them: audibility itself is an audiovisual form. And yet, the moment we concern ourselves with audibility, we are no longer concerned simply with the material life of the object, but also with its subjective and somatic possibilities for recognition. Audibility is not a purely material category that can be pluralised and distributed in a series as would a series of things: it is the ontological force by which consciousness can experience itself as such. Audibility is the supportive, yet occluded, function of the subject as the verb's mode of action.

The focaliser sees but does not 'say'. My concern here is not only the issue of confounding hearing and seeing, but also the distribution of the sensible by which politics determines aesthetics, or the threshold of an object's perceptibility.[23] Modernist scholar Melba Cuddy-Keane has also asked after the limits of focalisation in the account of sound, focusing in particular on what she calls a 'the new aurality' of technological modernity:

> Besides the problem of mediating sound through a visually oriented discourse, there is the fundamental problem of mediating sound through language at all – the inevitable translation of sound into a conceptual category that takes place in the process of verbalization.[24]

But is that not a problem with any sensation or perception? The literary can only become the site in which to recuperate such an object if it is to be understood as a purely representational space. Cuddy-Keane argues that rather than focalisation, terms such as 'diffusion and auscultation may thus help us both to focus on the presentation of sound in itself' (71).[25]

The gains of such a shift in focus to 'sound in itself' remain unclear, or rather, politically neutral. This neutrality defines the limits and scope of narrative theory in relation to audibility. Race, taken to be a purely visual phenomenon, has been largely absent from discussions of the sound object. Yet, race is not a content, a content that can be added and then removed through reduced listening. My insistence is on the 'audible', which is not prior to an act of reading. These questions become more vexed in moments of half-presentation and in the sound object that is its narrative 'voice', the very intersection of the linguistic, imagistic, psychic and sonorous. Judith Butler writes of a 'racially saturated field of visibility'.[26] We might say in turn: race determines in advance the field of audibility.

Narrative voice is no voice at all or lacks sonorous substance. As a grammatical category, it is *desonified*. Someone is speaking (in the case of the first person) or reporting speech (in the case of the third person). This 'voice' bears no relation to timbre, which immediately gives rise to the question of a point of audition, a someone who is listening. Narrative voice also bears no relation to phenomenological voice as the animating intention of *logos*. Again, it is merely the 'narrating instance', that blank neutrality of the space of narrative. How are we to anatomise a series of auditory thresholds that determines narrativity? I take narrativity here to be not only the presumed narratability of an object that makes it available to focalisation, but also the supposed neutrality of narrative voice as grammatical agency: voice as it brings into existence, as it signifies, but is not itself retrievable. Narrative voice is a figural voice that displaces, but cannot fully overcome, its acoustical associations.

Who hears?

In relation to this difficult-to-narrate region of audibility the prologue to Ralph Ellison's *Invisible Man* (1947) stands as a primal scene. The title of the novel would indicate a problem with vision alone. The novel's narrator describes himself only as 'invisible', or 'the product of a "refusal" on the part of others to see him'.[27] Because he is invisible, light, he tells us, 'confirms my reality, gives birth to my form'.[28] Light is that which gives birth to form, form here taken to be the outline of the body, the very shape of what would otherwise be a 'formless mass' (7). But his form reflexively indicates a structuring omission in the ontology of form as such, its manner of appearing as if from nothing. While the emergence of any literary world posits a ground against which figure appears, here ground persists as that against which a body resists manifestation, even against so many lights. As in Kabnis' room, ground is figured. 'There is a certain acoustical deadness to my hole', he explains – there is a resistance, then, even to echo of the voice as auditory reflection of the self (8). There is a fundamental gesture of disappearance in the will to escape, to re-determine determination.

As this unnamed narrator addresses us, some reality of voice, one not without its own skin, remains. David Copenhafer writes of Ellison' prologue:

> Insofar as the narrator is able to speak, to write, to *figure* his condition, his invisibility would appear not to be absolute . . . A mouth, a face, may tend to stubbornly persist. Beyond this particular figure, however, the simple fact of narrative voice, what we might call an irreducible acoustic remainder in the text, tends to bring the blackness of the narrator into visibility. Someone is speaking. And it is difficult not to confer a 'raced' body to a voice despite the massive epistemological uncertainties of such a conferral. Oddly, voice translates a measure of vision.[29]

The 'measure of vision' in which the black body of the narrator appears is perhaps only a measure because it cannot be sustained, that is, made properly substantive. It disappears as quickly as it appears. A measure of vision of course has musical and rhythmic implications – a sequence, a series of beats, a unit of protraction in time. If *legein*, the Greek root of *logos*, means speaking, gathering, binding, joining, but also 'to count' and 'to recount', *logos* also requires 'a sequence, or chain that is developed temporally'.[30] This chain is between single words, a chain that gives them meaning. As I will return to, this sequence would seem to forbid anything like an ellipsis, for each dot is a unit of the same. If there is always a space between words that holds together their meaningful sequence, the ellipsis is a pure holding together, a pulse.

In the translation of voice into a measure of vision, it is as if audibility, visibility and legibility coincide along a certain threshold. I cannot claim to 'see' the body of narrator, just as I cannot claim to hear his voice. I can only claim to do so to the extent that a written figure might facsimile something other than what it is.

In an invisible man's room,[31] it is difficult to know if voice only translates a measure of vision because someone – who wishes to be anonymous – is speaking in the first person. Decades of post-structural narrative theory, from Barthes to Genette and Gates, would encourage us not to seek out anyone speaking behind the first-person voice. 'Writing is that neutral, composite, oblique space where our subject slips away, the negative [*le noir-et-blanc*] where all identity is lost, starting with the very identity of the body writing.'[32] If in Kabnis' room, there are two entities (one a disembodied narrator, the other the body it narrates into existence), in an invisible man's room there is one entity. An 'I' addresses, seemingly directly, a 'you' who cannot possibly respond.

But Ellison's unnamed narrator draws the conditioning disappearance of the third-person voice into his own being, wishing to overcome its intractable determination. He cannot perfectly imitate its force, displaced as it is onto a series of prosthetics under his tight supervision. He lives in a dark hole artificially illuminated by 1,369 pilfered lights. Ellison borrows the structuring omission of the third-person to lend it architectural and technological proportions; in that gesture its sly force becomes figured as his room (invisible, at least to us). Yet, who could forget that his narrator sits not only amongst the artificial lights, but also with the disembodied voice of another? The singing voice of Louis Armstrong, who 'made poetry out of being invisible', floats from out of a radio-phonograph.[33] In the phonographic voice, there is a doubling of the imaginary body of the narrator, but also of the very force of narrative.

At the end of this essay, we will have occasion to return this scene that has borne so much critical repetition – making what follows something of an ellipsis itself – but suffice it to say that the title of the song Armstrong sings dramatises the difficult to retrieve bracketing of the agential force of third-person narrative voice: '(What did I Do to Become So) Black and Blue'. I say 'bracketing' of the third-person because though the first part of the title avows an 'I', it is an 'I' that poses a difficult-to-answer question. The parenthesis acknowledges that the agency lies with someone else who is not there or, what's more, fundamentally unavailable.[34]

We should leave for a moment the song as described by the narrator to consider the song as sung by Armstrong. Reading Ellison invites moving between these two regions. After a protracted instrumental introduction, Armstrong finally sings. Ellison does not transcribe the lyrics of the song. While we must go outside of the novel, as listeners, Armstrong again forces us to become readers, reading and listening being enjoined in his voicing of the problem of legibility. At the bridge, that part of any song that is cast between its beginning and return, Armstrong sings:

> I'm white inside but that don't help my case
> 'Cause I can't hide what is in my fa . . .[35]

I borrow this transcription from Copenhafer's 'Invisible Music (Ellison)', a title whose own punctuation dramatises a missing voice (illegible and inaudible). The standard transcription of the song provides the full word 'face', but that belies Armstrong's performative omission. For, just then, Copenhafer notes, Armstrong begins to scat, transcribed here as an ellipsis. Ellison, Copenhafer convincingly argues, could only have been referring to a 1929 recording, in which Armstrong replaces the original lyric, 'on my face' with 'in my face' (177). The grammar of that substitution claims to convert the surface of the skin, as if form to an imputed content. Such a claim is simultaneously undone by its own articulation in (or as) Armstrong's voice. He refuses to articulate the phoneme and digs up sounds secreted within or rejected by the word as it has shaped itself. Again, content stands in disarticulated and transmuted relation to form. 'In fact', Copenhafer writes, 'he never completes the world, never completes the rhyme with "case" that might bring some kind of closure to the bridge' (177). Ellison's unnamed narrator concludes the novel with an elementary blues lyric, one that completes the very phonetic structure of rhyming that, Copenhafer suggests, had been occluded in the revelatory moment of Armstrong's performance (185).[36] The narrator intones: 'Being invisible and without substance, a disembodied voice, as it were, what else could I do? What else but try to tell you what was really happening when your eyes were looking through?'[37] The narrator then culminates with a single, dangling line: 'Who knows but that, on the lower frequencies, I speak for you?' (581). He suggests, then, something of his inaudibility.

He ends with a rhetorical question, figuring a direct address and with it, the reader's conjectural hearing. I agree that the rhyme is fundamental to blues musicality and that his particular rhyme is one that ironises his racialised condition. Yet, the narrator's address figures its somatic and acoustical collaboration with the timbre of reading. Does not the reader begin to transmit rhythm to his word, translating word into song? These frequencies and rhythms suggest something of the material process of traversing an invisible distance between text and consciousness. It is a paradoxical site – paradoxical, because nowhere locatable – for word to become rhythmicised as song. Simultaneously, or at least structurally inseparably, these lower frequencies function on the baritone register of a male voice, a timbre that is often racially stereotyped and therefore functions in advance of his individual speech. The narrator tells us that his invisibility is 'a matter of the construction of [people's] *inner* eyes, those eyes with which they look through their physical eyes upon reality' (3). Yet, at issue in the space of narrative is the threshold of audibility, or what I have called the stratification of the ear: the inner ears with which we hear through physical ears. A white woman at one point says to the narrator that his voice has 'primitive' associations: 'no one has told you, Brother, that at times you have tom-toms beating in your voice?' (413). It is a timbre that he himself does or cannot hear: the narrator ironises something of the act of reading, for even in his reduced space of disembodiment, he is given black skin within the ear of a (white?) reader. There is, then, a kind of fulfilment of voice by a reader who might provide both the sensuous, yet structural archive of timbre, the reader perhaps recalling a series of phantasmatic voices to suture to this narrating instance.

The lower frequencies are lower still, beneath even that threshold that gives the lowest range of human audition, and yet more intimately travelling: his voice might in fact line and people the inner speech of reading. The threshold of audibility concerns the very voice that might be recognised as the immediate, internal voice of reading, a voice presumed to be racially neutral. It is as if the narrator asks, if this space is so fungible that you can continue to attribute to me a race, then how do you know that you are where and who you are when you hear yourself?

Not all voices of reading translate a measure of vision. Some readerly voices occlude, vex, or hyper-accentuate that translation and in different somatic sites of animation. There is a voice that a reader might lend to writing, a voice that might efface, misappropriate and misconstrue. The voice without a mouth is not without reference to a situation. Rather, it is with an elided or half-presented situation. Richard Dyer writes, 'white power secures its dominance by seeming not to be anything in particular ... [moreover] when whiteness qua whiteness does come into focus, it is often revealed as emptiness, absence, denial'.[38] Consciousness itself – the very 'site' of the word's animation and shelter – is a racial formation. The act of reading, in traversing an invisible distance, traverses not an emptiness of immediacy, but a virtual and yet no less material and racialised space.

The challenging issue of focalisation or selection in the space of reading remains to be considered within this nexus.

The deselected object

Language knows a 'subject', not a person, and this subject, empty outside of the very enunciation which defines it, suffices to make language 'hold together' . . .

Roland Barthes[39]

I have been suggesting that the category of narrative voice is structured by auditory elision. I have also considered the possibility of a mode of omission that is vexed in its play of appearance and disappearance in part because a series of graphic omissions are made to stand in for auditory thresholds, both physical and what Frantz Fanon might call 'historico-racial'.[40] I turn now to an acoustical narrative space whose structure of selection will strike us as the kind inverted by Ellison.

Near the conclusion of Ernest Hemingway's *The Sun Also Rises* (1926), Lady Brett Ashley and her former love Jake sit at a café table with a young bullfighter, Pedro Romero, in Spain. Chapter 26 abruptly comes to end when Jake leaves the table for a moment, only to return and find that Brett and Romero are gone. 'The coffee-glasses and our three empty cognac-glasses were on the table. A waiter came with a cloth and picked up the glasses and mopped off the table.'[41] We have only metonyms, the empty table and glasses, to depict, vividly by way of narrative omission, that Brett and Romero have gone off together for the night. Fantasy must intervene where description will not. We come to know that something has happened, not because it is presented but by way of remainders, an affective halo around the scene of action that points towards it. Narrative that 'shows' by omitting, what Hemingway called 'the principle of the iceberg', here can be defined in rather visible terms.[42]

But consider another passing moment in *The Sun Also Rises* when Jake meets Brett in a jazz club in Spain. The moment is itself a passageway – a sonorous corridor – for larger themes of the novel concerning omission, but also reticence and repression:

The music hit you as you went in. Brett and I danced. It was so crowded we could barely move. The nigger drummer waved at Brett. We were caught in the jam, dancing in one place in front of him.
'Hahre you?'
'Great.'
'Thaats good.'

He was all teeth and lips
'He's a friend of mine,' Brett said. 'Damn good drummer.'
. . .
'Oh darling,' Brett said. 'I'm so miserable.'
I had the feeling of going through something that has all happened before.
'You were happy a minute ago.'
The drummer shouted: 'You can't two time – '
'It's all gone'
'What's the matter?'
'I don't know. I just feel terribly.'
'. . . . . .' the drummer chanted. Then turned to his sticks.
'Want to go?'
I had the feeling as in a nightmare of it all being something repeated,
something I had been through and that now I must through again.'
'. . . . . .' the drummer sang softly.
'Let's go,' said Brett. 'You don't mind.'
'. . . . . .' the drummer shouted and grinned at Brett. (69–70)

A selected sound object is 'audible' to the focaliser; a selected visual object is 'visible'. This scene forces us to ask, what is a *deselected* object? Are its axes purely silence and invisibility, or rather a more fraught sensory and political territory delimiting speech from noise, image from its occlusion, a location in which seeing and hearing are co-produced in the somatic act of reading?

Brett knows one of the musicians and while she does not say more, in a novel that is fundamentally about words withheld or omitted, they perhaps know one another from America. We know from other moments in the text that Brett has left a long line of lovers, the implication here being that Brett and the unnamed drummer have been sexually involved. The racial epithet serves the psychic function of neutralising Jake's anxiety in this interracial space. Already displaced away from the American scene, the presence of jazz speaks to an America abroad in suspension. But the scene, as presented by Jake, is notably disfiguring. The body of the drummer, in a measure of vision, is corporealised by the epithet as a black body. But that body is immediately reduced, disappearing behind two remaining figures (teeth and mouth) that hang suspended. A floating mouth absorbs and stands in place of the rest of the body. Jake's mode of narrative is not only reductive, but also aggressive, disfiguring the drummer's face.

And yet, not only is seeing the drummer not at issue, but also hearing him. An essential violence is happening at the level of reported speech. The drummer's speech is rendered in vernacular, which is perhaps how Jake hears it, that is, through racist filters. But this violence is happening in the apparatus of reporting itself. For, while the scene is focalised through Jake, he is also one of the scene's objects. The apparatus must overhear the characters as well as the music and drum-taps. There is some shift in attention: the narrative registers these sounds, but it increasingly attempts to banish the language of the drummer to non-narrative. Rhythm is the impetus for an elision in the ellipsis, which then comes to stand in for a voice. It is worth noting that another character in the scene is referred to simply as 'the count'. What begins as stenography of the drum-taps becomes overfull with displacement (by what force or from what point of audition, it is unclear). It is no longer sufficient to isolate the racist structures of representation within Jake. The well-worn literary question 'Who is speaking?' is perhaps best rendered here as 'Who is selecting?'

Perspective, narratologist Mieke Bal maintains, 'covers both the physical and psychological points of perception', but it has come traditionally to mean both the narrator and the 'vision'.[43] The term focaliser, meant to cover the act of vision alone, is drawn from the language of film and photography, preferred by Bal over something like 'perspectiviser' for being both subject-oriented while also technical. The examples that tether and elaborate Bal's theory of the focaliser are drawn from spectatorship for reasons that remain instructive in the case of the racial signifier: the focalised objects (another character, a landscape, a thing, or a voice or sound event) are fundamentally specular.

As Jake moves through the music of the jazz club, we are, despite an elision, in the realm of something that gains its narrative status from being seen: a body under the erasure of racist disfigurement, rendered and reduced graphically to a series of dots. But it also gains its status from being heard. Selection still remains in this instance an operative act. While a subject – who has been reduced to a (sound) object – is being heard, it is selected and unselected at the same time. That is not to claim that the drummer 'is not being heard', for the very structure of audibility here underscores that objects (who are also subjects) are not simply available to hearing. We are in the realm of *deselection* as the speech of the drummer moves further and further away from representation, being first a dialect rendering of a racialised timbre. It is perhaps even a Southern timbre, but it is made to take on black proportions: the matter of his voice is left unnarrated, calling upon the reader's inner sense of sound and that reader's archive of racial associations of voice. It is then a singing, a chanting, until finally it is an ellipsis, a spacing out within written discourse itself.

But while it is out of the ordinary for a drummer to sing, the ellipses stand in for a problem of description, as if the sound qualities of the drummer's singing cannot be graphically represented.[44] The very notion of timbre is premised upon a descriptive desire in relation to sound.

In one of few reflections on the incredibly difficult to define notion of timbre, Emily Dolan writes, 'to talk about timbre is to value sound as sound and not as a sonic manifestation of abstract principles'.[45] Timbre indicates an attention to what Dolan calls the 'eachness' of sounds (88). But how is eachness, or particularity, to be resolved with an attention to the *structural* levels that support the racialisation of timbre – the claim to reduce and therefore (mis)recognise a black voice or sound, in reading and in listening?

Certainly, the elision indicates a problem of acoustics, as Jake might not hear what the drummer sings (though the drummer's skin has silenced him in advance of speech and music). Perhaps Jake turns his ear elsewhere physically. The gap in both narrative and the grapheme might also be a kind of background noise, as if his emotional attention is drawn elsewhere in ways that he cannot quite articulate. If we return to Barthes's formulation of tragic listening, double meanings lend the scene its dramatic proportions: this scene unfolds principally as a failure of dialogue. Both Brett and Jake circle around some void in feeling they cannot say clearly or directly. But it is the body of the drummer that indicates something of that circle. He was there, in the scene, for a moment, just before marking its borders of inclusion. The novel has rich technical resources internal to itself for omission. What work is he – as a spectral, elliptical frame of dialogue – doing for narrative?

The acoustical pulses around narrative, just as the music pulses around dialogue: the music is represented *so as* to be marginalised. Yet, that narrative and textual labour is, nonetheless, unfulfilled. While the racialised sound object has been marginalised, it remains 'in' the narrative in elided and distorted (but also compressed) form. The racialised drummer is 'there', at the audiovisual margins of narratability: the ellipsis is a visualised fracture in articulation.

The two-time is in the text. It is the only thing that the drummer says: he is elided as a double elision, two-timed out of the narrative. It is possible that Hemingway here meant to say 'double time', a double time solo being the lingua franca of jazz of this moment, a remark about how early jazz was played. Perhaps the drummer is cautioning the player not to double the rhythm. The phrase 'two time' then takes on an ironic proportion as overheard by Jake who is, in a sense, asking Brett to two-time with him (she is engaged to Mike, a name with an easily substitutable phoneme). In Jake's impotence, an injury from the war, he could never fulfil that two time, where the drummer it seems, already has, making Jake painfully, or doubly secondary.

The elliptical sound, or the half-presentation of the music, indicates not only what the characters cannot hear, but also what narrative discourse itself cannot hear if it is to maintain its semiotic hold upon the affective limitations of its characters. The emptiness of the ellipses, or rather an emptying out of music by narrative and the grapheme, figures the characters' own sense of emptiness. But that emptiness is symptomatic of an absence already within and as whiteness, preserving its dominance. Jake cannot admit the drummer into his society if he is to preserve it; he can dance along to the music, but no more. But this emptiness is doubly empty, two-timing. The ellipsis is then over-full to double fully the convention of three dots. Jake and Brett are miserable, to be sure. But the narrative discourse borrows the authenticity of their emptiness from the erased music to communicate its own lack. The melancholy of the characters is borrowed, omitted music being its prosthetic.

Elision, all that dictates how the raced body is to be both seen and heard in advance of seeing and hearing, is an audiovisual form. Such labour cannot in itself be narrated, but supports narration. We can see, then, that this scene posits something of the exact inverse of Ellison's chamber, which borrows structural elision to displace it onto electric lights and the phonographic voice. What Hemingway elides, Ellison refigures.

The drummer indicates a rhythm, 'two timing', that is at the limit of narrative temporality and serial presentation. The narrative space is pulled in two directions – a syncopated rhythm stands as the limit of the linguistic representation of layered acoustical space. If narrative turns fully towards the drummer, it will negate the spoken scene, falling into the music that will become its primary object. Narrative is in the midst of a struggle to the death. In that moment, 'background noise' ceases to be an appropriate designation, for the written finds its limit in its capacity to represent these simultaneous sounds. The narrative struggles to represent what is underneath the spoken as its support. But, at the level of inscription, this support (of music) can only be *just alongside* of dialogue, visibly surrounding direct discourse. This proximity signals an acute danger: for what if narrative discourse were to turn its attention to this music?

As Hemingway's project of narrative omission reaches a certain limit, we might hazard that *The Sun Also Rises* would have to become *Invisible Man*, the two novels together being what Barthes had called 'the negative [*le noir-et-blanc*] where all identity is lost'.[46] I want, then, to conclude with a coda, a return to the prologue to *Invisible Man*. As the narrator listens,

the unheard sounds came through, and each melodic line existed of itself, stood out clearly from all the rest, said its piece, and waited patiently for the other voices to speak. That night I found myself hearing not only in time, but in space as well.[47]

He hears several layers of discourse beneath the lyrics, the voices of a congregation and then finally, of the ancestors. He begins to hear a more 'rapid tempo', perhaps as a compound rhythm. The ellipses are (in the) original, indicating a sound space in text, but also the logic of tautology as it eclipses genesis:

'Brothers and sisters, my text this morning is the 'Blackness of Blackness.'
And a congregation of voices answered: 'That blackness is most black, brother, most black . . .'
'In the beginning . . .'
'At the very start', they cried.
'. . . there was blackness . . .'
'Preach it . . .' (9)

In the beginning . . . there was blackness. How blackness came to be lies in the ellipsis, that invisible distance between matter and form. Here, a sonorous and non-verbal relation is performed. The ellipses are not a pause, but indicate the acoustics of their imaginary space, its resonance where the voice of one is ending and the voices of the others begin. The ellipsis, as antiphony, is a place of calling back. It is where the other lives, in resonance. The ellipsis is the only way, graphically, to indicate something of that interface between voice and space as a site of animation and circumscription.

But this relation, though difficult to narrate in its genesis, is not essential. Alexander Weheliye has persuaded us to hear the narrator's room as a fundamentally technological space, connecting its parameters to the trajectory of Afro-Futurism.[48] In that spirit, we should remember that the narrator tells us that he plans one day to have five radio-phonographs playing simultaneously. Such a device has a dual function; it both repeats and transmits. The narrator leaves unsaid how they, in his extreme solitude, could possibly be made to play the same record synchronously. Used as a radio, each device could tune in simultaneously to the broadcast, multiplying the same. Five records playing simultaneously would pose a different condition of listening: they would fall out of phase, echoing each other in odd and not fully determined intervals. The distinction between transmission (playing sound from afar) and reproduction (generating sound from within) is along the axis not of form or even 'format', but content.[49] Out of phase, the envelopes of words – their consonants and sibilance – would become prolonged . . . as *a whispering through its cracks* (we should hear, once again, the figural winds that give shape to Kabnis). The phase relations would return the words of the song into the sound of sibilance. In 1947, there were not yet stereophonics, but Ellison's narrator, a 'thinker-tinker', imagines dividing the unitary mono-sound not into two but *five* (7).[50] He is already beyond the fundamental units of dialectics, one and two, being amidst the many. For Plato, the number that gives reality to all things, because it gives dimension, is four. Perhaps, then, we are in an ultra-dialectical space, as it pushes out from the given.[51] The disarticulation of the phrase relations is not immediately immanent to the space as negativity: the phase relations do not neutralise, but multiply and expand.

The room, he tells us, is anechoic. It is through the technological addition of surround sound, phasing so many simultaneous recordings, that echo would be simulated rather than given in advance as a property of space. The work removes echo only to give it back as a facsimile, phase relations being the future of modernist music. It is a form of sound that had not yet been played, not yet heard, and perhaps, not even imagined.

Notes

1. Portions of this essay were presented the 'Techniques of the Listener' symposium at Yale University (2016) and the American Comparative Literature Association Convention panel, 'Sites of Sound' (2014). I wish to thank those auditors, Paul Nadal, Todd Barnes and the editors of this volume for their comments.
2. Toomer, *Cane*, p. 111.
3. Beckett, 'Company', p. 3.
4. Genette, *Narrative Discourse*, p. 27.
5. See, for example, North, *The Dialectic of Modernism*.
6. Toomer, p. 111.
7. Nancy, *The Inoperative Community*, p. 49. My aim here is to show how modernist voicing exposes tautologies within the very logic of racialised production.
8. I cannot address in the scope of this present essay the central importance of Mary Turner as an unfathomable presence in 'Kabnis'. Also see Julie Buckner Armstrong's *Mary Turner and the Memory of Lynching*. Confronting the social memory of Mary Turner, the prose of 'Kabnis' can appear to be what Armstrong calls 'an incomprehensible mess' (7).
9. See Henry Louis Gates Jr's monumental rethinking of narrative theory, *The Signifying Monkey*. Gates notes 'the privileged oral voice [of *Cane*] . . . and its poignant silences', describing at length a set of African American rhetorical strategies that both conceal and reveal (192). These strategies retain in their play a 'primarily antiphonal function' of a black oral tradition (192).
10. Cited in Novak and Sakakeeny, *Keywords in Sound*, p. 1. The editors begin, 'sound is vibration that is perceived and becomes known through its materiality' (1). This definition functions via a similar tautology.

11. Barthes, 'The Death of the Author', in *Image, Music, Text*, p. 142.

12. As Garrett Stewart asks, in one of few reflections on the question of sono-rousness in the event of reading, 'Where do we read?' Such a question, he suggests, immediately leads us to the 'reading body' as the 'somatic locus of soundless reception'. Stewart, *Reading Voices*, p. 1.

13. Riley, 'The Voice Without A Mouth', p. 58. In a recent discussion at the Whitney Humanities Centre meeting, 'Techniques of the Listener' (April 2016), Mara Mills noted that in nineteenth-century discussions of hearing and disability, it was thought that the deaf could not be taught to read silently, being without speech and therefore, without inner speech. So entrenched is the notion that written word must be silently articulated in mind.

14. Derrida elaborates this phrase across numerous works and evokes the double sense of the French verb écouter, both 'to hear' and 'to understand. '[To speak] produces a signifier which seems not to fall into the world, outside the ideality of the signified, but to remain there sheltered – even in the moment that it attains the audiophonic system of the other – within the pure interiority of auto-affection. It does not fall into the exteriority of space, into what one calls the world, which is nothing but the outside of speech.' Derrida, *Of Grammatology*, p. 166.

15. I borrow this phrase from Derrida's critique of Husserl in *Speech and Phenomena*. Derrida writes of 'the invisible distance held out between the two acts' of phenomenological reduction and between the transcendental and the world that requires it to appear (11–13).

16. 'The process of image-building begins . . . with the schemata of the text, which are aspects of a totality that the reader himself must assemble; in assembling it, he will occupy the position set out for him, and so create a sequence of images that eventually results in his constituting the meaning of the text.' Iser, *The Act of Reading*, p. 141.

17. In part, this space owes to Barthes's investments in certain models of psychoanalytic listening. See, for example, 'Listening' in *The Responsibility of Forms*, pp. 245–60.

18. Genette, p. 214.

19. Ross, *Fiction's Inexhaustible Voice*, pp. 7–8.

20. Genette, pp. 189–94.

21. Blanchot, *The Infinite Conversation*, p. 384. While Blanchot does not discuss focalisation per se, his parallel theory of narrative voice adopts *'il'*, often translated as 'he', but also indicative of a neuter 'it'.

22. I am grateful to the work of Pooja Rangan who recommends, in this vein, a related passage from Gilles Deleuze when he writes of 'visibilities'. These 'are not to be confused with elements that are visible or more generally perceptible, such as qualities, things, objects, compounds of objects. . . . Visibilities are not forms of objects, nor even forms that would show up under the light, but rather forms of luminosity which are created by the light itself and allow a thing or object to exist only as a flash, sparkle or shimmer'. Deleuze, *Foucault*, p. 45; Rangan, *Immediations*.

23. Jacques Rancière writes in *The Politics of Aesthetics*, 'the system of *a priori* forms determines what presents itself to sense experience. [Aesthetics] is a delimitation of spaces and times, of the visible and the invisible, of speech

and noise, that simultaneously determines the place and the stakes of politics as a form of experience' (13).

24. Cuddy-Keane, 'Virginia Woolf, Sound Technologies, and the New Aurality', p. 70.

25. Also see John M. Picker, *Victorian Soundscapes*. Picker discusses the Romantic and Victorian literary imagination in terms of auscultation, a technique whose history has since been richly explored by Jonathan Sterne in *The Audible Past*.

26. Butler, 'Endangered/Endangering', p. 17. In this seminal essay, Butler writes of the video of Rodney King being brutally beaten, as it was nonetheless marshalled as visual evidence of King being a threat. 'The visual field is not neutral to the question of race; it is itself a racial formation, an episteme, hegemonic and forceful' (19). Butler does not isolate the 'seen' as being prior to reading (17).

27. Copenhafer, 'Invisible Man (Ellison)', p. 172.

28. Ellison, *Invisible Man*, p. 6.

29. Copenhafer, p. 172.

30. Cavarero, *For More Than One Voice*, p. 43.

31. I use this rather awkward formation because the narrator says, 'I am an invisible man.' It would be misleading to substitute a definite article for what is persistently indefinite.

32. Barthes, 'Death of The Author', p. 142. It is a bit odd to translate the phrase 'le noir-et-blanc' as 'negative', though it is true that the contrast bears within itself a dialectical, and thus negating, relation. Barthes's original sense might have been the blank (white) page, which then bears black ink. But given that black-and-white is stated as if in union, it is difficult not to hear a prelude to Barthes's future thinking on photography. At the same time, given Barthes's silence on Algeria, it is also quite difficult not to hear an occluded racial other. This play is of course testimony to his central thesis.

33. Ellison, p. 8.

34. Also see Alexander Weheliye, *Phonographies: Grooves in Sonic Afro-Modernity*, in which Weheliye argues for the paramount importance of the subject position in Ellison's discourse. Judith Butler's *Giving an Account of Oneself* and *The Psychic Life of Power* are also foundational meditations on what in subject-formation cannot be narrated and is only figured.

35. Quoted in Copenhafer, p. 173.

36. Throughout his essay, Copenhafer shows how the narrator's language resists or forecloses rhyming more generally, making this final moment of rhyme all the more powerful.

37. Ellison, p. 581.

38. Cited in Jackson, 'White Noises', p. 51.

39. 'Death of the Author', p. 145.

40. Fanon, *Black Skin, White Masks*, p. 111.

41. Hemingway, *Sun Also Rises*, p. 191.

42. Hemingway, 'The Art of Fiction No. 21'. In the interview with George Plimpton, Hemingway states that only something that a writer knows can be omitted; anything else is a 'hole'.

43. Bal, *Narratology* (2009), p. 146.

44. For a related reading, see Benson, 'Gatsby's Tattoo', which argues for 'jazz under erasure' in *The Great Gatsby* (747). Benson compellingly highlights a moment of racialised foot tapping within the broader context of anthropology and ethnography.
45. Dolan, *Orchestral Revolution*, pp. 87–8.
46. Barthes, 'Death of the Author', p. 142.
47. Ellison, pp. 8–9.
48. See Weheliye.
49. For a discussion of the notion of format in relation to form and content, see Sterne, *MP3: The Meaning of a Format*.
50. So too does Toomer in 'Kabnis': 'Way off down the street four figures sway beneath iron awnings which form a sort of corridor that imperfectly echoes and jumbles what they say. A fifth form joins them' (143).
51. The novel begins with the end or the closest point of the present. I have tried to show how, in the musicality of the last line of the novel and its mode of address, the narrator and reader hear in ways not yet possible at the beginning of the book. He (and we) finally 'hears' his own self-alienation. This is the elliptical shape of Hegel's *The Phenomenology of Spirit*, one articulation of the modern predicament.

Part Three

Difficult Voices

Chapter 9

Harsh Sounds: George Gissing's Penetrating Literary Voice

Penelope Hone

In a 1912 review of George Gissing's career, Virginia Woolf draws attention to the late nineteenth-century novelist's treatment of the English lower classes. She notes how 'many writers before and after Gissing have written with both knowledge and sympathy of the poor . . . There was Mrs Gaskell, for instance, and Dickens; a score of writers in our own day have studied the conditions of their lives.'[1] While Gissing joins this rich and long history, his novels stand out for their lack of sympathy for their subject and as such, as Woolf observes, have a discomforting effect on the reader. 'The impressive part about Gissing', Woolf writes, 'is that knowing [the English lower classes] as he did he makes no secret of the fact that he hated them. That is the reason why his voice is so harsh, so penetrating, so little grateful to the ears.'[2] The harsh, penetrating effect of Gissing's literary voice is well recognised. Fredric Jameson proposes we read it as a 'conduct of *ressentiment*' against both the disenfranchised classes Gissing represents in his fiction and the middle-class bourgeois reading public for whom he writes.[3] More recently, Aaron Matz has argued Gissing's acerbic tone be understood as a form of 'vitriolic' and 'aggressive' realism.[4] Gissing's style can therefore be seen as a refusal to provide the nineteenth-century reader with an experience typically expected of the novel. Notably, in 'The Place of Realism in Fiction', Gissing resists the notion

> that a novel is written 'to please people', that disagreeable facts must always be kept out of sight, that human nature must be systematically flattered, that the book must have a 'plot', that the story should end on a cheerful note, and all the rest of it.[5]

Gissing advocates for an end to literary depictions of a world filled with pleasantries and shaped by happy endings. As he would have it, the novel should not show human nature in its ideal form, but instead expose its harsh and disagreeable qualities. In these terms, he looks to inspire a different kind of aesthetic for the novel and, in turn, appeal to a different kind of reader.

In her review, Woolf picks up on this desire to cultivate a different kind of reader. She notes how Gissing's novels would most likely find their way 'to houses where *very few novels* are kept. Ordinary culti-vated people will buy them of course, but also governesses who scarcely ever read; mechanics; working men who despise novels; dons who place [Gissing] high among writers of English prose.'[6] Gissing's challenge to the novelistic conventions of his day is a marker of his incipient modernity. Indeed, Woolf's particular notice of Gissing's fiction – well after his death – situates this lesser-known nineteenth-century novelist among the more established figures of literary modernism.[7] Gissing's standing as a proto-modernist figure is generally well recognised within critical studies of his work.[8] However, a connection is yet to be made between his modernist sensibility and his stylistic interest in how his 'harsh' and 'penetrating' voice would be read, if not heard, by the reader.

This chapter highlights Gissing's attention to how his writing sounds, and thereby challenges the assumption that a literary aesthetics attuned to the ear – particularly as it pertains to the novel – is a sensibility borne out of the twentieth century. The first section draws attention to the stress Gissing's critical writing places on cultivating a reading ear that is attuned to the acoustic qualities of literary prose, suggesting how this emphasis challenges the temporal limits critics such as Melba Cuddy-Keane place on intersections between theories of listening, literary mediation and sound.[9] Gissing promotes what might be understood as a literary form of listening. As such, his criticism looks for a new kind of reader, who considers not just what writing shows but also how it sounds.[10] With this in mind, the second part of the chapter examines how Gissing's acoustic sensibility sets out an ideal model of reading, with a particular focus on his 1891 novel about novel writing, *New Grub Street*. The commercial and populist drivers of the nineteenth-century literary market serve as a cruel and unremitting backdrop to the destruction of this novel's literary heroes, Harold Biffen and Edwin Reardon. *New Grub Street* uses these figures to describe a reading prac-tice that listens for the harmonies found in classical style.

Crucially, while novelists, neither Biffen nor Reardon are novel readers; their literary pleasures lie in reading the classics. On the one hand, this can be seen as a reflection of Gissing's own preference for the early nineteenth-century classical stylist, Walter Savage Landor. On the other, it reveals Gissing's ambitions for the novel as an aesthetic form. Through close readings, the concluding part of this chapter examines how Gissing's prose in *New Grub Street* denies those diligent readers whose ears listen attentively for pleasurable harmonies within his own fiction. Consequently, if this is a chapter about Gissing's cultivation of the reader's ear, it is also about how he uses his literary voice to do something more with the novel as a literary form.[11] In this respect, the acoustic refusal we encounter in *New Grub Street* is, I suggest, continuous with Gissing's efforts as a proto-modernist to have the novel do more than just "'please people" . . . and all the rest of it'.[12]

Auditory acuity in Gissing's criticism

The immediate context for Woolf's allusion to the 'harsh', 'penetrating' and 'so little grateful' effect of Gissing's voice on the ear relates to his treatment of the poor. Her comments also reflect an acute sensitivity to the acoustics involved in literary mediation.[13] Melba Cuddy-Keane has written extensively on Woolf's particular attention to sound, suggesting that her writing is layered with an 'intricate polytextural acoustic web'.[14] As Cuddy-Keane argues, Woolf's prose reveals an 'auditory acuity' that invites a different mode of reading, which listens for the sonic textures of literary prose and is attuned to narrative emphases on perceptual experiences (395). As such, Cuddy-Keane suggests that Woolf's writing 'calls for a shift in the way that we as readers perceive', wherein the reader must 'imitate that partially passive, partially active process [involved in listening], segregating and integrating the novel's voices to create a model of its complex world' (395). Writing in the 1880s through to the 1900s, Gissing falls within a period in which, according to Cuddy-Keane, literary responses to sound are limited to 'metaphor and analogy' (383).[15] By contrast, I would argue that while Gissing's writing may not attain the same kind of 'intricate' acoustics that Cuddy-Keane ascribes to Woolf's prose, his critical writing nonetheless reveals a notable sensitivity to how the acoustic qualities of literary form shape meaning. Gissing's interest in 'reading for sonics', that is, seeks a mode of reading that listens to the affective resonances of style (395).

Underlying Gissing's 'harsh' realism is a vested interest in how writing works as an aesthetic form. Pierre Coustillas and Patrick Bridgewater observe how Gissing's notebooks and annotations reveal an author 'highly responsive to brilliant use[s] of language'.[16] For Gissing, stylistic brilliance was less likely to be found in fictional prose than in the rich and established realm of the literary essay. Thus, when he advises budding young authors to scrutinise established literary works for their compositional techniques and stylistic qualities, neither Austen, nor Dickens nor George Eliot make Gissing's list. Instead, he suggests they read 'suitable portions' of late eighteenth- and nineteenth-century writers such as Walter Savage Landor, Thomas De Quincey and John Ruskin (amongst others), noting how such a practice would offer 'a special training valuable beyond expression'.[17]

From his list, Gissing draws special attention to the Golden Treasury imprint of Landor's *Imaginary Conversations* (1882).[18] Of this, Gissing wonders whether 'a young man whose thoughts are running on style [could] do better than wear the book out with carrying it in his side pocket, that he might ponder its exquisite passages hour by hour' (84). His particular admiration for Landor here is not altogether surprising. In the ficto-biography of Gissing, written by his close friend Morley Roberts, *Imaginary Conversations* is singled out as the work which, 'by its very nature and style appealed most of all' to Gissing. As Roberts adds, 'above and beyond [the] true and great feeling of Landor's for the past classic times there was [for Gissing] the most eminent quality of Landor's rhythm'.[19] Indeed, Gissing's admiration of Landor is vital to understanding his aesthetic interests in the sounds and acoustic effects prose can convey to the reader's ear.

It is worth noting that Gissing was not alone in his appreciation of the acoustic qualities of Landor's style. For those late nineteenth-century critics who were familiar with his work, there is scant interest in the message behind Landor's writing; of principle value was his skill in composing harmonious prose. The prolific literary critic George Saintsbury enthuses how Landor managed 'language literally as a great musician manages the human voice or some other organ of sound'.[20] Expanding on this musical metaphor, Saintsbury suggests that

> nowhere else perhaps in English does prose style, while never trespassing into that which is not prose, accompany itself with such an exquisite harmony of varied sounds; nowhere is there such a complicated and yet such an easily appreciable scheme of verbal music. The sense is, as has been said, just sufficient; it is no more; it is not in itself peculiarly arresting. Although the sentiment is heartfelt, it is not exactly passionate. But it is perfectly and exactly married to the verbal music, and the verbal music is perfectly and exactly married to it. (100–1)

As Saintsbury is careful to note, the musical beauty of Landor's style far overshadows – if not compensates for – the sentiments expressed by his writing.

A large part of the appeal of Landor's sonorousness lay in his ability to 'never [trespass] into that which is not prose' (100). In a similar vein to Saintsbury (and writing in the preface to the *Golden Treasury* volume of Landor that Gissing recommends), Sydney Colvin draws attention to the 'beauty of sound' that Landor achieves in 'single sentences'.[21] 'Such is the harmony of his best prose', Colvin continues,

> that strains of it haunt the ear and memory with an effect almost as pleasurable and stirring as strains of verse. At the same time few writers have been farther removed from the fault of breaking up their prose into the fixed and recurrent rhythms of verse itself. (xix)

While likening the musical pleasures Landor's prose conveys to those found in verse, Colvin maintains that such pleasures are formally distinct from the metrical rhythms constitutive of verse.

Colvin describes the beautiful effect of Landor's style as one that haunts the ear. This idea of an acoustic haunting seems to suggest that the harmonious qualities of Landor's writing may not be registered immediately, but instead can be heard and appreciated through a process of reflection. As such, the reader is encouraged to replay 'single sentences' and to listen for the pleasurable acoustics that will subsequently sound within their mind. The withheld, or even reticent, aesthetic affect conveyed through Landor's harmonious prose is a reflection of his classicist style. As Colvin explains, unlike the romanticist who 'eagerly proclaims the impressiveness of his own ideas as he presents them', a classical style of writing assumes that the 'reader will estimate for himself the ideas which are presented to him' (xx). 'Classical writing', Colvin adds, 'asks more of the reader than romantic, and in a certain sense does less for him' (xx). Understood in such terms, a classical style instantiates an austere literary manner that requires the reader's close attention – an affect that can be achieved through 'severely regulated and measured prose', as Colvin terms it (xvii).

These nineteenth-century critical evaluations of Landor help in identifying how Gissing carried his appreciation for Landor's measured and harmonious prose style into his own critical theory. In an indicative passage from his book-length *Charles Dickens: A Critical Study* (1898), Gissing calls attention to Dickens's 'habit of writing metrically'.[22] Aligning with Colvin's praise of Landor's ability to avoid 'breaking up [his] prose into the fixed and recurrent rhythms of verse itself', Gissing is highly critical of Dickens's tendency to mimic the rhythmic patterns of verse.[23] Indeed, he refers to Dickens's metrical prose as the 'gravest of his faults', and suggests it betrays 'an ear untrained in the harmonies of prose; the worst of it is, that many readers would discover it with delight, and point to it as admirable'.[24] In other parts of the *Study*, Gissing is more forgiving of how Dickens's writing appealed to popular sentiment. He even goes so far as to offer a critical defence of the famed novelist's 'touching deference to the voice of the crowd', such as his habit of altering character's fates and plot outlines in accordance with his audience's desires (56). Gissing's tone is, however, far less conciliatory when his critical ear turns to an analysis of Dickens's style.

He is particularly judgemental of how Dickens's metrical prose lulls reader and novelist alike into an unthinking relation to literary form. The balanced cadence of metre might charm and delight readers, but Gissing argues that this 'gravest of faults' also reflects an undisciplined, automatised form of writing and reading, especially in moments of emotional intensity (136). Gissing disapprovingly notes Dickens's awareness of this habit of writing metrically. He particularly dislikes the fact that Dickens speaks 'of it as something he cannot help, and is not disturbed by it. The habit', Gissing adds, 'overcame him in his moods of softness; and therefore is particularly noticeable towards the end of *The Old Curiosity Shop*' (136). Little Nell's death at the close of this novel famously produced a public outpouring of grief. Gissing coldly aligns this emotional response with Dickens's flagrant use of poetic metre in his prose. He disparagingly equates such instances of sentimental pathos with a type of rhythmic arrangement that coerces an unreflective and uncritical form of response in the reading mind.

According to Gissing, metrical prose reflects a too easily observed form of writing and encourages a too easily absorbed form of reading. Far better, he proposes, is a 'smoother' and 'closer' strain of narration (136). He praises a literary style in which 'there are no irruptions of metre; the periods are flowing, the language is full of subdued energy' (136). Gissing's suggestion that language contains a 'subdued energy' might be compared to Colvin's account of the 'beauty of sound' conveyed through Landor's prose, which 'haunts the ear and memory'.[25] In both is the suggestion of a literary affect that in order to be felt requires a thoughtful engagement on the part of the reader. In these terms, attending to the acoustic pleasures to be found in a writer's style requires a second-order relation to literary form. It asks readers to approach fiction in a colder light, to detach their attention away from what a writer says, and instead encourages them to listen for the rhythmic energy and acoustic resonances that sound from syntactical organisation and compositional style.

Reviewers of the *Study* were struck by how Gissing sought to encourage a kind of aesthetic training against the temptations of surrendering oneself to the sentimental coercion of Dickens's prose. William Archer, for instance, writes admiringly of how Gissing models a method of reading Dickens that avoids the usual 'dangers' of 'falling into excess, whether of praise or blame'.[26] Another reviewer notes how this detached method of reading helps reveal the 'true value' of Dickens's writing:

Read him swiftly, broadly, and with an eye to the broad impression he has to convey, and, curiously, the result is no unit; on the contrary, the mind is then left full of those contradictions and qualifications which make the true appraisement of Dickens so hard. Consider him in cold blood, after the fashion of Mr Gissing, and under the dry light one element of the subject after another comes up to be judged, at last, at its true value.[27]

Gissing's criticism solicits a method of reading that guards against the impressionistic responses elicited by the ebb and flow of Dickens's melodramatic plotting and his type-driven characters.[28] It encourages the reader to embody a classical frame of mind, which is attuned to the deeper, 'haunting' resonances that sound from the page.

Thus, while in some ways removed and detached, Gissing's critical ear also engages a more thoughtful approach to thinking about literary form. The type of reading Gissing invites might be understood as a form of close listening. To invoke Roland Barthes, listening, as distinct from hearing, 'is a psychological act'.[29] As a form of internalised acoustic registration, it suggests a conscious form of thought and not just a reflexive and unthinking mode of reception. Expanding on Barthes's explanation, Garrett Stewart suggests the concept of listening lends itself well to examining the 'phenomenality' of literary reading.[30] Stewart describes reading as a process in which the mind registers – or more aptly, listens for – the ways the text 'voices' itself: 'when we read to ourselves, our ears hear nothing. Where we read, however, we listen' (11). Understood in such terms, a literary form of listening associates reading with a form of acoustic registration that concentrates upon how the words, rhythms and the cadence of a text shape our reception of print media. Similar to Stewart, Gissing points to a perceptual mode of reading that listens for the harmonies (or, in the case of Dickens, the discordances) that are conveyed through written form. Therefore, and despite its roots in a nineteenth-century literary sensibility, Gissing's auditory acuity listens beyond a metaphorical or analogical attention to sound and provides a significant proto-modernist approach to reading sonically.

Ideal readers

The idea of a literary form of listening requires readers who are properly attuned to the cadence and harmonies of the literary voice. Indeed, Gissing was acutely aware of the need to cultivate a reading practice suited to his aesthetic ideals. By the end of the nineteenth century, fiction reading was at an all time high. Improved literacy rates, cheaper forms of print production and the growth of an educated lower-middle class (a veritable breeding ground for budding novelists and novel readers) culminated in a mass reading public and, in turn, a commercially driven literary culture.[31] Like many men of letters in this period, Gissing felt some concern over what this cultural change meant for the province of 'Literature'. Indicative of this concern is his warm response to literary critic Edmund Gosse's excoriating account of the broader English reading public's stunted – if not entirely deficient – appreciation of literature, published in an article for *The New Review* in 1892.[32]

Piqued by his impression that the public outpouring of grief at Lord Alfred Tennyson's death was far from genuine, Gosse observed:

> Since the pastoral days in which poets made great verses for a little clan, it has never been true that poetry of the noblest kind was really appreciated by the masses. If we take the bulk of what are called educated people, but a very small proportion are genuinely fond of reading. Sift this minority, and but a minute residue of it will be found to be sincerely devoted to beautiful poetry. (180)

The typically retiring Gissing wrote to Gosse to express his 'satisfaction' in reading these remarks and offer his fellow sympathy.[33] Gissing's letter proposed that the sincere devotion Gosse stipulated as necessary for literary appreciation be found amongst only those who read with a 'studious leisure' (329). Accordingly, Gissing describes his model reader: a commercial traveller he once encountered as a child. He fondly recalls how this 'man of samples' pulled a 'battered, thumbed, pencilled' copy of Horace out of his bag (330). 'Without this', Gissing adds, the commercial man 'never travelled. From a bare smattering obtained at school, he had pursued the study of Latin; Horace was dear to him; he indicated favourite odes——' (331). Unlikely figure though he is, the commercial traveller embodies a reading ideal in Gissing's mind. In part, this recollection is meant to demonstrate to Gosse that one's class was not a prerequisite for cultivating a 'sincere devotion' to literary form (180). But Gissing's stress on the travelling salesman's dedication of time and concentration – such as his efforts in marking up, rereading and selecting 'favourite odes' from within a classic work – also recalls the detached and thoughtful mode of reading required of a literary form of listening.

The connection I am drawing here between Gissing's conception of an ideal reader and his interest in how writing is read as an acoustic medium becomes clearer when one considers his depiction of model reading practices in *New Grub Street*. In this novel, Gissing transposes the diligent efforts of his travelling salesman onto the literary heroes of the narrative, Harold Biffen and Edwin Reardon. The novel depicts both men in scenes of reading in which they listen attentively for and are transfixed by the sonorous beauty of literary form.[34]

An early instance occurs in Chapter 9. Seeking to escape from his own struggles to write, Reardon reads from a volume of Homer's *Odyssey*. The beleaguered author savours the harmonious 'sounding of those nobly sweet hexameters', before he translates the Ancient Greek into English for Amy, his listening wife.[35] The short recital takes the couple back to a happier time before they were married, when Reardon would unexpectedly pull Homer out of his pocket to read Amy a beautiful passage. Amy's recollection of the since forgotten pleasures she found in listening to the reading voice of this man who had a 'habit of always carrying little books about' aligns Reardon with the ideal reader Gissing describes in his letter to Gosse and elsewhere (118). Here we have someone who pursues that 'special training valuable beyond expression', by carrying about classical works so as to 'ponder exquisite passages' and cultivate a sincere appreciation of their harmonious pleasures.[36]

There is an instructional tone underpinning this reading scene. The narrative voice used to describe Reardon's pleasure in Homer's verse hovers between direct and indirect discourse: 'Yes, yes', the narrator/ Reardon observes,

> *that* was not written at so many pages a day, with a work-house clock clanging its admonition at the poet's ear. How it freshened the soul! How the eyes grew dim with a rare joy in the sounding of those nobly sweet hexameters![37]

While clearly evoking Reardon's particular enjoyment, this string of observations is not ascribed solely to the character's thoughts. The use of free indirect discourse generalises this description of taking pleasure in the text, and thereby subtly guides readers towards the particular nuances and acoustic resonances they should listen for as they read.

The narrative's implicit instruction to read sonically is reiterated in a later scene, in which Reardon and Biffen read over a passage from Sophocles' *Œdipus Rex*. Here, the two men lose themselves in a technical debate concerning the variable rhythms one might use in reading the passage in question: where Reardon scans in choriambus, Biffen proposes to treat the chorus in question 'a Ionics a minore with an anacrusis' (134). As with Reardon's reading of Homer to Amy, this reading scene serves as an exemplary account of good reading habits. Following this account of the pair's technical sparring, reference is made to the particular pleasures Biffen finds in this rigorous approach to thinking about literary form. Then the narrator describes how Biffen proceeds to involve

> himself in terms of pedantry, and with such delight that his eyes gleamed. Having delivered a technical lecture, he began to read in illustration, producing

quite a different effect from that of the rhythm as given by his friend. And the reading was by no means that of a pedant, rather of a poet. (134)

Over the course of this description, the narrative voice moves from the third person to the more ambiguous mode of free indirect discourse, before finishing by assuming the perspective of a detached observer who is able to judge Biffen's poetic sensibility. This gradual distancing of perspective has the effect of reinforcing the authority of the narrative voice. Indeed, there is a gentle seriousness – felt especially in the concluding assessment of Biffen's reading as being 'by no means that of a pedant, rather of a poet' – that ensures this earnest tone is not missed, or that reference to Biffen's pedantry is not understood as a satirical jibe directed at the pair's arcane interests.

In both of these reading scenes, the narrative models an ideal reading practice that develops from a studious attention to the harmonious qualities of classical literature. One might go so far as to suggest that, as scenes of reading aloud, both instances depict an earnest and literal-minded conception of how the literary voice might be properly attended to. Garrett Stewart, we might recall, suggests that the references to classical works in Gissing's fiction represent a form of literary nostalgia.[38] In this context he proposes that texts such as Homer's *Odyssey* and Sophocles' *Œdipus Rex*, serve as stable points of literary reference for Gissing, and provide the late nineteenth-century reader with a 'common cultural heritage' (337). Beyond rehearsing this cultural heritage, though, these reading scenes also perform a form of literary engagement that is consonant with Gissing's interest in how a reader might listen studiously to the subdued harmonies resonating within literary form. By way of expanding on Stewart's reading, these earnestly meant citations might be understood, then, as a form of literary anthologising. In line with Leah Price's suggestion that anthologising practices in the nineteenth century are far from passive, Gissing's references to classical works in *New Grub Street* demonstrate what to read as well as modelling how to read.[39] It is a cruel irony therefore, that while these scenes work to train the reader's ear to listen for the subdued tones of his literary voice, Gissing's writing consistently fails – if not refuses – to generate any acoustic pleasure as part of this process of sincere reading.

Gissing's harsh and penetrating literary voice

Reardon's reading of Homer occurs in a chapter otherwise focused on the pressures of survival within a competitive market of exchange. The chapter opens with a quantified account of his literary output, where it is calculated that 'on an average he could write four ... slips a day', which would equal 'fifteen days for the volume, and forty-five for the completed book' (113). In the pages that follow, a series of adjustments ensue, first in response to Reardon's dwindling progress, then to the diminishing quality of his work. Despite bouts of anguish and despair, he persists, working away 'a fraction of the whole, a fraction, a fraction' (116). In the spirit of the narrative's taxonomic account of Reardon's writing process, this tripartite phrasing might be read as a tabulation of the intersecting pressures of work: time, productivity and value. Literary production is accordingly framed in similar terms to any other commodity produced within a capitalist system, with Reardon's labour and the varying crises that inhibit his writing being carefully accounted for as necessary interruptions.

In this way, the chapter can be read as an exposé of the decline in the quality of literary writing that ensues when serious-minded authors are subject to the exigencies of a modern literary system. We read of how the pressures placed upon Reardon produce 'intolerable faults of composition' (116). In similar terms to Gissing's disdainful account of Dickens's poor use of metre, the narrator draws attention to risible acoustic flaws occurring in Reardon's prose:

> He would write a sentence beginning thus: 'She took a book with a look of——;' or thus: 'A revision of this decision would have made him an object of derision.' Or, if the period were otherwise inoffensive, it ran in a rhythmic gallop which was torment to the ear. (116)

Reardon continues to turn out this inferior work, despite the fact that 'his former books had been noticeably good in style', and that he had 'an appreciation of shapely prose' (116). This decline implies that under the pressures of time and productivity, a modern writer has no capacity to sustain the craft and rigours required of good style. Reardon's literary voice is consequently silenced by the noise of bad style.

The episode in which Reardon enjoys Homer occurs shortly after this account of his struggle to control the acoustic matter of his writing. Notably, while contemplation of Homer's hexameters offers a 'rare joy' to the beleaguered novelist, this pleasure is made conspicuously unavailable to Gissing's reader, with the lines Reardon reads conveyed in 'free prose'.[40] Thus, we read:

> For never yet did I behold one of mortals like to thee, neither man nor woman; I am awed as I look upon thee. In Delos once, hard by the altar of Apollo, I saw a young palm-tree shooting up with even such a grace. (117)

Reardon's translation of classical Greek hexameters into English free prose no doubt prevents those unversed in Ancient Greek from feeling wholly alienated from this scene. Yet this translation also has a profound effect on the acoustic impression the reader is able to derive from the overall passage. Having effectively silenced the metrical pleasures to be found in Homer, the more striking sonic aspects of this scene sound from the narrator's preceding description of the 'intolerable faults' that trouble Reardon's prose (116). The easy stutter of took/book/look and revision/decision/derision recall an earlier moment in the novel, which draws attention to the efficiency and penetrating effect of a telegraphic style of writing.[41] Read with this in mind, the short and sharp echoic phrasing of Reardon's faulty prose works as a troublingly effective – and dominating – counterpoint to the elongated phrasing of the translated, unmetered passage from Homer. Thus, despite pointing to the pleasures found when one reads with an ear concentrated on the acoustic effects of literary writing, the narration of this scene limits the reader's access to this same harmonious effect.

This refusal of sonic pleasures is more blatant in the later reading scene between Biffen and Reardon. Consumed by the pleasures of pedantry, the two men lose track of time and place, talking 'Greek metres as if they lived in a world where the only hunger known could be satisfied by grand or sweet cadences' (134). From this allusion to their distracted enjoyment, the narrative focus moves on to describe the history of Biffen and Reardon's friendship. We learn of Biffen's 'dire poverty', as the narrator recounts in tawdry, if not satirical terms the 'preposterous ambitions' held by the only slightly less impoverished clerks who seek tuition from Biffen (134–5). Biffen's jobbing work is documented down to the most banal details, including descriptions of the methods of advertisement his students use to find a tutor, the fees they will pay and the number of students he might have on hand at any one time (134–5). While Reardon and Biffen are absorbed in the delights of Greek metre and are transported from the grim realities of their existence, the reader is held firmly in place by a bleak narrative voice, which relentlessly details the sad facts of their impoverished existence.

In the passage that follows, the narration turns to describe Biffen's practice as a writer. Before any progress on this matter is made, however, the narrative voice switches perspective in an awkwardly self-conscious manner: 'Then as to his authorship.—But shortly after the discussion of Greek metres he fell upon the subject of his literary projects, and, by no means for the first time, developed the theory on which he worked' (135).[42] The sudden, intervening em dash before 'But' marks a precipitous change of perspective from an impersonal narrative voice back to free indirect discourse. This abrupt insertion of that most notice-able of grammatical signs in nineteenth-century writing – the long dash – suggests a rupturing within the literary finish of Gissing's prose. The two vocal modes here jar against one another, as free indirect discourse rudely interrupts the narrative voice's descriptive flow. The usually silent work that effects transitions between voices within literary writing is, consequently, materialised on the page.

The awkward presence of the em dash suggests a rushed, somewhat self-consciously managed attention to the workings of narration. This sense of a metatextual self-awareness intensifies as we read on and learn of the literary theory Biffen is applying to his own novel writing. As Biffen explains to Reardon:

> What I really aim at is an absolute realism in the sphere of the ignobly decent ... I want to deal with the essentially un-heroic, with the day-to-day life of that vast majority of people who are at the mercy of paltry circumstance ... The result will be something unutterably tedious. Precisely. That is the stamp of the ignobly decent life. If it were anything *but* tedious it would be untrue. I speak, of course, of its effect upon the ordinary reader. (135)

It is hard not to read Biffen's dedication to depicting the 'ignobly decent' as a reference to Gissing's own relation to realism. Biffen's focus on 'day-to-day life' and refusal to appeal to the reader's interests recalls Gissing's recommendation of a harsher, 'disagreeable' style of novel writing in 'The Place of Realism in Fiction'.[43] In this vein Aaron Matz suggests that Biffen's absolutist literary ambitions reflects Gissing's satirical take on contemporary debates about literary realism.[44] While this may be so, Biffen's comments also refer to the effect literary writing has on the reader. In this respect, these self-reflexive comments speak to a more immediate preoccupation with the process of narration itself. Biffen's recognition of the unutterable tedium an ordinary reader will encounter when faced with an overly descriptive literary style conse-quently reads as a direct commentary on the affective contrast between the process of reading *New Grub Street* and the reading experiences that the novel depicts.

Silent translation and such awkwardly managed transitions under-score an aesthetic failing in how the literary prose of this novel is 'heard' by the reader. These scenes of reading thus reveal a disjunction between Gissing's theoretical account of the harmonious qualities of literary writing and how he allows his own prose to sound. In *New Grub Street* Gissing, quite literally, crafts a literary voice that, as Woolf puts it, is 'so harsh, so penetrating, so little grateful to the ears'.[45] This refusal of prosaic harmonies in preference for a harsher literary voice might be read as indicative of his hostility towards the novel as an aesthetic form. For in a perverse manner, the discordance of Gissing's prose in scenes that insist upon the pleasures of classical form implicitly suggests that the harmonious tones he ascribes to the literary voice are not suited to the form of the novel – or at least to the form and function of the novel as it was generally conceived of and consumed at the close of the nineteenth century. A suggestion corroborated by the notable absence of novels in Reardon and Biffen's reading scenes. Writing of these contradictory impulses, Virginia Woolf constructs a typically evocative portrait of Gissing's increasingly rigid materialism in his late style. According to Woolf, Gissing's sole ambition was to '"manage a page that is decently grammatical and fairly harmonious" . . . [and that might] stand out like stone slabs, shaped and solid, among the untidy litter with which the pages of fiction are strewn'.[46] While evoking an artisanal mode of writing that seems out of time with modernity, Woolf's words nevertheless capture Gissing's acutely felt modern preoccupation with experimenting with the limits of literary form as a medium for the literary voice.

Notes

1. Woolf, 'The Novels of George Gissing', p. 677.
2. Woolf, p. 677.
3. Jameson, *The Political Unconscious*, p. 190.
4. Matz, 'Some Versions of Vitriol', p. 31. See also Matz's chapter on Gissing in *Satire in an Age of Realism*, pp. 70–104.
5. Gissing, 'The Place of Realism in Fiction', pp. 85–6. Gissing was not, of course, the first to express such sentiments. As Jacob Korg and Cynthia Korg point out in *George Gissing on Fiction*, his argument in this essay echoes Henry James's insistence that fiction be freed from established narrative moulds in his 1884 essay, 'The Art of Fiction' (Korg and Korg, pp. 82–3).
6. Woolf, p. 676, my emphasis.
7. On Woolf's writing on Gissing, see Coustillas, '"A Voice that Spoke Straight and Shapely Words"', pp. 1–29.
8. See, for instance, Ryle, '"To Show a Man of Letters"', pp. 119–32; McCracken, 'George Gissing Urban Modernity and Modernism', pp. 13–20.
9. Cuddy-Keane, 'Modernist Soundscapes and the Intelligent Ear', pp. 382–98.
10. Gissing's focus on the reader was, in part, typical of the 1880s. As Adrian Poole writes in *Gissing in Context*, 'the really crucial confrontation during the eighties . . . is the one between writer and reader' (p. 116). Dames also considers Gissing's attention to reading, but in this instance to the speed of reading, in *Physiology of the Novel*, pp. 207–46.

11. On Gissing's interest in the state of the novel, see also: Taft, '*New Grub Street* and the Survival of Realism', pp. 362–81 and Stewart's chapter on Gissing, 'Grubbing for Readers', in *Dear Reader*, pp. 329–42.
12. Gissing, p. 86.
13. Woolf, p. 677.
14. Cuddy-Keane, 'Modernist Soundscapes and the Intelligent Ear', p. 386; Cuddy-Keane, 'Woolf, Sound Technologies, and the New Aurality', pp. 69–96; Cuddy-Keane, *Virginia Woolf, the Intellectual, and the Public Sphere*, pp. 59–114.
15. Cuddy-Keane supports her point with reference to John M. Picker's thorough account of the ways in which developments in theories of sound in the nineteenth century heightened an interest in 'close listening' in Victorian fiction (Picker, *Victorian Soundscapes*, p. 9). While, to a certain extent I would agree with Cuddy-Keane's account of how Picker treats the intersections between sound and writing, her assumption that nineteenth-century literary aesthetics remains limited to a metaphorical and analogical treatment of acoustics is, as my reading of Gissing goes some way to suggest, open to debate.
16. Coustillas and Bridgewater, *George Gissing at Work*, p. 49.
17. 'George Gissing', in Bainton (ed.), *The Art of Authorship*, pp. 83–4.
18. Landor's *Imaginary Conversations* were first printed as a series of five volumes, between 1824 and 1829.
19. Roberts, *Private Life of Henry Maitland*, p. 226.
20. Saintsbury, *Essays in English Literature 1780–1860*, p. 100.
21. Colvin, Preface to *Selections From the Writings of Walter Savage Landor*, p. xix.
22. Gissing, *Charles Dickens: A Critical Study*, p. 136.
23. Colvin, p. xix.
24. Gissing, p. 136.
25. Colvin, p. xix.
26. Archer, '*Charles Dickens: A Critical Study*', *Daily Chronicle* (23 February 1898), 3; repr. Coustillas and Partridge (eds), *George Gissing: The Critical Heritage*, p. 320.
27. 'Rev. *Charles Dickens: A Critical Study*', *New York Tribune, Illustrated Supplement* (3 April, 1898): 16; repr. Coustillas and Partridge (eds), p. 330.
28. G. H. Lewes refers to the hallucinatory immediacy generated by Dickens's writing and characters in 'Dickens in Relation to Criticism', pp. 145–6.
29. Barthes, *Responsibility of Forms*, p. 245, emphasis in original. Jonathan Sterne makes a similar point, observing: 'Listening is a directed, learned activity: it is a definite cultural practice. Listening requires hearing but is not simply reducible to hearing.' Sterne, *Audible Past*, p. 19.
30. Stewart, *Reading Voices*, p. 3.
31. On this, see Brantlinger, *The Reading Lesson* and McDonald, *British Literary Culture and Publishing Practice*.
32. Gosse, 'Tennyson – and After', reprinted in Gosse, *Questions at Issue*, pp. 177–98.
33. Gissing to Gosse, 20 November 1892, reprinted in Gosse, *Questions at Issue*, p. 325.

34. Stephenson also addresses the 'complexity of reading', particularly as it relates to mass literacy, in *New Grub Street*, in 'Mr. Baker and Miss Yule', pp. 3–26.
35. Gissing, p. 117.
36. Gissing, in Bainton (ed.), *The Art of Authorship*, p. 84.
37. Gissing, *New Grub Street*, p. 117.
38. Stewart, *Dear Reader*, p. 337.
39. Price writes, 'anthologies are more than a referendum. They determine not simply who gets published or what gets read, but who reads, and how.' *Anthology and Rise of the Novel*, p. 3.
40. 'Free prose' is a term used in *New Grub Street* to describe Reardon's translation, p. 117. Gissing was particularly interested in how English translations could mimic the rhythms of Greek metre. See Gissing, 'The Pronunciation Of Greek', p. 13. In this respect he was attuned to broader cultural debates concerning hexametric translations of classical Greek, an account of which is found in Prins, 'Metrical Translation', pp. 229–56. Thanks to Sean Pryor for his help in thinking through this point.
41. See Jasper Milvain's account of the snappy title given to the journal he finds employment with ('The Current'), p. 70.
42. On Gissing's self-conscious style of narration in this novel, see also Christina Lupton and Tilman Reitz, '*New Grub Street*'s Self-Consciousness', in *Voices of the Unclassed*, pp. 133–44.
43. Gissing, 'Place of Realism', p. 85.
44. Matz, *Satire in an Age of Realism*, p. 74.
45. Woolf, p. 677.
46. Woolf, 'George Gissing', in *The Common Reader: Second Series*, available at: <https://ebooks.adelaide.edu.au/w/woolf/virginia/w91c2/chapter18.html> (last accessed 1 June 2016).

Chapter 10

Body and Soul: Modernism, Metaphysics, Rhyme

Sean Pryor

I

By the time Louis Armstrong recorded 'Body and Soul' in Los Angeles on 9 October 1930, thereby establishing Johnny Green's sinuous tune as a jazz standard, it was already a hit. But the words for the tune kept changing. 'My days have grown so lonely, / For I have lost my one and only', Armstrong pines. 'My life is sad and lonely; / I wait and sigh for you dear only', croons Pat O'Malley in the song's first recording, made in London in February with Jack Hylton and his Orchestra. Partly this is because three or four lyricists were involved in composing and recomposing the song over the course of that year, and partly it is because different versions were published in Britain and in America.[1] What's more, in rehearsing amorous banalities the particular words seem not to matter very much. 'My pride has been humbled', Armstrong continues, 'For I'm hers, body and soul'. That final phrase, the song's title, never changed. When Edward Heyman first proposed the title to Robert Sour and Frank Eyton, the three lyricists spent days deciding whether to use 'body and soul' at the beginning or the end of a line.[2] The result might have resembled the lyrics Frank Loesser wrote for Hoagy Carmichael's 1938 tune, 'Heart and Soul': 'Heart and soul, I fell in love with you, / Heart and soul, the way a fool would do'. Instead, each refrain of 'Body and Soul' returns inexorably to that culminating title phrase: 'I was a mere sensation; / My house of cards had no foundation; / Although it has tumbled, / I still am hers, body and soul'. Each refrain begins with its own rhyming couplet ('lonely'-'only', 'sensation'-'foundation') and a third rhyme then binds successive refrains ('humbled'-'tumbled'). None of these rhymes has the spark of those by a Cole Porter or an Ira Gershwin at his best. The lover's loneliness ironically matches the matchlessness of his one true love; only a common suffix sets the lover's past success against the substance which that success had lacked; and past participles determine both formulations of the lover's fall. But at last, as Green's melody finally resolves on the tonic, nothing rhymes with *soul* except for *soul*. No attempt at wit or charm, no sentimental rhetoric or romantic design affects the sense of this word with likeness or contrast. The soul of this poor lover is properly singular.

Body and Soul had been the title of Paul Robeson's first film, directed by Oscar Micheaux and released in 1925, as well as the title of silent films by George Irving (1915), Charles Swickard (1920), and Reginald Barker (1927). In 1921 Arnold Bennett used it as the title for a play. (It flopped.) The phrase was in vogue, though it had a long history. It appears in the 1549 Book of Common Prayer, and John Wesley and Charles Wesley often use it in their hymns: 'Waken'd by the trumpet's sound / Body and soul shall soon arise'.[3] But 'Body and Soul' seems to put asunder what history, fashion and grammar have joined together. By placing the title phrase at the end of the refrain, by refusing to find a regular rhyme for *soul*, and by having *soul* fall with the melody's closing perfect cadence, the song seems to privilege soul over body: I am hers not just in body but even in soul. Yet because *soul* rhymes only with itself, the song also suggests a union of soul and body. Whether in Armstrong's gravel tones or Billie Holiday's rasp, whether live or on record, the body of the word *soul*, its material being as sound, belongs only to this word's sense, the expression of our lover's inmost thoughts, of the immaterial soul itself. In contrast, the sounds of *lonely* belong to *only* too, and that correspondence counterpoints a woebegone narrative of cause and effect: I am lonely because I love you only. It would have been simple enough to find a rhyme for *soul*, and so to produce a comparable relation between senses. Loesser closes 'Heart and Soul' by finally letting its title phrase fall at the end: 'That little kiss you stole / Held all my heart and soul'. This rhyme, too, describes a neat if predictable correspondence: even more than hearts, souls are for stealing. And to establish that correspondence, the shared sounds of *soul* and *stole* belong equally to the two words' distinct senses. In rhyme, the shared sound, the body of language, seems to be emphasised and detached, sundered from the soul expressed in language, the specific sense. In moving from regular rhyme to identical rhyme, it is thus as though each refrain of 'Body and Soul' charts a progress from metaphysical dissonance to harmony, from division to unity.

In this essay I want to consider the relation of rhyme to metaphysics not in the popular song of the late 1920s and early 1930s, but in the poetry of that period, much of which explicitly invites comparison with song.[4] On both sides of the Atlantic, poets and critics debated the necessity and the meaning of rhyme at length. As free verse became increasingly dominant, modernist poems variously abandoned rhyme, parodied it and made it new. It is customary to think of modernist rhyme in terms of inheritance and innovation: 'rhyme is part of the Tradition that the Individual Talent embraces, but at arm's length'.[5] And it is customary to think of the modernists exposing the artifice or contingency of rhyme: they display 'the device as device ... showing it to be merely what it is, and thereby dispensable'.[6] I want to suggest that modernism also worked with and against rhyme because this seeming fetter or decoration, a matter merely of verse technique, was and had long been crucial to the representation and the understanding of bodies and souls. The relation between body and soul was a problem of some moment. 'Body and Soul' was banned in Boston for being too risqué, and for a time the NBC network refused even to name its title.[7] New technologies, new sexual freedoms, new race relations, new developments in brain science, the continuing vogue for spiritualism, the clash of religion with secularism or materialism – all put pressure on inherited conceptions of body and soul.[8] The problem exercised many British and American poets, from Mina Loy to Wallace Stevens, H.D. to T. S. Eliot. Some were eager to topple the traditional hierarchy of soul over body; some resisted the reduction of all spirit to mere matter; some wanted to break free from such dualisms altogether. And though it might seem in this context no more than 'a silly ornament',[9] rhyme was intimately involved in the metaphysics which underpinned moral, religious and philosophical systems.

Classical Greek and Roman poets did sometimes rhyme, but rhyme's ascendancy came with the shift from quantity to accent in the prosody of late antiquity. For Hegel, these developments participated in the shift towards a modern conception of body and soul. 'After the barbarian invasions', Hegel writes, came 'the corruption of accentuation' and 'the Christian emphasis on the personal inner life of feeling'.[10] In the quantitative metres of classical poetry, the 'corporeal side of the language' remains essential: every syllable is measured and arranged. 'But the more inward and spiritual the artistic imagination becomes', the more poetry 'emphasizes only that wherein the spiritual *meaning* lies for the purpose of communication' (2: 1023). Accentual prosodies harness correspondences between stress and significance: it's the *lone-* in *lonely* that matters, and with which a witty rhymester may play, not the *-ly*.[11] This is why rhyme fastens on stressed syllables; conventionally, you cannot rhyme *lonely* with *sadly*. This is also why alliterative metres fasten on stressed syllables: 'I shoop me into shroudes as I a sheep were, / In habite as an heremite unholy of werkes'.[12] The ascendency of rhyme or alliteration thus represents a new antagonism between sound and sense, matter and spirit, body and soul. In comparison to classical versification, 'rhyme is on the one hand more material but, on the other hand, within this material existence is more abstract in itself'.[13] Rhyme singles out and emphasises certain sounds, but only because they are the bearers of the sense. Verbal sound becomes a 'material medium', a vehicle (2: 1024). We listen for the recurrence of *lonely* in *only*, and we trace a narrative in their conceptual relation. As Simon Jarvis explains, the individual's new experience of interiority is thus set against the external world, and in particular against 'the sensuous and habitually sinful body of language'.[14] In this way, Hegel argues, 'rhyme is not something accidentally elaborated in romantic poetry' – by which he means post-classical poetry – 'but has become necessary in it'.[15] The rise of rhyme matches the prosodic shift from quantity to accent and, more fundamentally, the development and dominance of a modern metaphysics. For Hegel, Jarvis concludes, rhyme 'is part of what makes Christian and ultimately modern subjects possible'.[16] Rhyme expresses and participates in an epochal change in the shape of spirit.

Some years before the Visigoths sacked Rome, Augustine turned to the division between body and soul in order to understand the nature of language, and of the sounds of speech in particular. In *De doctrina christiana* Augustine urges that to tarry with the material of language, at the expense of the sense expressed in language, is a grievous error. When we interpret a figurative expression as though it were meant literally, we forget that 'the letter killeth, but the spirit giveth life' (2 Corinthians 3: 6); we understand the expression only in 'a carnal way [*carnaliter*]'.[17] To subject the intelligence 'to the flesh [*carni*] by following the letter', Augustine warns, is a 'death of the soul [*animae*]' (140–1). Augustine extends this metaphysical division when he argues that the material of language, whether in writing or in speech, is arbitrary, since language is socially constituted. The two syllables of *lege* mean one thing to a Greek speaker, he reasons, and another thing to a Latin speaker. The meanings of the sounds 'derive their effect on the mind from each individual's agreement with a particular convention', and people did not arrive at those conventions because the sounds 'were already meaningful; rather they became meaningful because people agreed to use them'.[18] Sense precedes sound, and body is subordinate to mind. Thus, when we speak,

> the word [*verbum*] which we hold in our mind [*corde*] becomes a sound in order that what we have in our mind [*animo*] may pass through ears of flesh [*carneas*] into the listener's mind [*animum*]: this is called speech. Our thought, however, is not converted into the same sound, but remains intact in its own home, suffering no diminution from its change as it takes on the form of a word [*vocis*] in order to make its way into the ears. (22–5)

Here, again, verbal sound is a material medium for the expression of an inner, independent and immaterial thought.

With this in mind, consider these five famous lines, traditionally attributed to the Emperor Hadrian, who died more than 250 years before Augustine began *De doctrina christiana*:

> animula vagula blandula
> hospes comesque corporis
> quae nunc abibis in loca
> pallidula rigida nudula
> nec ut soles dabis iocos.[19]

The prosody of this poem measures and arranges syllables according to their length. But the pressing question is how to understand and to judge the way, in addition to that quantitative metre, the poem plays with the sounds of its words, especially in the first and fourth lines but also in the other lines' repetitions of consonant and vowel. How does this loving attention to the body of language, to every movement of the tongue and the lips and the throat, reflect or affect the poet's fond address to his soul, soon to depart his dying body?

> Ah fleeting Spirit! wandr'ing Fire,
>   That long hast warm'd my tender Breast,
> Must thou no more this Frame inspire?
>   No more a pleasing, chearful Guest?
>
> Whither, ah whither art thou flying!
>   To what dark, undiscover'd Shore?
> Thou seem'st all trembling, shivr'ing, dying,
>   And Wit and Humour are no more![20]

First we need to note that both in the Latin original and in Alexander Pope's translation the soul expressed in language is not the 'animula' or 'Spirit' to whom the poem is addressed. Beyond *animula* and *corpus*, and beyond *spirit* and *breast*, the poet or subject is a third term or pole, implied in the Latin poem by the figure of apostrophe and named in Pope's translation as an *I*: 'my tender Breast'. The 'animula' or 'Spirit' is not the seat of identity and interiority. It seems to some extent a form of vital force, not unlike the notion of ψυχή or soul sometimes employed by Homer (see, for instance, *Iliad* 5.296, 11.334), though it does have its own particularity or character, having once been wont to jest ('ut soles dabis iocos', 'Wit and Humour are no more!'). The inmost thoughts of the individual, communicated through a verbal medium, reside not in the little soul or spirit but in that third term, the apostrophising subject.

In this light, it is possible to feel that the rhymes in Pope's translation trivialise the solemn moment of death with merely superficial and
adventitious correspondences. To figure the departing spirit (*spirare*,
to breathe) as a fire which inspires (*in* + *spirare*), and to figure the
spirit as a guest in the breast, might be to tarry culpably with the letter
at the expense of the poem's own animating spirit; it might even be
said to let the letter overrule that spirit, to let the sound lead the sense.
Though the subject in the Latin poem does address his little soul as
'hospes', a guest, that soul has been the guest of the whole body ('cor-
poris'), not of the breast in particular, whether that breast be a synecdoche for the body or the seat of life. Yet the original poem can, in
turn, seem even more trivial in its prosody. Its first line plays not with
the words' significant roots (*anim-*, *bland-*, *vag-*), but with the suffix
of diminution (*-ula*): this, some might complain, is mere homoeoteleu-
ton. To linger with the body of language in this way, in the very line
which addresses that wandering, pleasing little soul, might be judged
inept and inappropriate. Or it might, in a poignant irony, emphasise
the very scission of sound and sense, and so represent a last brave sally
of wit and humour against inevitable death, when body and soul shall
be sundered forever.

But Pope seems not to have read the Latin verses in either of these
ways. 'I was the other day in company with five or six men of some
learning', he recalls in a letter to Steele on 7 November 1712,

> where chancing to mention the famous verses which the Emperor *Adrian*
> spoke on his deathbed, they were all agreed that 'twas a piece of Gaiety
> unworthy that Prince in those circumstances. I could not but differ from this
> opinion: Methinks it was by no means a gay, but a very serious soliloquy to
> his soul at the point of his departure.[21]

Pope's companions censure the gaiety of the Latin poem's prosody, its
trifling with the body of language. But far from defending that gaiety
as irony, Pope hears gravity, solemnity, sincerity. (This, despite the fact
that a work like *The Rape of the Lock* plays precisely with the gravity
of levity, the profundity of superficiality.) 'The diminutive epithets of
vagula, *blandula*, and the rest', Pope adds, 'appear not to me as expressions of levity, but rather of endearment and concern' (149). That is to
say, Pope hears a significant sense in the Latin suffix and its repetition:
he hears endearment and concern. Pope thus seems to feel no antagonism, in reading these lines, between the body of language and the soul
expressed in language, because the body is properly, even virtuously
subordinate to the soul: the sounds serve the sense.

The Latin poem precedes by some centuries the invasion of the barbarians and the shift from quantitative to rhymed metres, but Pope's disagreement with his friends tells us not about the transition from classical to late Latin prosody, but about how, for many modern poets and readers, the sound of poetry is implicated in a metaphysics. As a consequence, religious and philosophical frameworks frequently shape technical decisions and aesthetic judgements. So, too, Hegel's arguments about the advent of rhyme in late antiquity represent a modern poetics, and one in which verse technique is intimately involved in the shape of spirit. This continued to be the case for many poets, critics and readers into the twentieth century. The rise of scientific measurement led acoustic scientists equipped with phonautographs, kymographs and other instruments to image and to study the performance of poetry and so to ground rhyme in its 'physical basis'.[22] Pursuing this approach in 1931, Henry Lanz chastised the 'superstition' that 'poets through their rhythms and rimes express the deepest moods and loftiest sentiments of their souls' (294). For Lanz, rhyme was first and foremost a physical phenomenon. And in his 1914 study of Thomas Hardy, D. H. Lawrence argued that the 'very adherence to rhyme and regular rhythm is a concession to the Law, a concession to the body, to the being and requirements of the body'.[23] Lawrence thus conceives of verse technique in biblical terms. 'But now we are delivered from the law', Paul writes in his Epistle to the Romans, 'that we should serve in newness of spirit, and not in the oldness of the letter' (Romans 7: 6). On the one hand, then, Lawrence means adherence to the regular rhymes of older, inherited verse-forms, and it is true that his poetry moved in time towards newer, 'freer' forms.[24] His 1928 *Collected Poems* is divided, according to a rough chronology, into two sections, the first entitled 'Rhyming Poems' and the second entitled 'Unrhyming Poems'. (Nevertheless, many of the later poems do rhyme.) In 1923 Lawrence praised Whitman's verse for springing 'sheer out of his soul, spontaneous, like the song of a bird. For a bird doesn't rhyme and scan.'[25] And as early as 1916, Lawrence was urging a friend that one should use 'rhyme *accidentally*, not as a sort of draper's rule for measuring lines off'.[26]

On the other hand, even accidental rhyme is a concession to the law and to the body. Irregular rhyme schemes, internal rhymes, alliterations, assonances and other forms of phonemic repetition all represent concession to the letter – to the material, the external, the inflexible, the body of language. Some concession is necessary, and even desirable, for Lawrence also celebrates the body. 'We have roots', he writes in the introduction to *Pansies* (1929), 'and our roots are in the sensual, instinctive and intuitive body, and it is here we need fresh air of open consciousness.'[27] Body and soul are essentially distinct, and both are essential to aesthetic success. 'Artistic form is a revelation of the two principles of Love and Law in a state of conflict and yet reconciled.'[28]

II

'We are dying', Lawrence urges in 'The Ship of Death', which he wrote in late 1929 as his health failed: 'we are all of us dying'.[29] Where the dying Hadrian had addressed his little soul, Lawrence addresses us all: 'Build then the ship of death, for you must take / the longest journey, to oblivion' (631). The poem imagines the soul's departure from the body, its voyage on the ship of death into nothingness, and its return into the body again; it is a poem of rebirth. The poem also rhymes, if only accidentally or occasionally, for before pressing us to build the ship of death it asks: 'How can we this, our own quietus, make?' (630). More often and more importantly, Lawrence's poem makes its metaphysics with alliteration, assonance and other forms of phonemic repetition:

> And in the bruised body, the frightened soul
> finds itself shrinking, wincing from the cold
> that blows upon it through the orifices. (630)

The poem thus figures the soul in the body and as a body, subject to and recoiling from physical sensation. This soul is itself twin: matter and spirit, cold and frightened, passive and active. (Its activity takes the form of self-consciousness: the soul *finds itself* shrinking and wincing.) This figurative or metaphorical body, as Augustine would put it, is the poem's own body, distinct from the bodies and souls it names. And this metaphorical body is mediated by the poem's material body, the sounds of its words. Much as Loesser's rhyme suggests that souls are for stealing, Lawrence's loving attention to verbal sound seems to suggest the soul's necessary or natural subjection to the cold that blows: the /əʊl/ in 'soul' sounds again in 'cold' and then is echoed, inverted, in the /ləʊ/ of 'blow'. To 'find' oneself is to be 'frightened' (/f/, /aʊ/, /nd/), or to be frightened is to find oneself. Bodies are for bruising; bodies are always already bruised (/b/, /d/).

But that is virtuously to subordinate the arbitrary body of language to the essential soul expressed in language; it is to make sound serve sense. We could instead insist that 'The Ship of Death' celebrates the soul's eventual return to body – 'and the frail soul steps out, into her house again / filling the heart with peace' (633). And we could in that case listen for sounds that lead the sense, though to do so in the name of the poem's narrative would be, nonetheless, to privilege an inner, independent and immaterial sense. Lawrence's poem can offer no easy solution to these dualisms; its narrative relies upon them:

> Already our bodies are fallen, bruised, badly bruised,
> already our souls are oozing through the exit
> of the cruel bruise. (631)

But though the poem can imagine souls surviving bodies, it cannot offer sense without sound. Lawrence's incantatory repetitions of phoneme, word and phrase emphasise the mutual mediation of that narrative and of verbal sound. Far from fallen as inanimate matter, the body of language is always already ensouled.[30] This means that the dialectic of the body of language and of the soul expressed in language is not a metaphor for or a repetition of the story the poem tells about bodies and souls. The dualisms do not coincide: Lawrence's poetry lives in the difference between them.

This difference animates a great deal of modernist poetry. It is crucial to the echolalic repetitions and the striving for repentance in Eliot's *Ash-Wednesday*, whose third section was published in the Autumn 1929 issue of *Commerce*, just as Lawrence was writing 'The Ship of Death': 'Blown hair is sweet, brown hair over the mouth blown, / Lilac and brown hair; / Distraction, music of the flute, stops and steps of the mind over the third stair'.[31] Eleven years earlier, the difference had been crucial to the rhymes, the assonances and the other echoings in Eliot's quatrain poems: 'He knew the anguish of the marrow / The ague of the skeleton; / No contact possible to flesh / Allayed the fever of the bone.'[32] One might also remember Stevens's 'Peter Quince at the Clavier': 'Beauty is momentary in the mind – / The fitful tracing of a portal; / But in the flesh it is immortal'.[33] But I want instead to consider the sequence of poems which W. B. Yeats began to write in 1929 and which would in 1932 be published as *Words for Music Perhaps*. These short lyrics are important first because they seem to turn away from Yeats's preoccupation, in *The Tower*, with the survival of the soul after death, and to turn instead towards the bodily, the sexual and the abject.[34] Yeats had made similar moves and countermoves before. In 1898 he opposed 'positive science' and 'exterior law' to a poetics of the inner and the spiritual, 'a rhythm too delicate for any but an almost bodiless emotion'.[35] 'Everything that can be seen, touched, measured, explained, understood, argued over, is to the imaginative artist nothing more than a means, for he belongs to the invisible life' (143). But in 1907 Yeats wrote that art 'bids us touch and taste and hear and see the world', that art shrinks 'from all that is of the brain only, from all that is not a fountain jetting from the entire hopes, memories, and sensations of the body' (212). As Denis Donoghue said long ago, Yeats had an 'intense and painful preoccupation with the seemingly irreconcilable claims of Soul and Body'.[36]

The poems of *Words for Music Perhaps* are important second because they return us to the question of rhyme's relation to music or song.[37] If modern music 'tries to find in sound the material most correspondent [to] subjective life', writes Hegel, and if rhyme specifically shapes those verbal sounds 'wherein the spiritual *meaning* lies', then rhymed 'versification approaches what is as such musical'; it approaches what Hegel calls 'the notes of the soul [*des Inneren*]', of interiority.[38] The short lyrics in *Words for Music Perhaps* all rhyme, some feature refrains, two are titled songs, and one is titled a lullaby. But the equivocation in the title of the sequence is significant; in September 1929 Yeats told Olivia Shakespear that '"For Music" is only a name' and that nobody would actually sing the poems.[39] That March he had explained that he conceived of them as poems for music, 'not so much that they may be sung as that I may define their kind of emotion to myself. I want them to be all emotion & all impersonal.'[40]

In October 1930, just as Louis Armstrong was recording 'Body and Soul', Yeats was revising 'Crazy Jane on the Day of Judgment', a poem he had begun drafting in October the previous year. In the first draft, Yeats had imagined a single refrain across three stanzas: 'Love is for wholes whether of body or souls.'[41] In the finished poem, that wholeness of body or of soul becomes the wholeness of body and soul together, and two refrains alternate across four stanzas. The poem begins:

> 'Love is all
> Unsatisfied
> That cannot take the whole
> Body and soul';
> *And that is what Jane said.*
>
> 'Take the sour
> If you take me,
> I can scoff and lour
> And scold for an hour.'
> *'That's certainly the case,' said he.*[42]

Here, too, it is easy to hear how rhyme establishes relationships of likeness or contrast. This has long been the customary approach to Yeats's rhymes.[43] It is sour to be loured at for an hour, and to take the whole means to take not just the body but also the soul. Then there is the passing implication that love is all – love is everything – when or because it takes body and soul together. For a moment 'all' is almost a noun, rather than an adverb, just as it had been a noun in early drafts: before settling on the line's final form, Yeats experimented with 'Passion asks for all' and then, more simply, 'Love asks all'.[44] A substantive *all* would have established another neat congruence with wholeness and with the soul. The adverbial *all*, in contrast, proves ironic: love is wholly unwhole unless it take the whole. And neatly enough the consonance of 'all' with 'whole' and 'soul', in place of a 'full' or 'perfect' rhyme, matches that ironic relation, that missed wholeness or dissatisfaction. (In 1914 Yeats remarked that he had, in revising a poem, removed a 'mechanical rhyme in the middle of carefully inexact rhymes'.)[45] Rhyme itself seems all unsatisfied when, in rhyming with 'Unsatisfied', the refrain finishes not with a resounding 'cried', but only with '*said*'. Nothing is more satisfying, to a metaphysical poetics, than these subordinations of sound to sense.

In 'Crazy Jane talks with the Bishop', Jane rises from a conversational 'said' to an impassioned 'cried', from 'I met the Bishop on the road / And much said he and I' to '"Fair and foul are near of kin, / And fair needs foul", I cried'.[46] But in 'Crazy Jane on the Day of Judgment', '*said*' is not Jane's verb; it is the refrains'. The prosaic verb belongs to that feature of the poem which most clearly associates it with song. Perhaps Jane can intend the congruence of 'whole' and 'soul', and can intend the irony of 'all', though '*said*' sets some distance between Jane's expression and the verse-form. Jane cannot in any case intend the irony of '*said*', or the unequal oppositions configured by 'me' and '*he*': taken and taker, first person and third person, speech and narration. If there is a soul expressed throughout this language, it is the poem's own soul. It is the spirit of song, or of poetry as song, of song as a modality of poetry.

To say so does not mean separating out and celebrating the poem's meaningless materiality, even as a riposte to strict or excessive idealism. Not even Jane's nonsense is strictly senseless: 'So never hang your heart upon / A roaring, ranting journeyman. / Fol de rol, fol de rol.' (509). Yeats was simplifying things when he said, in a letter in 1934, that there was 'no special value in "fol de rol"' and that 'any meaningless words would do'.[47] 'I put "fol de rol" at the end of the stanzas', Yeats added, to make the poem 'less didactic, gayer, more clearly a song'. There is a self-reflexive aspect to this – the refrain signifies the poem's quality as song – but it has other effects, too. As a conventional refrain, variations of which appeared as long ago as the eighteenth century, 'fol de rol' signifies its age: its nonsense has a history.[48] The 'rol' then rhymes, however 'imperfectly', with other rhyme words in the poem's two stanzas ('fool', 'bull', 'whorl', 'pearl'), and the 'rol' alliterates with 'roaring' and 'ranting', so that Jane's 'meaningless' refrain meaningfully matches Jack's sound and fury signifying nothing.[49] The spirit of song, then, animates general affects and specific meanings. It animates specific or local affects, too, if for instance we feel the small fall or check or deflation – no name is adequate – which happens as 'Crazy Jane on the Day of Judgment' moves from long vowel ('all') and diphthongs ('-fied', 'whole', 'soul') to short vowel ('*said*'). There is this spirit of song even when, as is often the case in *Words for Music Perhaps*, the whole poem is in the first person. 'I want them to be all emotion & all impersonal', Yeats said. In 'Crazy Jane and Jack the Journeyman', Jane imagines a final sundering: 'I – love's skein upon the ground, / My body in the tomb – / Shall leap into the light lost / In my mother's womb.'[50] But the spirit of song is always already and forever embodied, and it is collective.

It is largely an accident that 'The Ship of Death', *Ash-Wednesday* and *Words for Music Perhaps* were written and published at much the same time, though further examples from the late 1920s and early 1930s are not far to find. In 'The Widow's Jazz', which Mina Loy wrote in 1927 and which was published in 1931, Loy's typically rich repetitions of consonant and vowel are set against the music of a jazz club in an elegy for a lost lover: 'this cajoling jazz / blows with its tropic breath // among the echoes of the flesh'.[51] In 1925 Langston Hughes published 'The Weary Blues', in which the blues grounds the rhymes and rhythms, and in which body and soul ground the blues: 'Swaying to and fro on his rickety stool / He played that sad raggy tune like a musical fool. / Sweet blues! / Coming from a black man's soul.'[52] But the spirit of song is not a soul in the customary sense. It is not the soul of an individual. It is not an inner, independent and immaterial origin, which then finds expression in a body's movements or in language.[53] The spirit of song happens as rhyme, as rhythm and refrain, as alliteration, assonance and other forms of phonemic repetition. It is by no means particular to modernism, but modernist poetry does, I think, set it against the inherited metaphysics of moral, religious and philosophical systems with particular force. Hughes's poetics confounds what was then the routine reduction of blues, and of African Americans, to the bodily, the sexual and the abject. Crazy Jane pits her 'bodily lowliness' against the Bishop's 'heavenly mansion', her unrepentant sexuality against his pious moralising, but 'Crazy Jane talks with the Bishop' pits their dispute against its own dialectic of matter and spirit.[54] What matters most, for modernism, is that verbal sound is never mere matter and is as much a making as a medium.

Notes

1. Friedwald, *Stardust Melodies*, pp. 156–7.
2. Friedwald, p. 148.

3. Wesley and Wesley, *Poetical Works*, vol. 11, p. 176; Cummings (ed.), *Book of Common Prayer: The Texts of 1549, 1559, and 1662*, p. 37. The phrase recurs in the 1559 (pp. 137, 139, 162, 174) and the 1662 texts of the Book of Common Prayer (pp. 300, 360, 396, 403, 405, 433, 440, 456).

4. For a discussion of poetry's relation to popular song in this period, with particular reference to forces of assimilation and miscegenation, see Bernstein, 'Objectivist Blues: Scoring Speech', pp. 346–68.

5. Albright, 'Modernist Poetic Form', p. 26.

6. Wesling, *The Chances of Rhyme*, p. 40.

7. Friedwald, p. 148.

8. For a good survey of some of these and of related developments, see Bell, 'The Metaphysics of Modernism', pp. 9–32. For a key early study on modernism and the body, see Armstrong's *Modernism, Technology, and the Body*. Golston's *Rhythm and Race in Modernist Poetry* is rare in approaching the problem through the question of poetic technique.

9. Flint, 'Presentation: Notes on the Art of Writing', p. 19.

10. Hegel, *Aesthetics: Lectures on Fine Art*, vol. 2, p. 1025.

11. This depends on the phonological structure of the language in question, and so it is truer of English and German than French and Italian. 'Because most English rhymes involve the root rather than the inflectional ending or suffix', writes Derek Attridge, 'the semantic contrast or parallel between the two words is more prominent than it is in French' (Attridge, *Moving Words*, p. 61).

12. Langland, *The Vision of Piers Plowman*, p. 1. For Hegel's discussion of alliterative metres, see Hegel, vol. 2, pp. 1029–30.

13. Hegel, vol. 2, p. 1028.

14. Jarvis, 'Musical Thinking', p. 63.

15. Hegel, vol. 2, p. 1023.

16. Jarvis, p. 64.

17. Augustine, *De doctrina christiana*, pp. 140–1. Sigur Burckhardt echoed this argument, without the moral judgement, in 1956: 'Metaphors, then, like puns and rhyme, corporealize language, because any device which interposes itself between words and their supposedly simple meanings calls attention to the words as things.' See Burckhardt, 'The Poet as Fool and Priest', p. 283.

18. Augustine, *De doctrina christiana*, pp. 100–1.

19. Duff and Duff (trans.), *Minor Latin Poets*, p. 444, capitalisation and punctuation removed.

20. Pope, *Minor Poems*, p. 93.

21. Pope, *Correspondence of Alexander Pope*, vol. 1, p. 149.

22. Lanz, *The Physical Basis of Rime*. For accounts of the history of laboratory prosody in the late nineteenth and early twentieth centuries, see Hall, 'Mechanized Metrics', pp. 285–308; and Hall, 'Materializing Meter', pp. 179–97.

23. Lawrence, *Study of Thomas Hardy and Other Essays*, p. 91.

24. Many critics have emphasised and approved this narrative. See, for instance, Gilbert, *Acts of Attention*; and Sagar, *D. H. Lawrence: Poet*.

25. Lawrence, *Studies in Classic American Literature*, p. 417.

26. Lawrence to Catherine Carswell, 11 January 1916, in *Letters of D. H. Lawrence*, p. 503.

27. Lawrence, introduction to *Pansies* (1929), in *The Poems*, vol. 1, p. 664.

28. Lawrence, *Study of Thomas Hardy*, p. 90. Kalnins offers a detailed account of Lawrence's developing conception of body and soul, and in particular of his late turn from what he considered to be the metaphysics of Judaism, Christianity and the Orphic cults to the 'pagan' metaphysics of the Egyptians, the Chaldeans and the pre-Socratics. For Lawrence, the former conceives of the soul fallen into the body, redeemable only through departure from this world; the latter celebrates the mutual necessity of body and soul, and so conceives of cycles of rebirth. See Kalnins, introduction to *Apocalypse and the Writings on Revelation*, by D. H. Lawrence, pp. 3–24.

29. Lawrence, *The Poems*, vol. 1, p. 631. I quote from the second of three versions of this poem, all of which were published posthumously. See, also, 'Ship of Death' and 'The Ship of Death' (*The Poems*, vol. 1, 594–7, 633–4).

30. See Nowell Smith, *Sounding/Silence*, p. 121.

31. Eliot, *Complete Poems and Plays*, p. 93.

32. Eliot, 'Whispers of Immortality', in *Complete Poems and Plays*, p. 52.

33. Stevens, *Collected Poetry and Prose*, p. 74.

34. See Clark, introduction to *Words for Music Perhaps and Other Poems*, by W. B. Yeats, p. xxv. As early as 1927, Yeats remarked that his new poem, 'A Dialogue of Self and Soul', represented 'a choice of rebirth rather than deliverence [*sic*] from birth'. See W. B. Yeats to Olivia Shakespear, 2 October [1927], in *Collected Letters of W. B. Yeats*, #5034. Directly comparing 'Crazy Jane talks with the Bishop' and 'The Ship of Death', Marcus contrasts Yeats's vacillation between deliverance and rebirth with Lawrence's resolute desire for a reconciliation 'achieved not beyond but within the world'. See Marcus, 'Lawrence, Yeats, and "the Resurrection of the Body"', pp. 235–6.

35. Yeats, *Early Essays*, pp. 140–1.

36. Donoghue, 'The Vigour of Its Blood', p. 376.

37. For a recent discussion of song as an influence on and aspiration for nineteenth-century poetry, see Helsinger, *Poetry and the Thought of Song*.

38. Hegel, vol. 2, p. 1023.

39. Yeats to Olivia Shakespear, 13 September [1929], in *Collected Letters*, #5285.

40. Yeats to Olivia Shakespear, 2 March [1929], in *Collected Letters*, #5221. At first, however, Yeats does seem to have conceived of them as songs to be set to music. See Saddlemyer, 'Poetry of Possession', pp. 155–6. Yeats had long been interested in the relation between speech and song, and in the possibilities of performing poetry as musical speech or bardic chant. For a thorough account of this interest, see Schuchard, *The Last Minstrels*.

41. Yeats, *Words for Music Perhaps and Other Poems*, p. 351. This first draft is dated 29 October [1929]. A later draft, though not the last, is dated October [1930] (Yeats, *Words for Music Perhaps and Other Poems*, p. 361).

42. Yeats, *Variorum Edition*, p. 510.

43. Perloff anatomised the semantic relations generated by Yeats's rhymes in *Rhyme and Meaning in the Poetry of Yeats*. Vendler continues this approach to Yeats's rhymes in *Our Secret Discipline*.

44. Yeats, *Words for Music Perhaps and Other Poems*, p. 357. The sense of 'whole' also depends on Yeats's lineation. The word seems to be a noun, with 'Body and soul' in apposition, so that to take the beloved whole is to take body and soul together: 'take the whole[,] / [take both] Body and soul'. But 'whole' might instead be an adjective, so that Jane emphasises taking the whole body: 'take the whole / Body and [the whole] soul'. The phrase would then suggest divisions within body and soul, as well as the division between them. This was Yeats's original thought. In the first draft Jane urges Jack to 'touch – all pōtions [portions] of / my body – every plane & mound – omit / but one I shall think of Jim or John / or some that might take your place' (Yeats, *Words for Music Perhaps and Other Poems*, p. 351). Not taking the whole body thus means not receiving the whole soul.

45. Yeats to Lady Gregory, 14 March [1914], in *Collected Letters*, #2417.

46. Yeats, *Variorum Edition*, p. 513.

47. Yeats to Margot Collis, 23 November [1934], in *Collected Letters*, #6134.

48. Yeats would very probably have known Robert Browning's 'Mr. Sludge, "The Medium"' (1864): 'Fol-lol-the-rido-liddle-iddle-ol!' See Browning, *Complete Works*, p. 288. Yeats might also have known George Farquhar's *Sir Harry Wildair* (1701):

> *Lurewell*: I tell you, Sir, your Wife was a Jilt; I know it, I'll Swear it. – She Vertuous! She was a Devil.
> *Wildair [Sings]*: Fal, al, deral.

See Farquhar, *Sir Harry Wildair*, p. 34.

49. The effect is different in 'The Pilgrim', whose refrain of 'fol de rol de rolly O' rhymes with no other line (Yeats, *Variorum Edition of the Poems of W. B. Yeats*, pp. 592–3).

50. Yeats, *Variorum Edition*, p. 511.

51. Loy, *Lost Lunar Baedeker*, p. 96.

52. Hughes, *Collected Poems*, p. 50. Gordon E. Thompson has recently argued for understanding African American poetry as fundamentally lyric, not least in its responses to and adaptations of spirituals, blues, jazz, funk and other musical forms. For Thompson, emphasising the 'lyricism' of African American poetry attunes us to 'the power of sound and feeling over the power of words as rational signs'. See Thompson, 'Introduction: Lyrical Aesthetics in African American Poetry', p. 10.

53. Culler persuasively argues against reducing lyric poetry to expression, though of course expression remains important in certain works and traditions. See Culler, *Theory of the Lyric*, pp. 73–85.

54. Yeats, *Variorum Edition*, p. 513.

Chapter 11

Listening to the Late Cantos

Kristin Grogan

Titter of sound about me, always
                    (Canto 5)

In the early 1950s, Ezra Pound, a seasoned student of languages who had famously brought a copy of Confucius and a Chinese-English dictionary to the Disciplinary Training Centre outside Pisa in 1945, complained of the difficulties he was experiencing in learning to speak Chinese. In a letter to the Harvard-based Sinologist Achilles Fang, Pound wrote that he found Chinese to be 'fer somethings the most precise and, in fact, only satisfactory medium for making certain statements', but that it was also 'the most damblasted and DAMbiguous modus loquendi, wot yu cant bust open with a meat AX'.[1] Only late in his life, with all the spare time that incarceration in a psychiatric hospital allowed, did Pound make a serious attempt to learn the spoken words of a language that he had been reading and translating for over thirty years. By 1951 he included himself among the number of 'pore mutts trying to learn a little chinese, esp/ SOUND'.[2]

Pound's awareness that Chinese can indeed be spoken was, to be sure, a belated revelation. The cantos that Pound wrote in the 1950s constitute one of the last seismic shifts in *The Cantos* as a whole: for the first time, the Chinese character is present not only as an organisational concept or a structural principle, but as a major medium of writing and representation in its own right.[3] This new awareness of Chinese phonetics is part of a broader restructuring in the late poems of the role and possibilities of sound. Yet when writing about the late cantos, and especially their heavy use of Chinese characters, critics have tended to think of the late poems in terms of a divide between the aural and the visual, which has meant that sound in the late cantos has received little critical attention. In an early review of *Section: Rock-Drill*, Dudley Fitts wrote:

The Chinese, like the (I suppose) Egyptian hieroglyphs at the beginning of Canto 93, the medieval musical notation in Canto 91, and the fragments of Greek, Latin and other languages disject and stream throughout the text – these . . . are romantic doodles – like the compulsions of a man so fascinated by the contours of a Greek word that he is constantly jotting it down on envelopes and tablecloths and the rocky skulls of his children.[4]

Fitts was one of the first to think about the late poems in terms of a conflict between 'lyric interludes', 'flashes, unsustained and unsustaining' and the late poems' 'romantic doodles'. Massimo Bacigalupo writes that in the early cantos of *Rock-Drill* 'the English text is overshadowed by large, silent, Chinese characters', which, as a result of their material presence, 'preserve their magic appeal'.[5] This is to create and uphold an ontological difference between textual forms that are silent and magical, and those which are spoken, and, by implication, average or everyday. In her study of lyricism in *The Cantos*, Mutlu Konuk Blasing creates a similar divide by contending that the ideograms block the eye's access to the circuit between the mouth and the ear, and suggesting that 'ideograms have an undeniable material presence, but for the Western reader, they also present a principle alien to the materiality of spoken language. They represent a disembodied materiality.'[6] Blasing goes so far as to suggest that for the non-Chinese reader, Chinese is 'purely a visual language . . . a language purged of sounds, cleansed of the body and its vicissitudes' (169). Blasing's reading restricts our understanding of Pound's audience to a sort of uncurious anglophone reader, yet this restriction is one that Pound actively resists throughout both his criticism and the poem itself. More recently, new readers who come to Pound by way of Peter Wilson's *A Preface to Ezra Pound* will be told of the 'visual richness' of the late poems' ideograms and hieroglyphs.[7] In *The Buddha in the Machine*, R. John Williams concludes his analysis of the relationship between the ideogram and the machine by superimposing a page from Canto 85 against a sketch of Jacob Epstein's sculpture 'Rock Drill'.[8]

What is missing here is a full discussion of the sound of the late poems. In various ways, these readings all think about the late cantos in terms of a conflict between sound and image, and tend to equate Pound's use of Chinese characters and other non-textual forms with the visual and, in turn, with moments of silence or inaccessible sounds. Williams's overlain diagram is only the most recent and most unambiguous example of a longstanding critical tendency: to read the late poems the way we read images.[9] Taking the Chinese character as Pound's major formal renovation in the late poems and thus as a useful starting point, this chapter revisits the question of sound in Pound's late cantos. My intention here is not to document Pound's complex and lengthy relationship with sound media: his career as an opera writer, a music critic, or indeed a Fascist radio broadcaster. Rather, my aim is to rethink some of the critical tendencies that have shaped the way we think about sound in the late cantos, and to revisit some of the contests that have structured our readings of the late poems: between the visual and the aural, between sound and silence, and between accessible and inaccessible poetic material. By the time of the late cantos Pound's view of sound has changed – and we, as attentive readers, ought to keep up.

'One's opinions change as one progresses', wrote Pound to the doctoral student Angela Jung: '[A person] should not be held responsible for what he said or wrote decades earlier.'[10] Certainly, by the time of the late cantos Pound's approach to Chinese sound – and sound in poetry more broadly – had shifted. Pound's initial approach to the sound of Chinese was shaped in large part by his encounter with the work of Ernest Fenollosa, whose *The Chinese Written Character as a Medium for Poetry* argues that Chinese characters constitute a new medium but that medium is, above all, visual and pictorial.[11] This view has, of course, been widely criticised by Sinologists as a misrepresentation of the language, just as Pound has attracted his share of criticism for his use – or misuse – of the language. In Fenollosa's reading, each individual character 'is based upon a visual shorthand picture of the operations of nature'.[12] Pound, following that line, accepted that there was a motivated relationship between the signified and signifier, and was thus convinced that it was possible to interpret the characters without any prior study of Chinese by relying on visual literacy alone. He famously wrote of Henri Gaudier-Brzeska that

> he was so accustomed to observe the dominant line in objects that after he had spent, what could not have been more than a few days studying the subject at the museum, he could understand the primitive Chinese ideographs (not the later more sophisticated forms), and he was very much disgusted with the lexicographers who 'hadn't sense enough to see that that was a horse', or a cow or a tree or whatever it might be, 'what the . . . else could it be! The . . . fools!'[13]

Pound's praise of the sculptor's eye champions a particular type of intelligence and interpretative skill – a way of seeing that perceives a relationship between language and nature. By the 1930s, Pound was arguing not only that a character is 'the picture of a thing', but that 'the Chinese still use abbreviated pictures AS pictures, that is to say, [the] Chinese ideogram does not try to be the picture of a sound, or to be a written sign recalling a sound'.[14] Even after two decades of studying Chinese, Pound remained uninterested in the sonic elements of a language that had been so crucial to the development of his early poetics.

By the time of the composition of the late cantos, however, Pound was engaged in an enthusiastic and rigorous attempt to school himself more fully in Chinese, and especially in its sounds, which he had belatedly recognised as, firstly, extant, and, secondly, poetically important. That this development in his thinking is traceable is due in large part to a 2008 collection of letters edited by Zhaoming Qian, *Ezra Pound's Chinese Friends: Stories in Letters*. The volume shows how throughout the 1950s Pound corresponded extensively with Chinese scholars and poets and attempted to learn conversational Chinese from visitors to St Elizabeth's. Pound admitted to Achilles Fang in 1952 that 'for years I never made ANY attempt to hitch ANY sound to ideograms, content with the meaning and visual form'.[15] In January 1951 Pound sent a 45-page typescript to Fang entitled 'Preliminary Survey' which shows his efforts to understand the development of Chinese sound as 'not only inflected but also agglutinative'.[16] Moreover, Pound's translation of the Confucian *Odes* was initially intended to appear as a three-way 'scholar's edition', which was to include character, translations and Pound's own sound key for the characters.[17] In 1952 Pound was so convinced of the unbreakable link between the Chinese character and its sound that he proposed to Fang that 'ten deaths, the execution with 34 cuts or some other ADEQUATE punishment shd/be held over the neck of anyone who attempts to separate these phonetic . . . expositions from the Chinese text'.[18] What follows, then, can be read as an effort to avoid that punishment by paying the sounds of the late poems due attention.

While the late cantos were composed under the sign of intellectual renewal, they were equally affected both by the particular auditory conditions of St Elizabeth's and against the landscape of the mass media of mid-century American capitalism such as it was filtered through to Pound. Richard Sieburth describes the 'oppressive acoustic environment' of Pound's life at St Elizabeth's. Pound had little control over the sounds surrounding him in the hospital; outside his room, patients would make noise or watch television. Sieburth suggests that *Rock-Drill* and *Thrones* 'are probably the only two major American poems ever written with a television running continually in the background'.[19] Nurses at the hospital noted that while in his room, Pound would 'constantly hum . . . appears at times to be singing . . . At times have heard him humming some kind of tuneless chant at night.'[20] Barbara Holdridge and Marianne Mantell witnessed these conditions when they visited Pound to record him reading in 1952. Mantell described their first encounter as such:

We came to Pound, as most people come to Pound's poetry, with uncertainty and a feeling of less than total sympathy. Pound came to us as a teacher to his disciples. To him we looked exactly like two girls who had spent close to their last $20.00 on the midnight bus to Washington. . . . By the afternoon, he was ready to record – in Provençal, and on our promise not to release the recording while he was confined. 'Bird in cage does not sing,' he said, many times. The machine was set up on the lawn, and Pound began to recite. These lyrics are onomatopoetic, and as he sang of birds, the birds perched overhead and sang too. In the background, inmates hooted.[21]

Sound, then, was a significant feature of Pound's intellectual and epistolary life, and a key component in the intellectual activity that fuelled the composition of the late poems. At the same time, however, Mantell's description points to a tension between that intellectual rejuvenation, and Pound's powerlessness over his lived conditions and auditory environment ('bird in cage does not sing'). Caught somewhere between the reinvigoration and constraint that defined Pound's late life, in the late poems, sound takes on the full weight of both.

What does it mean to sound out a poem? In what ways do we think of our reading of a poem as also involving the ear? 'I listen the way I read', wrote Roland Barthes, distinguishing between the physiological process of hearing and the psychological and interpretative act of listening.[22] Reading can be likened to listening because both involve a hermeneutics and attention; the production or anticipation of sounds aligns reading closely with speaking. We might say that a poem can be sounded if it can be read aloud or if we can anticipate a reading aloud by internally processing the words (this is partly what Jeremy Prynne has called our 'mental ears'). Written poems not only register sound, but they organise it in certain ways. A written poem (and its reading) might fall somewhere between the upper limit of music and lower limit of speech that Louis Zukofsky sets out in his calculus in 'A'-12. Thus prosodically even or metrically stable poetry has been said to resemble music, and free verse to resemble speech – Tennyson is closer to music; Whitman to speech.[23] In either scenario, poetry is attempting to replicate on the page a way of organising sound that we hear and use in life. Thus when critics describe the late cantos as having blockages and periods of silence, or forms of expression that cannot be spoken, the underlying anxiety is that Pound's late poems have broken a contract or a pact that poets and readers have long since implicitly agreed upon and maintained. If that relationship was altered with the early revolutions of modernism and with the advent of free verse and the broken pentameter, by modernism's late stages that contract is subject to yet another renegotiation.

Always reaching towards the condition of songs by virtue of their title, *The Cantos* are in general concerned with the nature of sound, different types of sound, and the ways in which poems can organise, record, mimic or produce sound. These efforts take on new importance and new forms as the long poem moves into its late stages. After seven lines of poetic text, the second canto of *The Pisan Cantos* switches to the violin line of Clément Janéquin's *Le Chant des Oiseaux* arranged by Pound's friend, the German pianist Gerhard Münch.[24] This is to leave poetry aside altogether, however briefly, and to push against or past that upper level limit, music. Similarly, the beginning of Canto 91 of *Rock-Drill* consists of a two-line melody written in medieval musical notation, a code that will be inaccessible to most readers and that Pound makes no effort to teach us (91/630). We might be more likely to recognise the violin line of Canto 75 as music, or even to be able to read it ourselves, whereas Canto 91 relies on a familiarity with medieval song. Sound, and access to sound, is thus bound up with the late poems' dynamics of power and knowledge. At other points the poem presents us with symbols or icons that can be sounded, but matches them instead with other words – as in the playing card symbols that end Canto 88. How do we deal with the suits? Do we sound out the unnamed *heart / diamond / club / spade*, or do we read 'And / fifty / 2 / weeks / in / 4 / seasons', knowing that they describe and match the suits, but that doing so will leave the symbols *as* symbol, and silent symbol as that? (88/609) Here there is a disjunction between image and word offered. In response, we can either implant a signifier that is not written out in the poem, or we can read the text offered, embracing the disjunction – and most of us, probably unthinkingly, would opt for the latter. This is one of the ways in which disjunction becomes a fundamental, not only an incidental, principle in the late poems.

What, then, of the Chinese character? At least initially, much of an Anglophone reader's ability to sound out the figure will depend on its attachment to a transliteration. Most of the time Pound keeps the character and its corresponding transliteration close together. This is not so much to make a distinction between ideogram as visual form and Romanisation as sounded form – and thus to imply that they must always be together in order to be aurally comprehensible – as it is to create a bond in which they are mutually reinforcing. With enough time and familiarity, to subtract one element will not be to subtract the other. We see this effect most clearly in the characters that Pound leans upon most heavily. By the end of *Thrones*, we can all recognise *pen yeh* 本 業 ('a developed skill from persistence', as Pound glosses the characters in Canto 99) in either its ideogrammic or transliterated form; to experience one is always to conjure up and experience the other (99/718).

That relationship is why we read some instances of separation between ideogram and character as a loss. One of the things that this can do is offer us lessons in reading. Sean Pryor has shown how the late poems endeavour to teach the reader and how this pedagogical relationship in turn shapes the late poems. This teaching is sometimes done through processes of repetition and subtraction. In Canto 91, for example, Pound includes the character 旦 glossed as 'tan, the dawn' (91/635). When we next encounter it a few cantos later, the word is simply 'tan': transliterated but not translated; it is up to us to recall the meaning.[25] Sometimes Pound offers us lessons not only in how to read, but how to read aloud or to speak. He is extraordinarily attentive to the tonal features that distinguish Chinese words, drawing our attention to 'ching / in the 4th / tone' (88/601). But he also leaves us with a half or incomplete knowledge, such as this lesson in listening and speaking:

> 尸   to act that, training the child as
>
> 尸   shih, in the 1st tone
>
>   (88/602)

Pound's character shih is a slight variation of *shih* 尸, meaning corpse. Within the context of a canto that describes a Mencian conflict over the respect owed to the living and the dead, the character opens up questions of inheritance and intergenerational transmission of knowledge. Here the reader is placed in the position of the child; we are trained through repetition to read *shih* correctly, in the high and level first tone. Except that we are not: that the first tone is high and level is left unsaid. The poem only meets us halfway in its teaching, telling us which tone to use, but not what the tones themselves mean or do. Without that lesson – which we can imagine Pound easily providing, given his proclivity for including musical scores or the fact that he requested musical approximations of the tones from Fang – we are left with the promise of understanding dangling, pledged and only half fulfilled.

Elsewhere those lessons in sound are entirely lacking and the ideogram is left to speak for itself. But in many cases I would argue that the effect of withholding a transliteration is linked to the forms of power and control that the late poems create, such as in Canto 98 of *Thrones*:

> She being of Cadmus line,
>   the snow's lace is spread there like sea foam
> But the lot of 'em, Yeats, Possum, and Wyndham
>   had no ground beneath 'em.
>
>   Orage had.   不
>
>   (98/705)

The character is *bù*, a negating word (not), which is left conspicuously untransliterated. One reading would be to match the refusal or negation denoted by the word with the denial of its sound. Declining to give us the character's sound is part of the late poems' claim to authority, for to give us an easy understanding of the character would be to cede ground, to relinquish the clout that Pound and A. R. Orage, the editor of *The New Age*, have claimed and must continue to assert. This is a dynamic of power, both over his peers and, by association, his readers. Sound, when withheld deliberately, is used as a tool and bargaining chip in those particular competitions of authority. The late cantos sometimes use silence for pedagogical or poetic effect, turning it into a medium in its own right – but this is not to say, as other critics and indeed a younger Pound have claimed, that the Chinese character is always silent. Instead, the ideogram becomes workable material, used to mediate the relationship between sound and silence and between reader and text.

If Pound sometimes uses the ideogram without transliteration, he also does the opposite. There are extensive passages in the late poems where the Chinese character is absent and the Romanisations stand alone. This is particularly true of Canto 99, where sound and speech are at stake in both the poem's form and themes. The canto reformulates the Kangxi Emperor's *Sacred Edict*, a seventeenth-century series of sixteen maxims designed to instruct the people in Confucian values. Pound had access to two versions of the *Edict*, collected in a 1907 edition: a literary text produced by Kangxi's son, Emperor Yongzheng (Yong Tching in Pound's spelling) and a vernacular version from 1726 written by the Salt-Commissioner Wang Youpu. As a reformulation of a vernacular text that aims to instruct a populace, this canto focuses on 'speed in communication', 'public teaching' and 'taking the sense down to the people'. In such a context, the poem's sound becomes all the more essential, and all the more contested.

There are just four characters in Canto 99. Without the character, Pound does new things with sound, and sound in turn is able to do new things. Within a canto about clarity and efficiency of verbal communication and instruction, the poem's sound facilitates a countervailing tendency towards wordplay and experiment. This wordplay, as with much of Pound's polyglot wordplay, hinges on a relationship between the sound of a word bearing a similarity to words in another language, and either a difference or similarity of meaning. It hinges, too, on the disjunction between the freely available experience of sound and withheld or specialised knowledge. Thus we find examples such as a line in Canto 99 which describes 'meng^2, the people, the many, the menée / the perishing' (99/715). Each iteration of 'people' has a slightly different valence. The

English *many* places the emphasis on multitudes, the French *menée* from *mener*, to lead, suggests a passive crowd; *meng* is glossed as 'the people', which might feel like the emphasis is on social or national ties, rather than quantity; and they all imply an opposition to a few. If the many can see and hear the alliteration, only the few can make full sense of it. Sound without meaning creates a confidence or secret that sits in tension with the efficiency and clarity of speech and its social role that Canto 99 advocates. It allows for a sort of negative capability that might help us better understand the frequent discrepancies we feel between Pound's stated aims and intentions and the actual results: it helps the poet to hold two things at the same time, however contradictory, without one fully undercutting or neutralising the other.

Elsewhere the balance tips more heavily towards sound for its own sake, or towards a fetishisation of sound and its relation to the world:

> Tinkle, tinkle, two tongues? No.
> But down on the word with exactness,
>   against gnashing of teeth (upper incisors)
>   chih, chih!
>   wo chih^3 chih^3
>   wo^4 wo ch'o ch'o, paltry yatter
>   wo$^{4\text{-}5}$ wo$^{4\text{-}5}$ ch'o$^{4\text{-}5}$ ch'o$^{4\text{-}5}$
>   paltry yatter.
>   (99/722)

The primary mode of this passage is onomatopoeia, the collapsing of sense into sound and sound into sense.[26] *Chih*^{3} is a soft consonant sound which means upper incisors, or to gnash the teeth; while *ch'o*$^{4\text{-}5}$ refers to grating teeth, and *wo*$^{4\text{-}5}$ means 'paltry'.[27] When those single-stressed beats are repeated they create the sounds they evoke. So too do 'tinkle' and 'gnashing' imitate their referents. The lines create a single bilingual mouth ('Two tongues') and briefly makes our mouth, as well, bilingual. But it is resistant to its own effects: it is abruptly stopped, 'No. / But down on the word with exactness'. The passage declares itself *against* those gnashing teeth, the yatter it describes is 'paltry'. Yet, against its own intellectual argument, the poem's sonic texture pushes towards that yatter (as if to describe a thing is always to revel in that thing). And, of course, these words are exact, for onomatopoeia brings us away from a Saussurian arbitrariness of the sign and towards a mimetic relationship between sound and word. This is a form of sound symbolism or iconicity. But for Pound, it is also part of a tendency that dates back at least as far as his first encounters with Fenollosa, to make a fetish out of forms of language that preserve a 'natural' link with the world. In the ordered social world of Canto 99 and its edicts, that link between language and nature participates in another organic relationship between proper social behaviour and good governance, which all depends on the clarity of spoken language. It is no surprise, then, that the figure whose oratory power looms largest over this canto is Mussolini.

Pound's recorded readings, made freely available thanks in large part to Pennsound, might inform the way we think about sound in the late poems. Here Charles Bernstein's 1998 edited collection *Close Listening*, which 'attempt[s] to rethink prosody in the light of the performance and sounding of poetry' and to find a 'prosody for the many poems for which traditional prosody does not apply' is a useful model.[28] Unsurprisingly, given its argument in favour of verbal authority, Canto 99 was the only poem from *Thrones* that Pound chose to read as part of the Caedmon recordings which took place at St Elizabeth's in June 1958 and which Harper Collins eventually released on cassette as *Ezra Pound Reads*.[29] It is an extraordinarily energetic reading of the poem, in which Pound adopts his characteristic chant-like persona cultivated early and modelled largely after Yeats. Pound's pronunciation and accent are often inexpert (although a generous interpretation might suggest that this is a product of his infamous tone deafness and notorious lack of musical ability). Pound was never one to be discouraged by lack of experience, and the reading is strikingly active and enthusiastic. That we lose little and gain much in the transition from page to recording shows the limitations of the argument that the late poems are primarily visual; those late recordings show Pound as a seasoned broadcaster, making his speech purchasable and available to be heard, his lessons to be learned.

Sound performs certain types of work, and one of the things it can do is act as a structural agent. Sound can bind words more closely together, or push them away from one another. In the paratactic landscape of late modernist verse, and in the late cantos in particular, this is all the more pressing. One of the critical orthodoxies of the late cantos has to do with coherence, or the way that the line, the canto, or the volume, fall together. The late cantos, we are often told, do not hang together in the way that poems ought to hang together. Reviewing *Rock-Drill* in 1956, Randall Jarrell wrote that the volume was made up of 'indiscriminate notes' – and we might be tempted to hear a musical pun in that description.[30] Similarly, in a 1960 review of *Thrones*, John Wain argued that 'to call the Cantos a long poem is perhaps stretching the word "poem"' because 'a good deal of the Cantos, as one leafs through them page by page, consists of notebook jottings and other material which bears no relationship to verse'.[31] Wain describes the late cantos as having 'fewer lyrical passages and more doodling' and argues that reading them is like listening through the keyhole to some grand old scholar, working on a vast theory of history, muttering to himself as he moves about his study, trying to put his hand on the right book, repeating dates and quotations to himself, suddenly bursting into oratory. (454)

Our response to this might then be to deny this charge of poetic laziness, to assert that the notes are not just 'doodling', but rather a particular type of verse that requires its own methods of interpretation. Or, we might affirm that the late poems are indeed just notes, but that this is, in fact, fine and acceptable – and thereafter we can offer new ways of navigating those notes.

Critics have thought about this problem of coherence on various scales and often in relation to sound. For Hugh Kenner, the late cantos 'put on display discrete elements, phrases, single words', and force us to focus on each word, each syllable, slowly and one at a time; this is also what Bacigalupo has called the 'microscopic feasts' of the late poems.[32] More recently, Michael Golston has approached this issue on a macro level. Picking up on Pound's theory of the 'great bass', Golston argues that the late cantos are structured around a series of inaudible codes and rhythms, which form part of the totalitarian political strategy of the late cantos. 'It is as if, in order to anchor the unordered fragments comprising the text', Golston writes, 'Pound has placed a meticulously measured *beat*, a repetition stitching the fragments into a fabric.'[33] Golston's aim is, in part, to 'rescue Pound from any charges of compositional carelessness or undue haste', but also to remind us that this inaudible rhythm forms the 'unconscious heartbeat of a corporate, blood-based State' (145).

The poems are 'microscopic' or they are 'inaudible': either way, we are at the very limits of what we can perceive. When the poem's structure, coherence, and its very status as a poem are in question in such a way, sound and its functions take on new weight. Sound becomes a way of mediating between factors and relations that become more urgent and more tense as the poem progresses – for even if we reject the claim that the late poems are 'doodlings', their formal contours do fundamentally change. Will sound work with or against the poem's inconsistencies and ambiguities? Will it smooth, exacerbate, or mask the poem's conceptual and formal tensions? Will it help its fragments to cohere, or deepen the cracks between them?

Let's look, for example, at the opening lines of Canto 106:

AND was her daughter like that;
Black as Demeter's gown,
                    eyes, hair?
Dis' bride, Queen over Phlegethon,
        girls faint as mist about her?

The strength of men is in grain.   管 Kuan
NINE decrees, 8th essay, the Kuan
    子 Tzu
So slow is the rose to open.

(106/772)

These lines are some of the most sonically and rhythmically consistent of the entire volume. They are dominated by the same repeated consonants: daughter/Demeter/dis/decrees; gown/grain; 'Queen' is almost perfectly repeated in 'Kuan'. We might read 'Kuan Tzu' as its own line, just before the final line; it forms a heavily stressed parallel stand-alone to 'eyes, hair'. All of these sounds are neatly concluded with the vowels of the final line, which reads like something of a defence of the poem's own slow composition. The effect of its sound, then, is to create something tightly woven. At the same time, this section presents two coincident principles of coherence: its alliterative and rhythmic texture forms one ordering principle, which meets and is matched by the principles of Pound's ideogrammic method, whereby details from the Eleusinian mystery rites can sit alongside references to the work of pre-Han economic and political theory, the *Kuan-Tzu*. This is a canto that carefully weighs certainty against uncertainty. On the one hand, the canto opens with questions, and unstable questions at that. Is the 'her' of those lines Demeter, and therefore her daughter is Persephone, or is the unknown and unknowable woman's daughter simply 'like that', or like Persephone? It is not until we arrive at 'Dis' bride, Queen over Phlegethon' that this is more clearly elaborated, and then that clarity is quickly undercut by the 'girls faint as mist' of the next line. On the other hand, the *Kuan-Tzu* is there to assure us of the existence of masculine strength, contained within grain (and within its cultivation), to remind us of the authority of an ancient text, and the precision of a decree or an essay (and precision, as Pound might tell us, is itself a kind of authority). The rhythmic consistency of the opening lines might, then, bring this balance down slightly on the side of certainty. But this is not consistent across the canto as a whole. The poem's two hymnal refrains – 'this is grain rite', which continues the agricultural theme set up by Demeter and the *Kuan-Tzu*, and 'helpe me to neede', taken from Layamon's *Brut* – form two four-beat parallels, one an assertion and the other a supplication.[34] Sound will not solve the problem for us. It refuses to adjudicate, to make either the certainty of the *Kuan-Tzu* or the uncertainty of Layamon and the faint, misty girls of the underworld win out.

It is striking, then, that in his recorded reading of the poem from 1967 Pound leaves the words 'Kuan Tzu' unspoken. It is unclear how to account for that omission as anything other than an idiosyncratic choice, but even an inattentive listener will notice the differences between that reading and the Caedmon recording of Canto 99. Pound's volume is lower, his pace slower, and it is hard to imagine him having skipped over those crucial words in an earlier reading. We might also point to his inconsistent hard and soft pronunciations of Circe as evidence of an indeterminacy at play. Does this undercut the authority that the canto proposes? And does it bring us closer to a point in which silence will not only be present in the poem as a medium, but will overtake or engulf the poem altogether?

That unspoken *Kuan Tzu* is a silence, sounded and soundable in the poem but left conspicuously unsaid in its performance. It is also, then, a marker of disjunction between the ways we read and the ways we speak, listen and hear. This is perhaps where we arrive at a limit of Bernstein's argument in favour of close listening.[35] Pound's quiet, slow, late recording of Canto 106 risks leading us down the path of thinking about the poem's form as mimetic of the poet's failing health, his depression and his refusal to speak during his final years: in short, as a retreat into silence and, eventually, death. By his own admission the poet's paradise will be 'A nice quiet paradise' (Notes for CXI/803); 'this is a dying', we are told not long after (113/806). For many critics, encountering the late poems is to come face to face with poetry that has almost given up on being poetry. Peter Nicholls has observed that 'the privileged scenes of *Section: Rock-Drill* and *Thrones* are studiously quiet', and, as a result, 'the overall effect . . . is one of a procession of interiors, of private spaces where the self is mirrored back to the self'.[36] Peter Stoicheff's analysis of *Drafts & Fragments* implicitly follows the poet's biography and approaching death, writing that the late poems seem to draw ever nearer to 'the point where the incoherence of poetic language is exchanged for silence'.[37]

The incoherence of poetic language: positioned in this way, against silence, this suggests that silence is stable and coherent, whereas poetic language (as sound, as not-silence) is incoherent, chaotic, unmanageable. We manage sound – as poets or writers, we manipulate sound, make it workable, and put it to work – but sound also manages us, guiding our reading and our relationship with texts. That we desire to speak of silence when talking about the late cantos speaks volumes about our reading: we would prefer that silent stability to the power that sound has over us and that we cannot always, in turn, exercise over it. Decades earlier, Pound had written to Margaret C. Anderson of his 'desire to hear the music of a lost dynasty'.[38] In the 1950s Pound makes one last effort to compose that music himself – the question then is whether we can hear it too, whether Pound will let us, and whether we let ourselves.

Notes

1. Ezra Pound to Achilles Fang, March 1951, in *Ezra Pound's Chinese Friends*, p. 58.
2. Pound to Achilles Fang, 3 February 1951, in *Ezra Pound's Chinese Friends*, p. 54.
3. That the characters appear for the first time in *Rock-Drill* is in large part the fault of the late poems' complex textual history. Ronald Bush has outlined how the Chinese characters that Pound inscribed on his typescript of *The Pisan Cantos* never survived into the published volume. See Bush, 'Confucius Erased', pp. 163–92.
4. Fitts, 'Prelude to Conclusion', *Saturday Review of Literature* 39 (12 May, 1956), 18–19; repr. in Erkkila (ed.), *The Contemporary Reviews*, p. 355.
5. Bacigalupo, *The Forméd Trace*, p. 233.
6. Blasing, *Lyric Poetry*, p. 169.
7. Wilson, *Preface to Ezra Pound*, p. 185.
8. Williams, *The Buddha in the Machine*, pp. 125–6.
9. There have, of course, been some exceptions. See Zhaoming Qian's introduction to *Ezra Pound's Chinese Friends;* see also Liu, 'Pharmaka and Volgar' Eloquio', pp. 179–214.
10. Pound to Angela Jung, 1952, in *Ezra Pound's Chinese Friends*, p. 89. Jung wrote her dissertation at the University of Washington, entitled 'Ezra Pound and China'.
11. In his introduction to *Ezra Pound's Chinese Friends,* Qian revisits this argument, levelled by George Kennedy and James Liu among others, and lays somewhat more of the blame at Pound's feet: Qian points out that Pound removed passages that concerned the sound and rhythm of Chinese from the 1919 published version of *The Chinese Written Character as a Medium for Poetry*. Qian, Introduction to *Ezra Pound's Chinese Friends*, p. xix.
12. Fenollosa, *The Chinese Written Character*, p. 51.
13. Pound, *Gaudier-Brzeska: A Memoir*, p. 46.
14. Pound, *ABC of Reading*, p. 21.
15. Pound to Fang, February 1952, in *Ezra Pound's Chinese Friends*, p. 77.
16. Pound, 'Preliminary Survey', in *Ezra Pound's Chinese Friends*, p. 207.
17. This never eventuated, and its failure to appear marked the end of Pound's correspondence with Fang. See *Ezra Pound's Chinese Friends*, pp. 107–9.
18. Pound to Fang, 31 July 1952, in *Ezra Pound's Chinese Friends*, p. 115.
19. Richard Sieburth, 'The Sound of Pound', available at: <http://writing.upenn.edu/pennsound/x/text/Sieburth-Richard_Pound.html> (last accessed 10 May 2016).
20. Quoted in Sieburth.
21. Quoted in Sieburth.
22. Barthes, *Responsibility of Forms*, p. 245.
23. The comparison between poetry and music, as Craig Dworkin points out in his introduction to *The Sound of Poetry/The Poetry of Sound*, comes up against the instability and tenuous definition of the term 'music', and of how the expansion of what we mean by music in the twentieth century can

lead to an expanded definition of poetry. See Dworkin and Perloff (eds), *The Sound of Poetry*, p. 15.

24. Pound, *The Cantos*, Canto 75, p. 470. Subsequent references will cite canto and page numbers parenthetically.

25. Pryor, '"Particularly Dangerous Feats"', p. 31.

26. Pound's 'Preliminary Survey' includes several references to onomatopoeia, as he attempts to uncover sound symbolism from the language. The 'Preliminary Survey' is reprinted in *Ezra Pound's Chinese Friends*, pp. 207–28.

27. Terrell, *Companion*, 641.

28. Bernstein, 'Introduction', in *Close Listening*, p. 4.

29. Available at: Pennsound, <http://media.sas.upenn.edu/pennsound/authors/Pound/1958/Pound-Ezra_14_Canto-XCIX_DC_1958.mp3> (last accessed 2 May 2016).

30. Jarrell, 'on the extraordinary misuse of extraordinary powers', from 'Five Poets', *Yale Review* (September 1956) xlvi, p. 103; repr. in Homberger (ed.), *Ezra Pound: The Critical Heritage*, p. 438.

31. Wain, 'The Shadow of an Epic', Spectator (11 March 1960) cciv, p. 360; repr. in Homberger, p. 454.

32. Kenner, *The Pound Era*, p. 92; Bacigalupo, p. 335.

33. Golston, *Rhythm and Race*, p. 143.

34. In his 1967 reading of the poem, Pound pronounces 'helpe me to neede' as four syllables.

35. Bernstein, 8.

36. Nicholls, 'Lost Object(s)', p. 173.

37. Stoicheff, *The Hall of Mirrors*, p. 151.

38. Pound to Margaret C. Anderson, January 1918, in *Selected Letters 1907–1941*, p. 128.

Part Four

Modern Rhythm: Writing, Sound, Cinema

Chapter 12

The Rhythms of Character in Katherine Mansfield's 'Miss Brill'

Helen Rydstrand

In the early decades of the twentieth century, many writers and critics saw rhythm as being able to mediate between world and text. A number of modernists were also thinking about subjectivity in terms of rhythm, with some even considering rhythm to be the very essence of being. Prose was often considered the best medium for expressing these rhythms of subjectivity in literature, and Katherine Mansfield's short fiction is a significant example of this tendency. Her perception of the rhythmic qualities in speech, thought, emotion and indeed being pervades her *oeuvre*, and is particularly evident in those stories that are primarily studies of character. In her 1920 short story, 'Miss Brill', the title character is mediated through rhythms.[1]

As this essay will demonstrate, while Mansfield does evoke the sonic rhythms of Miss Brill's voice and thought, her ultimate aims in this are to limn the complexity of a character's emotional state and even being through rhythmic mediation. The resolute cheerfulness of Miss Brill's voice, which reaches us through free indirect discourse, is repeatedly undercut by a discordant undertone of melancholy. This bifurcation of the protagonist's voice can be productively understood, making use of terminology from Henri Lefebvre's *Rhythmanalysis* (1992), as 'arrhythmic'.[2] Lefebvre explains arrhythmia as a situation in which rhythms are 'discordant', causing 'suffering, a pathological state (of which arrhythmia is generally, at the same time, symptom, cause and effect)' (16). This concept helps us to recognise the two currents of cognition apparent in Miss Brill's voice as discordant and perhaps even bordering on the pathological. This contributes to a pattern of habitual self-deception that recurs at multiple levels of the story. The influence of the relatively new field of psychology is apparent in the story's exploration of consciousness, personality, emotion and the relation between self and world. In addition, Mansfield's use of rhythms to mediate character serves a political purpose. It enables a deeper portrayal of the loneliness experienced by her marginalised subject (a single, childless, older woman), and the exposure of the social structures that lead to it.

Mansfield's experimentation with rhythm can be located within a wider tendency during the modernist period. At this time, there was a strong trend of understanding the operation of thought as rhythm and therefore of viewing literary rhythms as key to its representation. At the same time, the growing attachment of prose to the everyday, the natural and even the real, meant that prose rhythms were of particular interest. Two texts that point to a significant level of attention to this subject in British modernist literary discourse are *English Prose Style* (1928) by poet and critic Herbert Read, and *Modern Prose Style* (1934) by Bonamy Dobrée, Professor of English Literature at the University of Leeds.[3] Both Read and Dobrée were well connected to mainstream British modernism as close friends of T. S. Eliot, with Read's journal *Arts and Letters* being one of the first venues to publish Eliot's work. Although they appeared several years after Mansfield's stories, these primers on style can be seen to codify notions arising from literary discourse of the preceding decades, making them a fitting context for Mansfield's earlier experimentation.

Read's ideas about prose rhythm revolve around its relation to thought. His book begins by placing rhythm at the heart of prose style. One of prose's distinctions from poetry, Read claims, is that while the essence of poetry can be contained in a single word (his example is Shakespeare's 'incarnadine'), prose is a form of constructive expression, which 'does not exist except in the phrase, and the phrase always has rhythm of some kind'.[4] He likens rhythm to a *gestalt* (a German word meaning form or shape), since the rhythm of either verse or prose can be seen as a unique entity that has 'shape or form as one of its attributes' (60). However, he also insists that rhythm 'is not an ideal form to which we fit our words' (61). Instead, prose rhythm is a more natural, spontaneous phenomenon; it is 'born, not with the words, but with the thought, and with whatever confluence of instincts and emotions the thought is accompanied' (61). So for Read, pre-linguistic mental activity has a rhythm, and he sees it as identical with that of prose.

Read applies his *gestalt* theory of rhythm to the technicalities of prose writing, focusing in particular on the paragraph, which he considers to be a transcription of the rhythm of a thought. According to Read's guide, a well-written paragraph does not simply explore or expound an idea. It is 'a plastic mass, and it takes its shape from the thought it has to express: its shape *is* the thought' (61). Read insists that in a prose piece, the rhythm of each sentence 'must be dissolved in a wider movement and this wider movement is the rhythm of the paragraph – a rhythm that begins with the first syllable of the paragraph and is not complete without the last syllable' (59). The assumption underlying this formal theory is that an idea can be accurately, completely expressed in writing, but that rhythm is more fundamental in this process than language.

Dobrée emphasises rhythm's perceived potential for the mimesis of mental processes as a whole, rather than simply the expression of an idea. This brings us closer to Mansfield's interest in evoking character through rhythm. Dobrée links modernist experimentation with prose rhythm to an increased desire to mimic the passage of thought as a way into understanding the mind. He sees this as continuous with traditional aims of prose writing, however: he claims that 'the original prose writer' has always aimed to 'give objective reality to things, translate sight into sound'.[5] The mimesis pursued by the modern writer, though, is concerned with more abstract phenomena than the visible world. Dobrée suggests that 'the experimenter of today' wants to 'follow all the curious transitions of the mind, its evolutions, its twists, so as to give a closer illusion of reality' (233). This is an understanding of reality that stresses the mediating role of the mind. Dobrée cites Gertrude Stein's work (along with that of John Rodker and John Dos Passos) as a notable example of writing that makes use of syntactical experimentation to develop for the reader the hypnotic effect of being inside the mind of her characters (240). Like Read, Dobrée emphasises a particular capacity in prose for mediating the inner life through rhythm, but he additionally links this to an affinity with everyday speech. He explains this 'return to speech rhythms' as part of an attempt by modernist writers to develop 'a style that will faithfully reflect their mind as it utters itself naturally' (217). Thus attention to closely rendering the way people speak – their accents, habitual vocabulary and syntactical patterns – may be understood as allowing in turn the replication of their habits of mind. Voice is seen as having an intimate connection to the self.

Similarly, other critics also saw prose as being particularly able to express emotion because of this perceived connection with speech and hence the body. Frederic Manning makes this argument in 'Poetry in Prose', his essay for the *Chapbook*'s 1921 special issue on prose poetry.[6] His overall argument rests on explicitly following Plato and Aristotle in defining poetry as 'mimesis, its object as katharsis', merged with contemporary scientific interest in the rhythms of the human body (11).[7] Manning proposes that 'the rhythm of prose depends entirely upon breathing, [so] it reflects perfectly the physical distress of one labouring under any passion, or touched either by sorrow or joy. It may be completely mimetic' (15). In this statement, a single rhythm erupts out of emotional experience, running through the body, out of the mouth and onto the page. Through a conflation of spoken and written voice, rhythm is presented as a medium that can convey emotion from the body into the text.

For some, an even more abstract dimension of the self – the essential being – could be perceived as rhythmic. Mansfield's husband John Middleton Murry directly expresses this conception of rhythm as an essential quality of the individual. Murry had a pivotal role in the history of British rhythmic modernism. Most celebrated during his lifetime for his modernising editorship of the *Athenaeum* between 1919 and 1921, Murry began his career as an editor by launching the little magazine *Rhythm: Art, Music, Literature* (1911–13). Mansfield worked as a contributor and eventually co-editor and financial supporter of the magazine from spring 1912. Murry writes in his autobiography, *Between Two Worlds* (1935), that around 1911, one of the 'tremendous significances' that he found in the word 'rhythm' was sparked by his friend, the Scottish colourist painter, J. D. Fergusson.[8] Murry writes, 'his being had natural laws which it obeyed: mine had none. So rhythm came to mean for me that essential living positive thing – whatever it might be – which I was acutely conscious that I lacked and F— possessed' (156). Murry's conception of rhythm as a vital dimension of human being bears notable similarities to the way that Mansfield writes about her aims in Miss Brill, which I discuss below.

Murry also connected this conception of the rhythms of being to the possibility of expressing this quality in art. Fergusson, who later became *Rhythm*'s art editor, also introduced the young Murry to the idea that rhythm 'was the distinctive element in all the arts, and that the real purpose of "this modern movement" . . . was to reassert the pre-eminence of rhythm' (156). Fergusson assigned Murry the role of bringing this 'new doctrine of rhythm into literature' (156). Murry can be seen carrying out this task many years later as an established editor and literary critic, in his essay 'Romanticism and the Tradition' (1924), first published in Eliot's *Criterion*. In this essay, Murry maintains that to fully understand a work of art we must consider it 'a manifestation of the rhythm of the soul of the man who created it'.[9] At its most conventional level, this claim defines the ideal work of art as a personal expression of feeling, experience or being. But more than this, Murry describes the 'soul' in rhythmic terms, and posits the artwork as a physical version or extension of that personal rhythm. In this conception, then, the rhythm of a literary work is continuous with the individual rhythm of its author.

Mansfield was always concerned with the nature of the subject and with questions around its evocation in fiction. She frequently acknowledged a sense that there are certain registers of human experience, or dimensions of human being, that are inaccessible to language. This is evident in a 1921 letter from Mansfield to her friend Lady Ottoline Morrell:

> How strange talking is – what mists rise and fall – how one loses the other & then thinks to have found the other – then down comes another soft final curtain . . . But it is incredible, don't you feel, how mysterious and isolated we each of us are – at the last.[10]

Knowledge, in particular of the other, is here a kind of intermittent and incomplete vision. Nancy Gray explains this sentiment in Mansfield's writings as a tension between the desire for a 'true' self, consistent and knowable, and a reality in which the self is a changeable, complex multiplicity.[11] In the above passage, Mansfield is plainly alert to the complexity of the self, and even more so, its irreducible isolation. And yet, her understanding of the self seems less characterised by yearning for a stable truth which does not exist, and more to rest on the assumption that behind these 'mists' or 'curtains', there are 'true' selves to be found that language is just unable to articulate. It is for this reason that Mansfield insisted, as Sydney Janet Kaplan puts it, on 'ineffability as a necessary component of the modernist aesthetic gesture'.[12]

However, Mansfield always considered the task of the author as being to convey wisdom, to express some deeper 'truth' about existence. She celebrates this quality in the writing of Anton Chekhov, one of her most prominent influences. She wrote to Murry in 1920 that Chekhov's stories 'are true. I trust him. This is becoming most awfully important to me – a writer *must* have knowledge – he must make one feel the ground is firm beneath his feet.'[13] On the one hand, this remark indicates that Mansfield's ideal writer must be able to convey a sense of the materiality of experience. On the other, this firm ground must also include deeper knowledge or wisdom to offer. She felt that it is possible to approach this 'truth', to evoke the vital essence of things through art, as she felt Chekhov had done. She explains this in a letter to the painter Dorothy Brett, in which she describes a two-stage creative process: the 'seeing-and-feeling' followed by the 'grasping'. She writes to Brett,

> I know that when I write stories if I write at the seeing-and-feeling stage they are no good & have to be scrapped. I have to go on almost squeezing them in my hands if you know what I mean until I KNOW them in every corner and part.[14]

For Mansfield, then, simply recording immediate sensory experience is not the ultimate object of art. It is instead the communication of the kind of 'knowledge' she admires in Chekhov. But she recognises that this kind of knowledge, or 'truth' cannot be directly articulated, so an expanded formal approach to representing what she saw as 'true' is required.

Mansfield often describes the process she uses in order to 'grasp' this knowledge as involving an intensely sympathetic becoming: an imaginative, intuitive impersonation of characters and objects. Most famously, she writes to Brett in 1917 that 'when I pass the apple stalls I cannot help stopping and staring until I feel that I, myself, am changing into an apple, too'.[15] This is clearly a form of mimicry, but one that captures more than the merely tangible. It is a mimesis of being itself. This imaginative mimetic process is creative as well, because it leads her to feel 'that at any moment I may produce an apple, miraculously, out of my own being like that conjuror produces the egg' (330). She describes this moment of creation further as being one 'when you are more duck, more apple or more Natasha than any of these objects could ever possibly be, and so you create them anew' (330). Mansfield was constantly engaged in trying to develop a literary form that could enable these imaginative impersonations to reach her texts.

Prose was for Mansfield the form best equipped for this task, not least because of its associations with the real. Her nervous excitement about what she saw as prose's potential for evoking subjectivity is palpable in a 1921 letter to her brother-in-law, Richard Murry:

> But you know Richard, I was only thinking last night people have hardly begun to write yet. Put poetry out of it for a moment & leave out Shakespeare – now I mean prose. Take the very best of it. Aren't they still cutting up sections rather than tackling the whole of a mind? I had a moment of absolute terror in the night. I suddenly thought of a *living mind* – a whole mind – with absolutely nothing left out.[16]

One of the things that this passage conveys is a typical modernist sentiment in its sense of the possibilities achievable through new artistic experimentation. Indeed, in the reference to brain dissection, Mansfield can be seen thinking about writing as experimentation in scientific terms. More importantly, in this passage she also implicitly suggests that prose is the medium best equipped for capturing this whole, '*living*' mind. These interests in prose's ability to capture not just thought, but an expansive conception of mind, clearly dovetail with those expressed by contemporaries like Manning, Read and Dobrée.

Mansfield also shares with these critics a conviction that rhythm is vital to evoking the mind, and even, like Murry, the core of one's being. In the same letter, Mansfield moves from this musing on prose's ability to capture the whole mind to explain how she attempts to achieve this in the short story that is the focus of this chapter:

> In Miss Brill I chose not only the length of every sentence, but even the sound of every sentence – I chose the rise and fall of every paragraph to fit her – and to fit her on that day at that very moment. After Id written it I read it aloud – numbers of times – just as one would *play over* a musical composition, trying to get it nearer and nearer to the expression of Miss Brill – until it fitted her. (165)

Thus, by Mansfield's own account, in this story she uses linguistic cadences to develop character; how this is approached will be investigated more closely below. Here, I want to draw attention to Mansfield's declared focus not just on evoking the sound of Miss Brill's voice, but on 'the expression of' her, and on 'fitting' the sound and cadence of her text to the character. Thus, the story as a whole is imbued, or indeed impersonated, with Miss Brill at the level of form. So, Mansfield uses rhythm to mimic something intrinsic to the 'whole mind' of Miss Brill, rather than merely the external or even conscious manifestations of her personality.

This is not to say that Mansfield was unconcerned with the power of vocal mimesis. As I show below, Miss Brill's voice is certainly central to that story. Mansfield was fastidious about the technical rendering of vocal character in her work. There are several instances in her letters that demonstrate the care she took to get the voices of the characters right, in particular through certain spelling, typographical or word choices. For example, in 1921 she writes to her literary agent, J. B. Pinker, worrying whether such choices in 'At the Bay' would be correctly retained in published form: 'There are several words which appear to be spelt wrong – i.e. emer*al* for emer*ald*, ninseck for insect and so on. . . . But my hand on my heart I mean every spelling mistake!'[17] Mansfield explains that she has not marked these words with inverted commas or italics because she feels that this treatment 'interferes with the naturalness of children's or servants' speech' (286). In citing 'naturalness' as the desired effect, she refers both to the representation of a particular quality of the characters' speech and to the reader's experience of it. She aims for her text to provide as 'noise'-less an acoustic transmission of the cadences of characters' speech as possible. That is, she hopes that textual form will act as a medium for the direct communication of material experience, in this case clearly encoded with cues about social power, and hence politically charged. Yet Anne Besnault-Levita argues that Mansfield's voices do more: they are 'often associated metonymically with the "self"'.[18] This points to a sense that less external or social aspects of subjectivity might also be captured through voice. Thus Mansfield's careful attention to voice should be seen as part of a wider strategy that aims to develop and express deeper registers of character through rhythm.

Mansfield's short fiction plainly exhibits the desire to 'follow all the curious transitions of the mind' that Dobrée described as characterising the prose 'experimenter of today'.[19] Likewise, as evident in her non-fiction writing on her art, she shares with him that certainty that it would allow a closer representation of reality. She is particularly interested in the ways that mental habits can offer insight into subjectivity; many of her stories are structured through rhythms that bring out this aspect of mind. In 'Miss Brill', rhythm is used to evoke the title character's internal as well as her outward habits, becoming a way into a sympathetic but complex portrait of the psychological effects of social isolation.

As is evident in the letters discussed above, Miss Brill, and consequently the story that concerns her, is conceived rhythmically. The text is centrally concerned with a study of character and psychology, and Mansfield considered the cadence of the character's voice and the story as a whole as integral to her evocation. Written in November 1920, the story was first published in the *Athenaeum* that same month and collected in *The Garden Party and Other Stories* in 1922. Mansfield seems to have thought of this story in musical terms from its conception. During composition, she wrote to Murry that 'Last night I walked about . . . – and lamented there was no God. But I came in and wrote Miss Brill instead, which is my insect magnificat, now & always.'[20] This statement relates the story to the 'Magnificat', an ancient Christian hymn attributed to the Virgin Mary, which celebrates God's mercy to the weak and humble. This allusion implies the author's desire to 'magnify' or elevate the importance of a subject often skimmed over in literature. Mansfield wrote to Murry again a week later to say 'I am very glad you liked Miss Brill. I liked her, too. One writes (one reason why is) because one does care so passionately that one must show it – one must declare ones love.'[21] Mansfield's desire to pay tribute to ordinary, marginalised women is apparent in the writer's effort not just to give Miss Brill a voice, but to make her manifest through careful, laborious modulation of technical rhythm. J. F. Kobler has observed that 'the story *is* so completely the language with which Miss Brill records her world'.[22] But, more than the language itself, this character piece is achieved through how language is arranged.

In 'Miss Brill', Mansfield invokes the familiar rhythm of human routine to economically portray the eponymous character's life. The story describes, through free indirect discourse, Miss Brill's solo Sunday afternoon ritual, which is to attend a public concert in a park. Although it is a routine activity, Miss Brill takes an active interest in everything around her, noting the weather, the flowers, the music, and watching people avidly. The pace of her thought is quick, lively and controlled, with sentences tending to be short, or tightly punctuated. Many begin with conjunctions or words and phrases that seem to indicate a response ('Yes, she really felt like that about it'), as though she is holding up one half of a conversation in which she hopes to entertain her interlocutor.[23] Her animated diction is supported by exclamation marks throughout as she repeatedly reiterates her enjoyment. However, the intimation that her bright tone covers a pervasive melancholy is evident from the first word of the story, which begins 'Although it was so brilliantly fine', the negative conjunction undermining all the asserted pleasantness that follows (250). The echo of Miss Brill's name in the adverb connects her persona to this illusory quality, and this arrhythmic duality continues throughout.

The doubleness that characterises Miss Brill's voice is accentuated by a recurring pattern of comparison. The suggestion that Miss Brill is attempting to divert herself from her loneliness is strengthened by her mental habit of describing things to herself using amusing or fanciful similes. She describes the conductor of the band as 'a rooster about to crow', girls as 'little French dolls', a toddler's mother as 'a young hen' (251–2). As Miss Brill observes the crowd around her, a relation of opposition is set up between the 'couples and groups' who are passing by, and those who sit on the benches with Miss Brill, watching the concert (252). The passers-by are dynamic, vital and connected with youth and growth, children and flowers (252). In contrast, those sitting with Miss Brill are static, or life-less: 'odd, silent, nearly all old, and from the way they stared they looked as though they'd just come from dark little rooms or even – even cupboards!' (252). Miss Brill does not consciously align herself with this latter group until the close of the story, but her spatial contiguity is enough to produce an immediate echo for the reader.

This failure of self-recognition is repeated when Miss Brill observes a chance meeting between an older woman and a male acquaintance who ignores her. The woman is

> wearing the same ermine toque she'd bought when her hair was yellow. Now everything, her hair, her face, even her eyes, was the same colour as the shabby ermine, and her hand, in its cleaned glove, lifted to dab her lips, was a tiny yellowish paw. (252)

Miss Brill's perception of the woman is dehumanising – she is morphed into an animal, and given the metonymic epithet 'ermine toque'. But she is a clear counterpart to Miss Brill herself, down to the old fur garment she wears and her response to the man's rebuff (252). Miss Brill fancies that the music responds to and echoes the woman's emotional state, at first comforting with gentle tones and then, as she leaves, covering her hurt under a smile, echoing her determined cheerfulness by playing 'more quickly, more gaily than ever' (253). Miss Brill, too, though avoiding conscious identification with the rebuffed woman, alters her diction to match this change of rhythm and makes a series of rapid, fiercely cheerful exclamations: 'Oh, how fascinating it was! How she enjoyed it! How she loved sitting here, watching it all!' (253).

The analogical pattern is again reprised in Miss Brill's notion of the scene at the public concert being a theatrical production in which she too is acting: 'even she had a part and it came every Sunday. No doubt somebody would have noticed if she hadn't been there; she was part of the performance after all' (253). By developing this fanciful, glamorous image of herself, and of her life as artistically ordered, Miss Brill gives meaning to her routine existence, and redresses her feelings of insignificance and isolation. At the same time, irony embedded in the free indirect discourse simultaneously acknowledges her self-deception. As she imagines the audience as a theatrical company, singing together, she creates the illusion of belonging and purpose:

> And then she too, she too, and the others on the benches – they would come in with a kind of accompaniment – something low, that scarcely rose or fell, something so beautiful – moving . . . And Miss Brill's eyes filled with tears and she looked smiling at all the other members of the company. Yes, we understand, we understand, she thought – though what they understood she didn't know. (253–4)

This passage ironically foreshadows Miss Brill's more painful confrontation with her real situation. In describing an apparently life-affirming experience, it syntactically echoes two other passages from earlier in the story, which instead connote the undercurrent of pathos that runs throughout the text. Miss Brill approaches and retreats from recognition of this twice. In the first paragraph of the story, a connection is made between the autumnal chill in the air and Miss Brill's melancholia: 'And when she breathed, something light and sad – no, not sad, exactly – something gentle seemed to move in her bosom' (251). This configuration is repeated and expanded in her description of the music: 'And what they played was warm, sunny, yet there was just a faint chill – a something what was it? – not sadness – no, not sadness – a something that made you want to sing' (253). Like the day, the music is sunny but with a faint chill, an ineffable 'something', which she refuses to identify as sadness and is conflated instead with beauty, movement and the body by syntactic resemblance. Thus rhythm, both biological and artistic, can be registered as converging the inner and outer worlds. It is these rhythms, not the artificial ones created by Miss Brill, which might offer a more authentic and rewarding connection to the world around her.

The denouement in 'Miss Brill' exposes the arrhythmic duality that characterises the story when her denial that this 'something' is sadness is unravelled by cruel comments that she overhears a young couple make about her. This moment forces to the surface the feelings that Miss Brill had been suppressing with her upbeat mental rhythms. The consequent disruption of her weekly routine – that she doesn't buy her usual treat on the way home from the concert – is representative of the dissolution of her defensive habits of thought. Thus the rhythm of an ordinary human routine functions metaphorically as both symptom of and remedy for loneliness.

As with much of Mansfield's work, this story is motivated by what she once called a 'cry against corruption'.[24] This is at once a passionate decrying of social injustice, and simultaneously a critique of personal inauthenticity. Miss Brill's eager observation of life going on around her veers into a bright artificiality that includes a deliberate othering of those – like the 'ermine toque' – with whom identification is painful. This failure to be 'true' to herself in fact serves to reinforce her isolation. In offering a sympathetic portrayal of the experiences and feelings of a typically marginal figure in both literature and society, Mansfield's attentive evocation of Miss Brill's mental and vocal rhythms undoubtedly serves political ends. But the competing, discordant rhythms at work in the story operate simultaneously to underscore the complexity of human psychology. Mansfield can be seen to use prose rhythms to evoke not only those aspects of identity that manifest in language, but those which remain ineffable. Through this, she contributes to wider ontological and aesthetic conversations surrounding rhythm in her time.

Notes

1. Mansfield, 'Miss Brill', pp. 250–5.
2. Lefebvre, *Rhythmanalysis*, p. 16.
3. *English Prose Style* was a popular guide: it had gone through two editions and nine reprints by 1956. Likewise, *Modern Prose Style* remained significant and was reprinted six times before a second edition was produced in 1964.
4. Read, *English Prose Style*, pp. x, xi.
5. Dobrée, *Modern Prose Style*, p. 232.
6. Manning, 'Poetry in Prose', pp. 10–15.
7. For recent investigations of the relation between these scientific interests and modernist literature, see Golston, *Rhythm and Race in Modernist Poetry* and Martin, *Joyce and the Science of Rhythm*.

8. Murry, *Between Two Worlds*, p. 156.
9. Murry, *Defending Romanticism*, p. 133.
10. Mansfield, *The Collected Letters*, vol. 4, p. 252. I have followed the editors of these volumes in letting stand the author's frequent divergences from spelling, grammar and especially punctuation conventions, and have not cited these '*sic*'.
11. Gray, 'Un-Defining the Self', p. 79.
12. Kaplan, *Katherine Mansfield and the Origins of Modernist Fiction*, p. 219.
13. 17 October 1920, *The Collected Letters*, vol. 4, p. 73.
14. 15 October 1921, *The Collected Letters*, vol. 4, p. 296.
15. 11 October 1917, *The Collected Letters*, vol. 1, p. 330.
16. 17 January 1921, *The Collected Letters*, vol. 4, p. 165.
17. 29 September 1921, *The Collected Letters*, vol. 4, p. 286.
18. Besnault-Levita, '"– Ah, what is it? – that I heard"', p. 90.
19. Dobrée, p. 233.
20. 13 November 1920, *The Collected Letters*, vol. 4, p. 109.
21. 21 November 1920, *The Collected Letters*, vol. 4, p. 116.
22. Kobler, *Katherine Mansfield: A Study of the Short Fiction*, p. 64.
23. Mansfield, 'Miss Brill', p. 251.
24. Mansfield to John Middleton Murry, 3 February 1918, *The Collected Letters*, vol. 2, p. 54.

Chapter 13

The Rhythm of the Rails: Sound and Locomotion

Laura Marcus

Rhythm-studies

Rhythm is the fundamental and vital quality of painting, as of all the arts – representation is secondary to that, and must never encroach on the more ultimate and fundamental demands of rhythm.

Roger Fry[1]

The critic John Middleton Murry, writing of his conversations with the Scottish painter J. D. Fergusson in the early decades of the twentieth century, recalled (in his autobiography *Between Two Worlds*):

One word was recurrent in all our strange discussions – the word 'rhythm'. We never made any attempt to define it; nor ever took any precaution to discover whether it had the same significance for us both. All that mattered was that it had some meaning for each of us. Assuredly it was a very potent word.

For Fergusson [rhythm] was the essential quality in a painting or sculpture; and since it was at that moment that the Russian ballet first came to Western Europe for a season at the Châtelet, dancing was obviously linked, by rhythm, with the plastic arts. From that, it was but a short step to the position that rhythm was the distinctive element in all the arts, and that the real purpose of 'this modern movement' – a phrase frequent on Fergusson's lips – was to reassert the pre-eminence of rhythm.[2]

In Fergusson's reported sentiments there is the suggestion that 'this modern movement' had come into being, or had found its true function, in the *reassertion* of 'the pre-eminence of rhythm'. In this account, modernism rediscovers or recovers a rhythm, whose centrality, it is implied, had become submerged. Fergusson (in Murry's account) represents 'rhythm' as the 'quality' which cuts across the divisions between the arts, although the fact that they made no attempt to define the 'quality' leaves open the possibility (perceived by the more cautious Murry) that 'rhythm' in the various and different arts is to be understood as a homonym rather than as an identity.[3]

The absence, or refusal, of strict 'definition' alluded to by Murry has as one of its contexts the vitalism (with its resistance to classification and differentiation) to which 'rhythm' was central, and which is part of that 'great hymn to energy', in Jacques Rancière's phrase, sung by artists and thinkers in the early twentieth century.[4] Rancière brings 'rhythm' into this energetic field in his quotations from the Swiss-born modernist writer Blaise Cendrars: 'Rhythm speaks. You are . . . Reality has no meaning any more. Everything is rhythm, speech life . . . Revolution. The dawn of the world today' (44). Rancière comments:

> The new common term of measurement, thus contrasted with the old one, is rhythm, the vital element of each material unbound atom which causes the image to pass into the word, the word into the brush-stroke, the brush-stroke into the vibration of light or motion. (44–5)

The transition from image to word to brushstroke to photographic/cinematographic image (these technologically mediated forms being one way of interpreting 'the vibration of light or motion') delineated by Rancière points to a more general desire to (re)connect artistic or aesthetic forms which had been artificially divided into the arts of space and the arts of time, or into the verbal and the plastic arts. (The desire for 'a new Laokoön' is one aspect of this newly constituted field of connections.)

Murry, Fergusson and Cendrars were writing from the perspectives of a modernity in which 'the dawn of the world today' was the beginning of a new century. Fergusson's 'little magazine' *Rhythm* (1911–13) emerged from this context, and reveals the influence of a vitalist philosophy shaped by the writing and thought of Henri Bergson. A full understanding of the meanings of 'rhythm' for the modern period requires, however, a longer historical perspective, beginning with exploration of the late nineteenth century in a range of contexts: philosophy, experimental psychology, science, music, aesthetics, art and literature. The analysis of 'rhythm' was central to all these fields. As or more significantly, 'Rhythmics' was in the process of formation at this time as an area of study, or a discipline, in its own right. As in the case of 'ethology' (the science of the study of formation of character, which John Stuart Mill had worked to develop as an independent discipline), 'rhythmics' could be understood as a field of thought or a science which failed to achieve the institutional or conceptual status imagined for it. It was at once all pervasive and, in disciplinary terms, homeless. It eluded definition in ways which, in the field of poetics as well as science, produced in some contexts ever more detailed and determined attempts to take its measure, though in others its very amorphousness as a concept was its most significant, productive and creative feature.

The concepts of rhythm as motion and as connectivity were two of the central topics to emerge in Herbert Spencer's influential writings on 'The Direction and Rhythm of Motion', in his *First Principles of a New System of Philosophy* (1862). In Chapter 10 of the volume, 'The Rhythm of Motion', Spencer argued for the omnipresence of rhythm, building up from the physical world and its laws to the realms of social organisation and human creative activity. Rhythmical action – initially defined through the terms of vibration and undulation – is to be found in the impact of a rising breeze on a becalmed vessel or, on land, in the 'conflict between the current of air and the things it meets': 'The blades of grass and dried bents in the meadows, and still better the stalks in the neighbouring corn-fields, exhibit the same rising and falling movement.'[5] For Spencer all motion is rhythmical, and the physical universe exists in a mode of perpetual motion which he defines in terms of 'a conflict of forces not in equilibrium': 'If the antagonist forces at any point are balanced, there is rest; and in the absence of motion there can of course be no rhythm' (254).

Spencer found rhythm not only at the largest levels (in, for example, geographical processes) but in the bodily processes – ingestion, excretion, pulsation – of each individual organism, and in human consciousness, whose rhythm he defined in the terms of a departure from and return to mental states and feelings. A more conspicuous rhythm, 'having longer waves', he argued, 'is seen during the outflow of emotion into dancing, poetry, and music. The current of mental energy that shows itself in these modes of bodily action is not continuous but falls into a succession of pulses' (265). The rhythmic dimensions of aesthetic expression start from the body, and the bodily discharge of feeling, and their naturalness is proven by the fact that they are also revealed in the cadences – the rise and fall – of ordinary speech.

Spencer's terms and concepts are important for two particular dimensions of 'rhythmics'. The first, exemplified in his focus on the bodily discharge of feeling, is the centrality of 'rhythm' to the 'kinaesthetics' and 'physiological aesthetics' which developed in the late nineteenth century, in the work of thinkers including the biologist Grant Allen, the psychologist Havelock Ellis and the philosophers and aestheticians Vernon Lee and Ethel Puffer. In Puffer's words:

When I feel the rhythm of poetry, or of perfect prose, which is, of course, in its own way, no less rhythmical, every sensation of sound sends through me a diffusive wave of nervous energy. I am the rhythm because I imitate it in myself.[6]

The second line of exploration is that of the impact of theorisations of rhythm, in its definitions as 'pulsation', 'conflict of force', 'continuous motion' and 'rise and fall', on the aesthetic theories and the literature of the period. Walter Pater, in the Conclusion to his collection of essays *The Renaissance*, famously described 'life' as consisting of a limited number of pulses, adding: 'For our one chance lies in expanding that interval, in getting as many pulsations as possible into the given time. Great passions may give us this quickened sense of life.'[7]

Concepts of 'rhythm' (often linked to 'periodicity', as in the theories of Wilhelm Fliess and Sigmund Freud) were also closely linked to models of sexuality and gender at the turn of the century. For Pater's contemporary, the poet Alice Meynell, writing on 'The Rhythm of Life' (and in a reinscription of Pater's call for an expansion of the interval and an intensification of pulsations) life is metrical, governed by the principle of recurrence. 'Life seems so long', she writes, 'and its capacity so great, to one who knows nothing of all the intervals it needs must hold – intervals between aspirations, between actions, pauses as inevitable as the pauses of sleep.'[8] 'The law that commands all things' is that of 'a sun's revolutions and the rhythmic pangs of maternity' (6). Marie Stopes used the concept of 'a fundamental rhythm of feeling' in women (to be represented as 'a succession of crests and hollows as in all wave-lines') to argue that

> woman has a rhythmic sex-tide which, if its indications were obeyed, would ensure not only her enjoyment and an accession of health and vitality, [but] would explode the myth of her capriciousness . . . We have studied the wavelengths of water, of sound, of light; but when will the sons and daughters of men study the sex-tide in woman and learn the laws of her Periodicity of Recurrence of desire?[9]

Stopes's insistent metaphorising of the concept of 'rhythm' in relation to waves and water indicates the widely held view that the etymology of 'rhythm' is 'rhein', deriving from the observed ebb and flow of ocean waves. In the later twentieth century, linguists (including Emile Benveniste) showed that 'rhythmos' was, in Ancient Greek tragedy and philosophy, synonomous with schema or form, but that whereas schema is to be understood as a fixed form, rhythmos is form in motion, fluid and changeable. 'Rhythmos' is thus to be understood as 'the particular manner of flowing' (though with a motion which is not that of waves in the sea).[10] This understanding of 'rhythm' as movement and 'becoming' can be traced through from Nietzsche to Bergson and his modernist followers and detractors in literature and the visual arts. The relationship of late Victorian and modernist writers and thinkers to classical aesthetics and culture also becomes crucial. It was fundamental to Nietzsche's distinctions between the 'rhythms' of classical and modern thought, which come to define the different concepts of time, historicity and cultural formation in the two periods.

The desire of writers and thinkers of the period to connect 'rhythm' (etymologically and conceptually) with natural and organic processes is highly significant. The metaphors of the 'pulse' and the 'heartbeat', as well as of waves, come to define concepts of 'rhythm' in a very wide range of contexts. It is my hypothesis that the fascination with rhythm in the period arose in substantial part from the desire to reclaim, retain or redefine human and natural measures in the face of the coming of the machine and the speed of technological development.

Many of the 'rhythm-scientists' of the late nineteenth and early twentieth centuries defined rhythm as the antithesis of both stasis and continuous motion: it was for them not a straight line but a wave. A similar distinction would later be drawn by Henri Lefebvre, whose 'rhythmanalysis' rests on a differentiation (though also a relationship) between linear and cyclical time. The work of art, he argued:

> displays a victory of the rhythmical over the linear, integrating it without destroying it. Cyclical repetition and linear repetition meet and collide. Thus, in music the metronome supplies a linear tempo; but the linked series of intervals by octaves possesses a cyclical and rhythmical character. Likewise in daily life: the many rhythms and cycles of natural origin, which are transformed by social life, interfere with the linear processes and sequences of gestures and acts.[11]

These complex processes would be the subject, for Lefebvre, of rhythmanalysis, 'a new science that is in the process of being constituted . . . [which] situates itself at the juxtaposition of the physical, the physiological and the social, at the heart of daily life' (130). In further and fuller writings in this field of study, Lefebvre argued that 'rhythm' was the most fundamental, and the most overlooked, of all the relations that define natural, social and cultural life. In music, he suggests, there is significantly more exploration of melody and harmony than of rhythm. In the broader experiential and phenomenological fields, we live within rhythms whose measure we have barely begun to understand. 'Rhythm enters into a general construction of time, of movement and becoming', Lefebvre writes.[12] His terms gather up those of Spencer, Bergson, Gaston Bachelard and other 'rhythmists' whose writings on the topic Lefebvre, insistent on the inaugural dimensions of his own rhythmanalysis, does not take up. To open up the longer history of rhythm-studies, however, is to see that it has had its own patterns of recurrence, appearing and disappearing as part of a conceptual history whose lineaments have indeed not been fully traced. Central to this history, and to the (re)emergences of 'rhythmics', are the models, or the utopias, of an interdisciplinarity and a synaesthesia in which connections become far more significant than divisions. As Lefebvre writes, the (future) rhythmanalyst 'will come to "listen" to a house, a street, a town, as an audience listens to a symphony' (22).

Rhythmics and locomotion

For the rhythm scientists of the turn of the century, the locomotive was a key image and exemplar. The American experimental psychologist Thaddeus Bolton – whose essay 'Rhythm' (originally a doctoral thesis from Clark University supervised by G. Stanley Hall) – set out to demonstrate that rhythm 'was a fundamental activity of mind'.[13] His lengthy article described a world defined by rhythm – the influence of Herbert Spencer is marked – with accounts of the origins of language in the rhythms of dance, and of the play of poetic rhythm. His scientific experiments entailed the observation of large number of experimental subjects (college students) who listened to a sequence of mechanically produced 'clicks' – described as 'auditory impressions' – relayed through a 'chronograph' (178–9).

The point of Bolton's experiments was to identify whether the subjects experienced the sequences as rhythmical – that is, whether they were grouping the individual sounds into rhythmical sequences. The identification of such sequences frequently followed, Bolton argued, from the subject's experience or habit of grouping the series of clicks according to rhythms which had been 'fancied or perceived' (205) in childhood:

> From early childhood the subject has observed the 4-rhythm in the puffing of the locomotive especially, and in later years the same rhythm has been observed by clocks, metronome, hammering, walking, and in all auditory impressions that approach a regularity in sequence. The rhythm is clearest in the sound of the locomotive. (203)

Bolton continues:

> Several of the subjects testify to have known of their tendency to group the puffs of the locomotive, even in early childhood, and they have taken great delight in it. With us this habit of grouping the puffs of the locomotive when it was starting slowly or pulling up a grade became so strong, even in early

childhood, that it led to all kinds of speculation as to the cause . . . Long association in early childhood with such rhythms stamps them upon the mind so firmly that they become a mental habit. Children either fancy or perceive rhythms in many sounds; they indicate this by their attempts to reproduce the sounds of machinery or of locomotives. Some railroad engineers believe their engines sing tunes. The same engine under like circumstances always sings the same tune. (205)

Bolton thus suggested that locomotive rhythm was for his subjects an ur-rhythm – an originary rhythm – which laid the basis for all subsequent apprehension of rhythmic forms. For his contemporary Sigmund Freud, trains had a foundational role (many aspects of which are outside the remit of this chapter) including the development of concepts of 'trauma' and 'hysteria' out of 'railway shock'.[14] Most fundamental is Freud's formation of the concept of the Oedipus complex through the reconstruction of an occasion

between the ages of 2 and 2 and a half, [when] my libido was stirred up towards *matrem*, namely on the occasion of a [train] journey from Leipzig to Vienna, during which we must have spent the night together and I must have had an opportunity to see her *nudam*.[15]

There is for Freud a marked focus on locomotive rhythms as foundational of sexual life (in particular for the male child), the 'compulsive link' between 'railway-travel and sexuality' being 'clearly derived from the pleasurable character of the sensations of movement'.[16] A more recent psychoanalytic commentator, Sylvie Nysembaum, has a similar conception of the train 'as the site of an excitation' for the child, who finds in it a 'fascinating mechanism: the track rods, rigid elements animated by a coming-and-going movement, transformed and transmitted to the wheels' in which 'you feel and hear the rhythm'.[17] This becomes identified with 'the representation of body parts, of the body in action, the repeated and noisy conduct of a sexual scene so engaging that the sight of the rhythm suggests the sound and vice versa' (154). The animation of the machine blurs, in Nysembaum's account, the boundaries between human and machine, animate and inanimate and creates a new relationship between the realms of sight and sound, in which 'rhythm' becomes both rhythmic sound or noise (that produced by the engine and by the pleasured body) and the machine/body in motion.

The experiments into rhythm-consciousness of the turn-of-the-century psychologists were innocent of this sexualised framework, although they were clearly fully engaged with questions of embodiment. Central to their explorations were questions of rhythm and the psychology of attention (drawing on the work of the nineteenth-century French psychologist Théodule Ribot) and of rhythm as predominantly auditory or visual. The issue of adaptation was also crucial. The apperception of rhythm brings external stimulus into subjective consciousness: the external world is adapted to our rhythms. There is a moulding of the external to the internal, whereby the external stimuli – the mechanically produced sounds – are transformed into subjectively experienced rhythms, patterned precisely by early 'rememberable sensation'. This drawing inward and the patterning of sound as rhythm is so frequently linked to the experience of locomotion (with the sound of the train as a clickety-clack) and of clock-time (the hearing of a clock's metronomic beat in the differentiated terms of a tick-tock) that we can reasonably say that it is the engines of movement and of temporality, and their incorporations and internalisations, which become the key terms of modern rhythm.

The central preoccupation in explorations of rhythm in the late nineteenth and early twentieth centuries is with the relationship between the organic and the mechanical, especially in relation to work rhythm. For the German psychologist Karl Bücher, in his *Arbeit und Rhythmus* (Work and Rhythm) of 1896, the 'festive' character of work in traditional societies was in symbiosis with the organic rhythms of the body, and this was expressed in music and in bodily movements (handclapping, foot-stamping etc.).[18] Industrial society, by contrast, made the human body subordinate to externally imposed, unrhythmic activity.

The German philosopher and psychologist Ludwig Klages (perhaps best known for his writings on 'The Science of Character') in his work on rhythm of the early 1920s, distinguished between Rhythmus and Takt (organic and machinic rhythms, or rhythm and something more like metronomic beat.) Rhythm is a general feature of animate (including human) and inanimate life, whereas Takt is a human product. For Klages 'the experience of Takt awakens us and keeps us awake', whereas 'the experience of rhythm set us into relaxed dreaming and finally into sleep'.[19] This is a general principle, but it is significant that Klages illustrates it with an account of train travel: 'Who has not often in a train sunk into relaxed dreaming and finally sleep through involuntarily listening to the mechanical beat of the wheels?' (29). To have this effect, however, the rhythm must be accompanied by the sensation of being moved forwards. If the train stops, the passengers rapidly become restless, even if a rhythmic noise continues (for example, from a nearby factory puffing out steam). Klages adduces from this a degree of interrelatedness between Rhythm and Takt: when the train is moving at a constant speed, it is the repetitive rattling of the wheels (Takt) which operates as a sign that the train is in motion, and it is this relation between sound (and perhaps vibration) and movement that composes the rhythm.

More generally, Klages argues that Takt is repeated, whereas Rhythm is renewed (32). He contrasts the ticking of the pendulum clock, which is essentially the same, with a wave of water, which is different each time. Yet, as his example of the train indicates, there are inconsistencies in his arguments. It is the experience of continuous motion that lulls the passenger to sleep, but it must be accompanied by the metrical beat of the wheels with which rhythm is otherwise contrasted. It would seem from Klages' account that the kind of vital rhythm he valorises is lost to modern man, for whom Rhythm would appear to be substantially dependent on Takt (as the metrics or measures of industrial modernity).

These relations would much later be taken up in the phenomenologically based psychoanalysis of Nicolas Abraham, who argues that the term 'rhythm' should be reserved for the organic and the perceptual – the machinic interval is defined as a 'periodicity' which has no relationship to experiential life. In his work on rhythm, Abraham writes of the ways in which train travel produces what he terms a 'rhythmitising consciousness'.[20] Echoing the terms of the turn-of-the-century psychological experimenters, he argues that

> the regular recurrence of intervals should not be mistaken for rhythm. Indeed, for the clatter of a train to take on rhythmic shape, a creative act is necessary. We must assimilate and, at the same time, transfigure the crude perception of intervals; the vocalic contrast in the words 'tick tock' bears witness to this type of assimilative transfiguration ... In the compartment of a train, distractedly contemplating the receding landscape, I feel myself surrounded by a whole world of presences: my fellow passengers, the windowpane, the rumbling of the wheels, the continually changing panorama. But for a little while now I have been nodding my head and tapping my foot, my whole body animated by movements and tensions. What has happened? A radical change of attitude must have taken place within me. A moment ago, too, I was perceiving the monotonous sound of the wheels, and my body was receiving the same periodic jolts; but in the interval between the sounds, I was taken hold of by a tension, an expectation, which the next shock would either fulfill or disappoint. And so the jolts, which were merely endured before, are now expected; my whole body prepares to receive them. My passivity of a moment ago has changed into an active spontaneity: I am no longer at the mercy of external forces; on the contrary, it is now they who obey me. At just the right time, I tap my foot – and instantly I trigger the event. My expectations have no other meaning: in reality they are desires, demands, incantations. When the event occurs, I experience the satisfaction of my efficacy. Thus, rhythmitising consciousness is apprehended as activity, as spontaneity. (108)

The head-nodding and foot-tapping are significant here, recalling the explorations of earlier psychologists into the role of kinaesthesis in the perception of rhythm. Thaddeus Bolton's account of the movements of what he calls the 'leg-pendulum' as a response to rhythm indicates both an apprehension of the automatic nature of the human organism and alerts us to a desire to connect the modern subject's responses to rhythms to their classical origins, with the foot-tapping or 'leg-pendulum' motion forming the measures of the thesis and arsis, the accented and unaccented syllables, of verse.[21] Above all, however, it would seem that the locomotive was imbued with the capacity to mediate between inner and outer, subjective and objective, Rhythmus and Takt. Two particular reasons for this could be adduced. Firstly, there is the chiasmic structure of the railway and railway travel, with its perceptually shifting relations between the internal and the external, stasis and mobility. (As we experience in an immobile train when the train alongside us begins to move.) Secondly, the locomotive railway was from the outset imagined as possessing organic or animal life – its speed tied to horse power, and its engine requiring fuel and water for sustenance and motion. In what he calls an 'extreme illustration' of the body/machine nexus, the scientific writer Grant Allen asked his readers, in his 1877 study *Physiological Aesthetics*, to suppose 'locomotive engines to have been evolved by natural selection, instead of having been consciously produced by the art of man'.[22] Here we have the image of the 'iron horse', central to nineteenth-century literature, as in writings by Dickens, Thoreau, Whitman and many others. In a chapter entitled 'Sounds' in *Walden*, Thoreau recalls the 'undisturbed solitude and stillness' of his first summer at the pond, whose 'days were not days of the week, bearing the stamp of any heathen deity, nor were they minced into hours and fretted by the ticking of a clock'.[23] Nonetheless, the modern world made itself heard. As he sits at his window 'this summer afternoon', there is not only 'the tantivy of wild pigeons [which] gives a voice to the air', but, 'for the last half-hour I have heard the rattle of railroad cars, now dying away and then reviving like the beat of a partridge, conveying travellers from Boston to the country':

> When I meet the engine with its train of cars moving off with planetary motion . . . when I hear the iron horse make the hills echo with his snort like thunder, shaking the earth with his feet, and breathing fire and smoke from his nostrils . . . It seems as if the earth had got a race now worthy to inhabit it . . . I watch the passage of the morning cars with the same feeling that I do the rising of the sun, which is hardly more regular . . . The startings and arrivals of the cars are now the epochs in the village day. (108–11)

In this chapter, Thoreau further describes the sounds of church bells, which produce a 'certain vibratory hum . . . All sound heard at the

greatest possible distance produces one and the same effect, a vibration of the universal lyre' and of birds and animals, the whip-poor-wills
'chant[ing] their vespers for half an hour', beginning 'to sing almost with
as much precision as a clock' (112). There is an exchange of terms here
between Nature, myth, technological modernity and commerce: both
the train and the whip-poor-wills mark time with a regularity equivalent to that of the absent clock whose ticking would have 'minced' and
'fretted' the days into hours and minutes. The locomotive – 'the iron
horse' – indeed sets the measure for clock-time.

Thoreau is of course describing a freight train, and it is indeed the
case that the 'romance of the rails' in the US most often attaches itself to
this type of locomotion, whereas the imagery of British and European
railways is as often based on the passenger train, and on the view (real
or imagined) from the train window. In the US context, the train tends
to be defined as a locomotive engine – the iron horse – pulling its burden
of railway cars behind it, whereas in the British and European contexts
the locus of attention is frequently the railway carriage or compartment,
with its single window. The US freight train – observed and/or heard as
it passes through a landscape – is strongly defined in aural terms. The
train whistle, 'high and piping' in European trains, 'low and powerful' in
those of North America, is, R. Murray Schafer argues, in his book *The
Soundscape*, a form of signalling which is 'a mystery code', known to
the train-men alone.[24]

Walt Whitman's 'To a Locomotive in Winter' is an ode to the railway
engine defined through rhythm and song:

> . . . thy measur'd dual throbbing and thy beat convulsive
> Thy black cylindric body, golden brass and silvery steel
> Thy ponderous side-bars, parallel and connecting rods, gyrating, shuttling at
>   thy sides,
> Thy metrical, now swelling pant and roar, now tapering in the distance . . .
> Thy train of cars behind, obedient, merrily following . . .
> Type of the modern – emblem of motion and power – pulse of the
>   continent,
> For once come serve the Muse and merge in verse, even as here I see thee.[25]

Carl Sandburg's poem 'Work Gangs' (from his *Smoke and Steel)* gives
voice to the box cars:

> I wonder what they say to each other
> When they stop a mile long on a sidetrack.
> Maybe their chatter goes:
> I came from Fargo with a load of wheat up to the danger line.
> I came from Omaha with a load of shorthorns and they splintered my
>   boards.[26]

and voice to the hammers and shovels of the work gangs –

> Then the hammer heads talk to the handles,
> then the scoops of the shovels talk,
> how the day's work nicked and trimmed them,
> how they swung and lifted all day, . . . (12–13)

'People singing', the poem concludes, 'people with song mouths connecting with song hearts; people who must sing or die; people whose song hearts break if there is no song mouth; these are my people' (13). Sherwood Anderson's 'Evening Song' creates railway rhythm as theme and as form:

> Back of Chicago the open fields – were you ever there?
> Trains coming toward you out of the West –
> Streaks of light on the long grey plains? – many a song –
> Aching to sing . . .
>
> . . . In the silence
> Always a song –
> Waiting to sing.[27]

For William Carlos Williams, the song is a dance – 'Gliding windows. Colored cooks sweating / in a small kitchen. Taillights – In time: twofour! In time: twoeight! . . . The dance is sure'.[28] Here 'railway time' commutes into dance time in a form of 'locomotive onomatopoeia'.[29]

Avant-garde contexts

I quoted earlier from Blaise Cendrars's 1917 prose-poem 'La profond aujourd'hui'. In this piece we see something of the ways in which the modes of vitalism represented by nineteenth-century thinkers such as Spencer – for whom the natural world was in a state of perpetual motion – and his successors in the sciences and philosophy, reappear in the work of avant-garde writers and artists, in particular those influenced by futurism and surrealism, of the early twentieth century. Representations of the accelerated 'tempo of life' in modernity come together with concepts (biologistic, and often sexualised) of the vibrations of the natural world. In 'Profond aujourd'hui', Cendrars extends the imagery of the iron horse: 'Since the origin of his species, the horse has been moving, supple and mathematical. Machines are already catching up with him, passing him by. Locomotives rear up and steamers whinny over the water.'[30] 'Where is man?', Cendrars asks:

The gesture of infusoria [acquatic microorganisms] is more tragic than the story of a woman's heart. The life of plants more moving than a detective story. The musculature of the back in motion is a ballet ... Everything changes proportion, angle, appearance. Everything moves away, comes closer, mounts up, fails, laughs, states its position and is enraged ... The sexual passion of factories. The turning wheel. The gliding wing. The voice retreating along a wire. Your ear in an ear trumpet. Your sense of orientation. Your rhythm. (229)

And at the close of the short piece:

You live. Off center. In complete isolation. In anonymous communion. With all that is root and crown and which throbs, enjoys, and is moved to ecstasy. Phenomena of that congenital hallucination that is life in all its manifestations and the continuous activity of awareness. The motor turns in a spiral. Rhythm speaks. Body chemistry. You are. (231)

Cendrars wrote this piece soon after he had been invalided out of his service as a legionnaire in the First World War: he lost an arm to a war injury. In one of his autobiographical pieces, 'In the Silence of the Night', he describes his war experience and, in particular, a solitary night patrol in 1915. The fear he experienced on this occasion produced, he later wrote, 'an eclipse of my personality'.[31] He had already witnessed what he described as 'the most appalling death ... on a battlefield': a legionary 'sucked up into the air, violated, crumpled, blasted in mid-air by an invisible ghoul in a yellow cloud, and his blood-stained trousers fall to the ground *empty*' (19). He heard the man's 'frightful scream of pain' continue to ring out 'for a long moment after the volatilized body had ceased to exist' (19). In Cendrars's account of his experience of the most acute fear on the Front, he hears sounds in the dark, including 'a sound like grass being crushed', which he initially interprets as an invisible enemy coming closer and closer to him, until he realises that 'the trembling of my hand, transmitted along the butt of the rifle, was causing it to describe a fairly wide quivering motion amongst the weeds where the point was entangled' (33). The 'ecstasy' of motion, the continuum of body and world, and the decentred consciousness described in 'Profond aujourd'hui' have their darker correlatives in the representation of the experience of war.

In the year preceding the outbreak of war Cendrars had published his long poem 'The Prose of the Trans-Siberian and of Little Jeanne of France' (1913), whose subject is a journey on the Trans-Siberian Railway. The poem has received a great deal of critical attention, including discussion of the relationship between word and visual image. My focus is more precisely on the 'locomotive' dimensions of the poem and, as I discuss a little later, its relationship to film and film aesthetics.

And still, and still
I was as sad as a little boy
The rhythms of the train
What American psychiatrists call 'railroad nerves'
The noise of doors voices axles screeching along frozen rails
The golden thread of my future[32]

It could be said that the poem is driven by the forward momentum of the train rather than by any attempted correlation between locomotive and poetic metrics, though Birgit Wagner argues convincingly that the text directly incorporates

> the panoramic perception of the outside world of the windows through the telegraph masts racing by, and the rhythm of the shaking of the ties, which is transferred to the body of the traveller and eventually to the language of the writer.[33]

While the correlation between train and poetic rhythm would be seem to be less direct than in the poems I have mentioned (including Whitman, Sandberg, Anderson, Stevens), Cendrars plays fully with its possibilities. In a later piece of prose writing, 'Third Rhapsody: the Open Road', Cendrars describes 'the cry of the locomotives'. The trains 'speak' the word 'Revolution', bringing together its dual meanings of political overturning and the movement of wheels. In 'The Open Road' Cendrars writes:

> 'Revolution . . . revolution' breathed the machines. It was the very breath of the night. The cry of the locomotives of the 'Train Bleu' or the 'Golden Arrow' speeding at full steam between the signals and the semaphores, jumping over the points, shattering their way through steep embankments, plunging under bridges with the impact of a fist-punch: 'Revolution!' and 'Re-re-re!' repeated the distant engine-whistles of the great international express trains, vanishing into the depths of the night with a roar of wind and a great clattering of wheels: '. . . volution, volution, volution . . .' and this same word was stammered, stammered in the racket of the endless cortège of dust-carts that came up from the further bank of the night, carrying the dawn into Paris, 'Revolution!' they said at each jolt, the wagons in front and the wagons behind, their heavy chassis and their iron coffers shaken in the mare's nests of the badly-paved streets of the suburbs. It was like onomatopoeia, this word deciphered by the tensely listening ear. 'Revolution', announced the rattling motors.[34]

The reference to decipherment of the word by the 'tensely listening ear' is an echo of lines in 'The Prose of the Trans-Siberian': 'I deciphered all the garbled texts of the wheels and united the scattered elements of a violent beauty / Which I possess / And which drives me'.[35] 'It was like onomatopoeia', Cendrars writes:[36] the simile ('like') creates a gap between sound and sense. Something of the same mode of displacement, rendering (to borrow Gertrude Stein's term) an 'exact resemblance' a 'not-quite', is also found, in relation to railway rhythm and locomotive onomatopoeia in 'The Prose of the Trans-Siberian' (the title itself to some extent refusing the terms of the poetic).[37]

> And the bell of madness that jingles like a final desire in the bluish air
> The train throbs at the heart of the leaden horizon . . .
> Troubles
> Forget your troubles
> All the cracked and leaning stations along the way
> The telegraph lines they hang from
> The grimacing poles that reach out to strangle them
> The world stretches out elongates and snaps back like an accordion in the
>   hands of a raging sadist
> Wild locomotives fly through rips in the sky
> And in the holes
> The dizzying wheels the mouths the voices
> And the dogs of misery that bark at our heels
> The demons are unleashed
> Scrap iron
> Everything clanks
> Slightly off
> The clickety-clack of the wheels
> Lurches
> Jerks
> We are a storm in the skull of a deaf man . . .[38]

The rhythm, and the onomatopoeia, are 'slightly off'. The 'storm in the skull of a deaf man' places sound inside the head – as a rhythm or a commotion which is both and neither sound and sight. Towards the poem's close, Cendrars describes the shutting off of sight in order to release the other senses, and in particular to experience the rhythms and the languages of the rails:

> With my eyes closed I can smell what country I'm in
> And I can hear what kind of train is going by
> European trains are in 4/4 while the Asian ones are 5/4 or 7/4
> And there are some whose wheels' monotone reminds me of the heavy
> prose of Maeterlinck
> I deciphered all the garbled texts of the wheels and united the scattered
>   elements of a violent beauty
> Which I possess
> And which drives me. (28)

The final two lines of the poem are addressed to 'Paris / City of the incomparable Tower the great Gibbet and the Wheel' (29). It is these lines which appear in the French film director Abel Gance's *La Roue*

(*The Wheel),* premiered in 1922. Cendrars, who had also collaborated with Gance on the anti-war film of 1919, *J'Accuse,* was its assistant director. The naming of Gance's film as 'The Wheel' is said to have been at Cendrars's insistence: Gance apparently wished to call the film 'The Rose of the Rails', in a reference to the film's heroine, Norma, whom the engine driver, Sisif, discovers as a baby by a rose bush next to the wrecked train in which her mother has died. The two different names ('The Wheel' and 'The Rose of the Rails' – indicate something of the dual nature of the film, which is both a 'modernist' celebration of motion and locomotion – and a work of high melodrama (Sisif's growing desire for Norma as she becomes a young woman rendering him both suicidal and murderous). Gance himself suggested that the film was a compromise with commercial imperatives and that he had found it necessary to bring together the human drama with those of the natural and machinic worlds:

> I am searching for a more melodramatic motif, and at the same time an eternal subject which can use a world made for the cinema, the world of locomotives, rails, signal discs, smoke . . . To make the catastrophes of feelings and those of the machines go together, each as large and significant as the other; to show the ubiquity of everything which beats: a heart and a steam valve. The drama is created by the outside, by ambiances which gradually reveal (dégager) their hero, the opposite of theatrical drama.[39]

'The ubiquity of everything which beats.' The question of 'rhythm' was at the heart of the French avant-garde film criticism and theory of the first decades of the twentieth century. The film theorist Leon Moussinac drew a highly influential distinction between 'inner' and 'outer' rhythm in film: inner rhythm relates to the movement (of persons, objects, natural life) within the frame as well as to the camera's movements, and this is understood as the cinema's 'prosody'. Outer rhythm refers to the measurements of shot lengths, and the specification of the number of images (or photograms) within each shot, which create the film's 'cinematic bars' (akin to musical bars). Film sequences are thus structured 'according to simple and repetitive metrical patterns'.[40] The correlations are not precise, but we could think of this differentiation between 'inner' and 'outer' rhythm in relationship to the distinctions between endogenous and exogenous rhythms which I discussed earlier with reference to experimental psychology, or to the distinction between Rhythm and Takt, rhythm and metrical form, renewal and repetition.

La Roue (whose score was written by Arthur Honegger, who would go on to write the music for the train film *Pacific 231*) was central to definitions of film as an essentially rhythmic art: Bardèche and Brassilach, in their *History of the Cinema*, argued that it 'was the first work of any real scope to be composed to an exact rhythmical pattern', and claimed that

> Gance regarded the rhythm of film as being akin to that of Latin verse, with its long and short feet . . . La Roue was actually based on a careful metrical pattern, with blank film punctuating the end of scenes and sequences.[41]

Abel Gance himself wrote of the film:

> Is movement not, in fact, drama? Movement, in art, is rhythm. The possibility of inventing new rhythms, of encapsulating the rhythms of life, of intensifying them and varying them infinitely, becomes, at a given moment, the essential problem for cinematographic techniques. I think I resolved this by inventing what has since been called rapid montage. It was in *La Roue* that I think we saw on the screen for the first time those images of a runaway train, of anger, or passion, of hatred that follow one another with increasing rapidity, one image generating another in an unpredictable rhythm and order, an eruption of visions which, at the time, people thought of as apocalyptic and which are now as common in our cinematographic syntax as enumeration or exclamation in literary syntax.[42]

'Encapsulating the rhythms of life.' Gance gives a technical account of cinematic rhythm in this passage, but the broader implications – which my larger project is an attempt to pursue – are those of the stakes in 'rhythm' in the last decades of the nineteenth century and the first decades of the twentieth. 'There is no science of man', Cendrars wrote in his novel *Moravagine*, 'since man is essentially the bearer of a rhythm. Rhythm can't be analysed . . . In the beginning was rhythm and rhythm was made flesh.'[43]

Notes

1. Reed (ed.), *A Roger Fry Reader*, pp. 105–6.
2. Murry, *Between Two Worlds*, pp. 155–6.
3. Wendy Steiner uses these terms to explore 'interart analogies' – in particular the perceived relationship between painting and literature – in *The Colors of Rhetoric*.
4. Rancière, *The Future of the Image*, pp. 44–5.
5. Spencer, *First Principles*, p. 250.
6. Puffer, *The Psychology of Beauty*, p. 8.
7. Pater, *The Renaissance*, p. 190.
8. Meynell, *The Rhythm of Life*, p. 6.
9. Stopes, *Married Love*, p. 57.
10. Benveniste, 'The Notion of Rhythm in its Linguistic Expression', pp. 281–8.
11. Lefebvre, *Critique of Everyday Life*, vol. 3, p. 130.

12. Lefebvre, *Rhythmanalysis*, p. 79.
13. Bolton, 'Rhythm', p. 146.
14. For a fuller discussion, see Marcus, *Dreams of Modernity*.
15. Freud to Wilhelm Fliess, 3 October 1897, *Complete Letters of Sigmund Freud to Wilhelm Fliess*, p. 268.
16. Freud, 'Three Essays on Sexuality', p. 202.
17. Nysembaum, 'Une pensée qui va et vient', p. 154.
18. Bücher, *Arbeit und Rhythmus*, p. 413.
19. Klages, *Vom Wesen des Rhythmus*, p. 14.
20. Abraham, *Rhythms*, p. 108.
21. Bolton, p. 7.
22. Allen, *Physiological Aesthetics*, p. 19.
23. Thoreau, *Walden* (2000), p. 106.
24. Schafer, *The Soundscape*, p. 81.
25. Whitman, 'To a Locomotive in Winter' in *Leaves of Grass*, pp. 358–9.
26. Sandburg, 'Work Gangs', in *Smoke and Steel*, pp. 12–13.
27. Anderson, 'Evening Song', in *Mid-American Chants*, p. 69.
28. Williams, 'Overture to a Dance of Locomotives', p. 873.
29. This term is used by Albert Murray in his *Stomping the Blues*, pp. 117–26. Murray makes the link between locomotive rhythm and African-American music and culture – a topic fully addressed in Dinerstein, *Swinging the Machine*. See in particular p. 72.
30. Cendrars, 'Profound Today', in *Selected Writings*, p. 229.
31. Letter written in 1943, in Cendrars, *The Astonished Man*, p. 13.
32. Cendrars, *Complete Poems*, p. 18.
33. Wagner, *Technologie und Literatur im Zeitalter der Avantgarden*, p. 141. My translation.
34. Cendrars, 'Nights and Days (to be continued): The Nights', in *The Astonished Man*, p. 186.
35. Cendrars, *Complete Poems*, p. 28.
36. Cendrars, 'Nights and Days', p. 186.
37. Stein, 'If I Told Him: A Completed Portrait Of Picasso' (1923), p. 464.
38. Cendrars, *Complete Poems*, pp. 20–1.
39. Icart, *Abel Gance*, p. 131. My translation.
40. Guido, '"The Supremacy of the Mathematical Poem"', p. 150.
41. The British film historian Kevin Brownlow, who has been the key figure in the restoration and revival of Gance's films, disputes this account of the film's composition, arguing that the rhythm was created in the editing. See Brownlow, *The Parade's Gone By*, p. 554.
42. Gance, *The Cinema of Tomorrow 1929*, quoted from King, *Abel Gance*, p. 68.
43. Cendrars, *Moravagine*, p. 57.

Chapter 14

Two-step, Nerve-tap, Tanglefoot: Tapdance Typologies in Cinema

Steven Connor

Light fantastic

Of the three modes of musical sound production distinguished by musical historians, blowing, scraping and striking, it is the last that has come to the fore in modern music, perhaps in response to a world experienced as never before in the mode of auditory impact and concussion. If one were to think of modern sound as a kind of speech, it would be a matter more of consonants than vowels, of stops more than sustains, of beats more than melodies. Music and dance have responded in many ways to this world of incessant knocks, bumps, jostles, judders, rattles, clicks, cracks, bangs and blips, but nowhere as richly as in the practice of tap dance, which, in the decades before the Second World War, dominated popular music in film. If part of the work of music is to turn raw noise into information by articulating it as pattern, then we might see tap dance as increasing redundance, rendering the random concussions of modern sound purposively percussive.

Historians of dance are agreed that tap originates in a confluence of Northern European rural dance traditions instanced in the Irish and Scottish jig and Northern English clog-dance with African styles of dance retained and developed by slaves in American plantations. Tap retains from both currents the gravitational pull of the ground. Eleanor Powell recounts that, when she first began to learn tap dance, her coach, Jack Donahue, told her "'You're . . . very aerial; in tap you've got to get down to the floor.'"[1] Donahue came up with a surprisingly direct way of discouraging her balletic levitations:

> He had a war surplus belt, the kind that you put bullets in. There weren't any bullets, but on each side of the belt there were two sandbags – the kind they use to weigh down the curtains in a theater. I want you to know that with

that belt on I couldn't move off the floor and I haven't moved off the floor since. (x)

T. S. Eliot captures the clumpingly chthonic quality of the contact of foot and ground in country and traditional dances in 'East Coker':

> Round and round the fire
> Leaping through the flames, or joined in circles,
> Rustically solemn or in rustic laughter
> Lifting heavy feet in clumsy shoes,
> Earth feet, loam feet, lifted in country mirth
> Mirth of those long since under earth
> Nourishing the corn. Keeping time . . .
> Feet rising and falling.
> Eating and drinking. Dung and death.[2]

Of course the movement of tap, of which cinema really shows only the most perfected forms, is away from this kind of mortal shuffling. In becoming urban and sophisticated, tap had to minimise its contact with the ground. The values of lightness and flight had to prevail over the clinging cyclicities of country dances. As the dancer Paul Draper remarked: 'A heavy-footed tap dancer is a contradiction in terms, since 'tap' means to strike lightly.'[3] At the same time, the strongly vertical or pile-drivingly perpendicular orientations of country dances (recapitulated in primitivist reflexes like punk pogo-ing), in which all the energy may be driven down towards the ground and recoil in the same column away from it, is varied by lateral and radial movements. Most importantly, and definingly, for tap, the upper body, head and arms, are recruited to the dance. Where, in the earlier style known as 'buck and wing', the stamp is primary, and the little flutters and kicks (named after the flutter of the pigeon-wing) are snatched ornamentations, in fully fledged tap, the aim is to suggest an airborne dancer, who grazes and pecks at the ground only in passing. Tap is tact. W. C. Fields said of the performer Pat Rooney, who introduced a softer, more delicate style of tap dance: 'If you didn't hear the Taps, you would think he was floating over the stage.'[4] Cinema assists in the elevation of tap through a kind of pun, whereby the light fantastic toe merges with the evanescence of the flickering light that is the matter of cinema.

The recoil from the ground also has drearily predictable class and race analogies. As tap dance dwelt less and less on the earth, so it was also lifted up in the social scale. As the shifty clodhoppings of the rural folk dance gave way to the sophisticated struts and high kicks of urban dance, the clumping clown became the prancing toff, kitted out in spats, top hat and tails. In large part, this movement also meant a move from black dancers to white, though purist historians of dance will still often prefer the loose-limbed downward focus of a Bill Robinson to the exorbitant soarings and scissorings of an Astaire, O'Connor or Kelly. However, we might note that the air-walking associated with the aristocrat appears not second in the history of tap, but first, in the farcical high-stepping of the cakewalk, in which white slave-owners saw – or perhaps failed to see – their own dance movements mimicked and mocked by their slaves. Fred Astaire's aerial mode is therefore not so much a simple sublimation of the primitive buck and wing as a recapitulation of the modes of the 'class act' that emerged at the turn of the century, formalising and urbanising the plantation cakewalk, which was then itself taken over by white dancers. The aerial dancer both depends upon and is imperilled by the tug of the ground.

Adorno predictably saw the cakewalk and tap-dancing as the survivals of the original 'lament of unfreedom' which jazz never managed to transfigure, for

> everything unruly in it was from the very beginning integrated into a strict scheme . . . its rebellious gestures are accompanied by the tendency to blind obeisance, much like the sadomasochistic type described by analytic psychology, the person who chafes against the father-figure while secretly admiring him, who seeks to emulate him and in turn derives enjoyment from the subordination he overtly detests.[5]

This seems to be redoubled for Adorno in the adoption of jazz by the white lumpenproletariat, who 'participated in its prehistory during the period preceding its thrust into the spotlight of a society which seemed to be waiting for it and which had long been familiar with its impulses through the cakewalk and tap-dancing' (122). Clement Greenberg saw tap dance as one of the elements of kitsch, that assembly of 'chromeotypes, magazine covers, illustrations, ads, slick and pulp fictions, comics, Tin Pan Alley music, tap-dancing, Hollywood music, etc., etc.' that entertained the recent peasants who swarmed into cities to make up the proletariat and petit bourgeoisie, who had been educated to the point of being able to read and write, but had not the leisure to develop any really cultivated sensibility.[6] Tap dance is a kind of crippled transcendence.

But this, in a different sense from that meant by the austere kind of anti-modern modernism of Adorno and Greenberg, is precisely the point of tap. Tap dance reminds cinema of its origins in the turn-of-the-century vernacular of vaudeville, circus, carnival and other diffuse kinds of attractions and spectacles. In fact, one can make out in the difference between the smooth aerial flights of a Fred Astaire and the earthier moves of a Bill 'Bojangles' Robinson a rhyme with the struggle between the technical sophistication of the cinema in its developed form, and its lowlier, more vulgarly corporeal origins and appetites. The contrast between the clog-dancing rustic (black or Irish) and the sophisticated man-about-town testifies to a class ambivalence that is never quite resolved in tap dance, which always retains the traces of its ostentatiously corporeal origins, a kind of comic awkwardness that resists being lifted up into the condition of high art. Eleanor Powell relates how she had to say to a stiffly over-polite Astaire,

> 'Now listen. Fundamentally we're hoofers, right? We are the act that opens first with the flea circus. You may be the great Mr. Astaire and all that, but we are still hoofers, so can we get down to "Ellie" and "Fred?"'[7]

For all the air of sophistication of cinema's headline exponents of tap dance, Fred Astaire, Ginger Rogers and Gene Kelly, tap dance reminds cinema of its origin in the display of novelties and curiosities – the 'cinema of attractions', as, following Tom Gunning, it has come to be called.[8] Cutting athwart its slick syncopations, tap dance always acts like a kind decomposition of cinema to its elements of sound and movement, most importantly in its play with the mechanisation of human bodies. Tap dance therefore provides an elementary form of cinema's transaction between body and image, gravity and light.

Tap dance has another legacy from slavery, in the intense focus that it retains on labour. The gratuitous exhilaration of tap is always earned by toil and fatigue. Julian Marsh, the director in *Forty-Second Street*, famously barks at his cast:

> We're gonna rehearse for five weeks and we're gonna open on scheduled time. – And I mean scheduled time. You're gonna work and sweat and work some more. You're gonna work days and you're gonna work nights. And you're gonna work between time when I think you need it. You're gonna dance until your feet fall off and you're not able to stand up any longer. But five weeks from now, we're going to have a show!

Adorno is certainly right to see the leisure of tap dance grimly twinned with labour. And this labour is of an industrial kind, consisting of hours of regimented rehearsal – *Forty-Second Street* is built around the chorus line, which emerged during the First World War, and reflects the simultaneous industrialisation of war and the militarisation of work. But this irony is not an accidental analogy, apparent only to the irony-attuned eye of the cultural theorist, for it is part of the mythos of tap, and is time and again explicitly thematised within it. The defining dichotomy of tap dance history, between Fred Astaire and Gene Kelly, the one willowy and elegantly effortless, with wrists as loose and flappy as his trousers, the other squat, thick-necked and athletically straining against his T-shirts, is really the separation of this pairing of the *sprezzatura* and the blue-collar work ethic. Cyd Charisse, who paired with both of them, summed up the difference when she said 'My husband always knew who I was rehearsing with when I came home at the end of a day at the studio. If I didn't have a mark, it was Astaire; if I was black and blue, it was Gene Kelly.'[9]

I remember being struck by hearing a veteran saying the reason she enjoyed tap-dancing was because it had more 'attack' than other forms of dance. I was impressed by this term, because, though it flaunted a certain kind of technicality, it also named something almost embarrassingly basic about tap dance, namely the large amounts of aggression it displays and enables through its effecting of impacts and concussions. Though there are many dances in which formalised combats are acted out, there is no more immediate way of suggesting aggression than in bodily movements that mime actions of striking and impact. Much early tap-dancing took the form of competitions, and the tap challenge gives tone to the sexual sparring between Fred Astaire and Ginger Rogers that provides the unvarying template for the films they made together in the 1930s.

Tap and matter

This aggression is also visible in the relation between the dancer and the world of objects, and tap is more ambivalently entangled with matter than any other form of dance. Tap dancers repeatedly duet and duel with objects – Astaire's cane in *Top Hat* (1935), Astaire's dance with shadows, those most cinematic of quasi-objects, in his homage to Mr Bojangles in *Swing Time* (1936), or Gene Kelly's dance with newspaper and a squeaky board in *Summer Stock* (1950). Where ballet aims to shrink and immaterialise the shoe, in the process metonymically disavowing the baseness of the foot, tap glorifies it, and the metal prostheses that, from around the end of the 1920s, began to be added to it. In fact, shoes themselves were not always needed. The tradition of tap-dance roller skating is perhaps initiated by the roller skating sequence in Chaplin's *Modern Times* (1936), on which Fred Astaire and a rather wobbly Ginger Rogers elaborated in their version of George and Ira Gershwin's 'Let's Call The Whole Thing Off' from *Shall We Dance* (1937), and Gene Kelly superbly topped in *It's Always Fair Weather* (1955).

Perhaps tap is the first dance form to transform clumsiness into artifice without wholly purging that clumsiness. Tap is full of bungles and perilous flirtations with comically corporeal catastrophe. No matter how refined its techniques (and its discourse) may become, it can never entirely expunge its associations with the freakish, the decrepit, or the ridiculous. This is sometimes encoded in the contrast between the cretinously slurred shuffle, that fails to break with the surly bonds of earth, and the cleanly starched pizzicato of tap proper. The comedy of Wilson Keppel and Betty's sand dance depends a great deal upon this contrast between the shuffle and the tap. The *OED* rather sniffily defines 'tap-dancing' as 'a form of exhibition dancing characterised by rhythmical tapping of the toes and heels'.[10] All forms of dancing involve some kind of exhibition, one might reasonably think, but it is certainly the case that tap dance is much more exhibitionist than other forms of dance. 'Tap dancing is nothing if not virtuosic', remarks Joseph Epstein, 'by which ugly and awkward word is meant, not to put too fine a point on it, showing off'.[11] The exhibition involved often suggests a kind of mild monstrosity, the word monster being related to demonstration, as suggested by the scene from Mel Brooks's *Young Frankenstein* in which the education of the monster is proved by his capacity to perform a song-and-dance routine. There can be few dance forms in which disability or bodily anomaly can have been so prominent, marking the risible Bergsonian collision of the organic and the inorganic. In a publicity poster of 1892, T. F. Grant was described as 'the champion one-legged clog dancer of the world'.[12] You could be forgiven for thinking that there would be limited competition for such a title, but you would be mistaken. One Robert Stickney danced on stilts, the Purcella Brothers appeared as convicts with their legs chained together, and Harper and Stencil performed a one-legged double act, their amputations, one of them missing a left leg, the other a right, being complementary (140). The extra limb represented by the dancer's cane, and the recruitment to the dance of other parts of the body, such as hands and fingers (one performer won a tap dance contest by flipping into a handstand and patting out the finale with his palms) reflect a certain Sphinx-like uncertainty about the exact complement of limbs required to perform tap. The most astonishing exemplification of the link between impediment and tap is the career of Clayton 'Peg Leg' Bates. At the age of twelve, in 1919, he caught and injured his leg in a conveyor belt in the gin mill in which he was working; his leg was amputated on his own kitchen table. Bates, who was already a dancer, set about relearning how to dance with one leg, and built a career on Broadway in the 1930s, and subsequently on TV, making more than twenty appearances on the *Ed Sullivan Show*, which culminated in an astonishing tap challenge with Conrad Buckner in August 1965. Bates's opening number on TV would announce: 'Folks my name is Clayton/Peg Leg Bates to you/I'm always syncopating/ And doing something new.'[13] He is also said to have capitalised on the musical possibilities of the 'rhythmic combination of his deep-toned left-leg peg and the high-pitched metallic right-foot tap' (186–7).

Tap dance is both closer to mechanism than any other mainstream dance and also, for what is in fact a closely related reason, highly individualistic. Tap seems designed to amplify the idiosyncrasies of individual physiologies, which not only resist the formalising disciplines of the dance, but are amplified by them. Many tap performers acted as their own choreographers, and there is an enormous premium in tap placed on the production of new and original steps. And yet, at the same time, there is no dance that has been so caught up in popular pedagogy, or so systematically taught and learned, as tap. We may say that tap involves a paradoxically simultaneous intensification both of the individual idiom and the stereotype, there being no form of dance to which the idea of the 'routine' seems to be more appropriate. The tapping part of tap is anonymous, abstract and impersonal. Bill Robinson used to challenge the judges in tap dance competitions to sit underneath the stage and try to distinguish the sounds made by his left and right feet. Tap aims for atomic exactitude and equivalence. Rather than from drawing on a spectrum of expressive moves, the versatility of tap is combinative, with moves being genetically modified by the addition or subtraction of molecular elements. Tap is automatic not just because it mimics mechanical procedures, but also because it isolates and amplifies those individualising automatisms, the subliminal twitches that distinguish individual bodies. Even Astaire's canonical blending of ballroom, ballet and tap styles has been characterised as a kind of 'outlaw' style.[14] Tap dance is regulated eccentricity.

The matter and mechanisms with which tap traffics are, like tap itself, noisy. Jerry Ames and Jim Siegelman note the relation of adversarial mimicry between tap and the increasingly cacophonous material world of the twentieth century. Tap dancers, they say,

> want to blast out and express themselves in a blatant racket, they want to fight back against the roar of jets, the boom of factories, the whirr of air conditioners, the slamming of doors, the battering of jackhammers, the car horns, doorbells, telephones, stereos, barking dogs, alarm clocks, screaming babies, ambulance sirens, whistling teakettles, banging garbage can lids . . . and dripping faucets in the night.[15]

Joel Dinerstein has placed the relation between the tap dancer and the mechanical world at the heart of his reading of popular dance in the interwar years. For Dinerstein, the tap dancer does not merely fight back with noise against noise; rather, he transforms noise, and in the process, himself:

> the tap dancer was a vision of the industrial body retooled for a rootless, mobile future . . . the tap dancer took the speeded-up machine-driven tempo of life and the metallic crunch of cities and factories and spun it all into a dazzling pyrotechnical display of speed, precision, rhythmic noise, continuity, grace, and power.[16]

So, if in one sense, tap represents the iron entering the soul, with tap dancers 'taking the industrial soundscape into their bodies', this landscape is at once sublimated and humanised (228); 'tap's primary message is one of *industrial power under individual control*' (223). Dinerstein's primary exhibit is the 'Slap That Bass' routine from *Follow the Fleet*, set in the engine room of an ocean liner, in which Fred Astaire is travelling to Europe in pursuit of Ginger Rogers. The point of the dance, for Dinerstein, is to show that '[a] human being is more *expressively* energetic than a machine. Unlike a machine, a human body can display grace, elegance, humor, surprise, spontaneity, and rhythmic control' (243). But I think there may be more reciprocity than Dinerstein allows between the human and the inhuman engines. I think we can say that, if tap spiritualises matter, it may be with the cost, or profit, of a materialisation of spirit.

Tap sounds

Tap dance of course involves a kind of self-accompaniment. A tap dancer busking in a doorway does not need a boom box to draw the attention of passers-by, because the dance provides its own soundtrack. This is one of the most striking ways in which tap dance seems to recall the world of novelties, stunts and exploits rather than the arts of dance; providing your own soundtrack resembles the art of the one-man band. But if tap turns the body into an instrument, it is an acoustically very limited one, much more limited in fact than most percussion instruments, despite the claims sometimes made by jazz percussionists to have listened to tap dance for new ideas. Indeed, there was a movement in tap away from styles that emphasised the variety of percussive sounds – scrapes, slides and shuffles participating with stamps and tinging raps – towards a style in which the tap is reduced to ripples of dry, homogenous clicks. Cinema participates in this, in that early sound-recording techniques were in any case inadequate to pick up and reproduce much timbre or resonance. The only forms of variation that tap really permits are in amplitude and speed: you can tap louder, or you can tap faster, and these two parameters seem to have an inverse ratio to one another – a loud stamp will usually slow the sound, or halt it altogether, while fast passages diminish the volume.

Ordinarily, to make any sound at all in dance is a kind of accident or transgression. Those who, like me, prefer to sit near the front to watch ballet, in order to catch the wafts of heat, and even the occasional whiff of animal effort, from all that whirling and leaping, are indulging a somewhat perverse desire to restore the density of the body to the weightless image, to apprehend the grossness of mass and matter in line and form. The grunts and pants, and the thump of the ballerina on the boards, are corporeal sound becoming the sound of corporeality itself, which the dance-image must strive to sublimate. Of course almost all dance is accompanied by sound, in the form of music, but the point of that sound is precisely to drown or displace the actual sounds of the moving body, thereby replacing accident with intention.

There was almost no accidental or incidental sound in early cinema, the attention of sound engineers being focused almost exclusively on the sound of speech and, in the case of musicals, of song and music. When trouble was taken to capture incidental sound, it almost always had a diegetic purpose, to focus the attention of the audience on some narrative element of the scene – a train pulling in to a station, the blare of a siren, the clink of a glass, or the creak of a door. Sound tends to act as a kind of acoustic captioning of significance, or, as we may as well say, it captions itself, as 'the sound of' (a door, a train, a busy street). By folding hearing exactly over seeing, sound doubles seeing, instructing the viewer to look at what they can see.

In one sense, tap conforms docilely to this economy, for it gives us the sound of dance, as though dance were being accorded some kind of authentically self-designating voice. Tapping says, tautologically, this is dance you're seeing here, look at all this dancing you can see, just as the creaking door says, look here at this door you can see opening. But the sound of tap is also an anomaly within this economy, precisely because the only sound that dance is supposed to have is not endogenously made by it, but produced alongside it in the form of song or music. The sound that dance itself produces, as opposed to a sound which it accompanies, or to which it responds, is, in every other case than tap dance, the sound of accident or excess – the clatter of a fall, the growl or giggle at a mistake. In formalising these contingencies, tap dance is the essentialising or apotheosis of accident.

Synchronicities

The form of apparatus with which tap has its most insistent affinity is the semi-immaterial apparatus of cinema itself. This is most apparent in the play that tap, like cinema, effects between the divisible and the indivisible. These two principles are made to collude in the person of Astaire, who developed a highly distinctive blending of ballroom, with its long, sweeping, skating curves, and tap, with its sharp angularities, which chop up those contours into their elements. Astaire aims to bring the viewer to the tipping point between these two orders, as the divisible and individually audible forms of the tap come close to being indiscernible. The important factor here is speed. Astaire recalled that when he was a radio tap dancer for *The Packard Hour* in 1935 the limitations of the microphone meant that he had to perform on a mat four-feet square, which encouraged density and speed of taps rather than graceful and expressive movement.[17] Since it was not possible to hear leaps Astaire had to provide the show's listeners 'a lot of taps close together – a string of ricky-ticky-ticky-tacky-tacky steps'.[18] Speed is correlated here not with movement, but with the simultaneous condensation and agitation of place. Speed becomes a principle of introversion, of an energy that turns in on and regenerates from itself. Speed both thickens matter, and also pushes it towards immaterialisation – the blur of the propeller, or the illusion of matter in movement produced by the moving matter of cinema itself.

For the most important feature of tap is that, for all its demonstrative extravagance, it is designed to elude or outdo the eye. This kind of deception has been at the heart of tap dance; one early tap dancer was found to have hollowed out her heels and inserted bullets in the metal-lined cavities, to double up the taps. And many choreographed tap dances escape the eye of the camera in a more literal way, since the sound of the tapping is dubbed on after the performance. Ginger Rogers's tap steps were overdubbed by Hermes Pan (Panagiotopoulos), Fred Astaire's long-term choreographing partner. Eleanor Powell, who choreographed her own dances, also overdubbed them herself, not just to ensure her signature crispness of sound but also to allow her to wear more attractive shoes than she could otherwise have done. There were three stages in the recording process. After the dance had been developed in rehearsal, Powell would dance it silently on a mattress in the sound room while the orchestra recorded the music, to ensure that they had the right tempo. The dance would then be filmed, with the recording being played, but again only for synchronisation purposes, since no sound was recorded. Finally, Powell performed the dance again in a sound studio, on a wooden mat, so the tap steps could be added to the recording, and the three laminations, of dance, music and tap-sound at last locked together.[19]

The question of integration is always to the fore in speaking and writing about dance numbers. Jerome Delamater argues that the song-and-dance number is an 'integration of the entire cinematic process'.[20] Yet the song always marks a more-or-less violent break of continuity in terms of plot, which many musicals attempt to overcome by making the characters dancers, or setting the story in a theatre in which lots of dancing is going on. Fred Astaire spoke in 1937 of the challenge of smoothing out this discontinuity:

> I think the audience always slumps – even more in the movies than on the stage – when they hear an obvious dance cue, and both the picture *and the dance* seem to lose some of their continuity. Each dance ought to spring somehow out of character or situation, otherwise it is simply a vaudeville act.[21]

Astaire also reacted against the tendency for the camera to dance along with the dancer – 'Either the camera will dance, or I will',[22] he said – and rehearsed his dances so intensively that they were able to be shot in one take:

> In the old days . . . they used to cut up all the dances on the screen. In the middle of a sequence they would show you a close-up of the actor's face, or of his feet, insert trick angles taken from the floor, the ceiling, through lattice work or a maze of fancy shadows. The result was that the dance had no continuity. The audience was far more conscious of the camera than of the dance . . . I have always tried to run a dance straight through in the movies, keeping the full figure of the dancer, or dancers, in view and retaining the flow of the movement intact. In every kind of dancing, even tap, the movement of the upper part of the body is as important as that of the legs.[23]

And yet, tap always cuts into this smooth suture, asserting the order of the discontinuous over that of the continuous. Discontinuity is never overcome, if only because the more thoroughly the big dance number may integrate all the elements of cinema, the more discontinuous it will then seem with the rest of the movie which does not exhibit the same saturation of elements. Within cinema, we suddenly break into pure and integrated, but for that very reason, also abstract, 'cinema' *en-soi*. Michel Chion points to tap-dance numbers in 1930s monaural cinema as displays of sonic fusion or 'a continuum of dialogue, music and sound effects', suggesting that, everything today tends on the contrary to separate the sounds from one another; their dispersion across several tracks, their precision, the differences in contrast and the gulfs of silence between them, etc. Apart from that, we no longer believe in a rhythmic unity of creation. We live in a world in which the rhythms overlay one another without blending.[24]

In fact, Chion here seems to be describing very aptly the tendency of tap, which is to produce a sort of superfluous, or unintegrated sound that is always a sort of sonic surplus to the audiovisual composite, and right from the very beginning.

Tap is concerned, not just with the world of matter, but also with the kind of materialised temporality that Bergson found exemplified in the cinematographic apparatus. For Bergson, this materialisation took the form of discontinuity introduced distortingly into the 'suppleness and variety of life' and the 'inner becoming of things'.[25] Tap dance provides such a striking exemplification of this materialising discontinuity because it is a matter of numbers. All dance involves counting, and the greater the number of dancers, in the hugely expanded chorus lines of the 1930s, for example, and the greater the intricacies of synchronisation required, the more exacting considerations of number and quantity became. Given the way in which tap seems to produce its own accompanying soundtrack, as it were auto-synchronising its own movements with finite numbers of divisible beats, tap might be said to be the apotheosis of corporeal number. Itself reducible to number, it can be seen as a way of reducing contour, flow and quality to pure quantity or enumeration. More than other kinds of dance, tap is full of counting. Biographical accounts of tap dancers like Fred Astaire and Eleanor Powell emphasise the fanatical austerity of their work ethic, usually rendered in time-and-motion terms of the number of hours put in each day. It is apt that the most basic step in tap is known as the 'time-step'. The pursuit of dizzying speed in tap dance produced an obsession with counting the number of taps that performers could produce in a given time, as though it were an athletic event rather than an art form. Ann Miller took on the expert typist Ruth Myers in a radio speed contest in 1946, and out-tapped her at 627 taps a minute as against Myers's 584,[26] while the world record for tap-speed, established in 1973 by Roy Castle at over 1,400 taps a minute,[27] works out intriguingly at around twenty-four taps a second, the same as the standard frame-rate of cinema. There is no dance that corresponds as closely as tap to Walter Benjamin's characterisation of cinema as detonating 'the dynamite of the tenth of a second'.[28]

Clickety-click

The sound of the click became ubiquitous in the early twentieth century. It marked the possibility of the abrupt and absolute alternation from an off state to an on, a new experience made possible by the switch, and transferred quickly to psychological states: William James evokes in 1880 a 'state of *consent* [in which] the passage from the former state to it ... is ... characterized by the mental "click" of resolve'.[29] But the click exhibited and effected the many forms of synchronicity that modern coordinated life required. The synchronised sound of the cinema comes late in a process whereby the things and processes of the world were increasingly required to be got, and kept 'in step', as we say, with each other. But synchronicity was allied to, perhaps in a certain sense produced, its apparent opposite, namely syncopation. Synchronicity and syncopation, the on- and the off-beat, were themselves synchronised, as Adorno's snarls about the ersatz pseudo-surprises of jazz syncopation seem to make clear. Not only were devices and mechanisms subject to temporal regulation, they became, so to speak, timepieces. Everything told the time, and kept the beat, in a literalisation of Bertrand Russell's explanation in his *ABC of Relativity* (1925), that

> there is no longer a universal time which can be applied without ambiguity to any part of the universe; there are only the various 'proper' times of the various bodies in the universe, which agree approximately for two bodies which are not in rapid motion, but never agree exactly except for two bodies which are at rest relatively to each other.[30]

It was the century, not just of time, but, more specifically, of *timing*. Tap dance required tight synchronisation, but might also be seen (and heard), as a kind of auto-synchronisation of film. Indeed, the 1930s marked the development of two devices for synchronising sound and music that seem to have a family resemblance to tap dance: the clapperboard, whose sharp spike of sound was easily detectible in the soundtrack, and what become known as a 'click track', in which holes would be punched in the optical soundtrack at specified intervals (once every twenty-four frames would give sixty bpm), which, when light shone through it, produced a sharply audible click on the soundtrack.

For all its fierce energy, tap aligns itself with the electronic mechanisms of the second industrial revolution rather than the thumping shafts and pistons of the first. Even the engine room in which Astaire dances in *Follow the Fleet* seems more like an art deco office than the sooty satanic mill we might expect. Tap dance is a magical transfiguration of the phenomenology of the click that became so ubiquitous in the early twentieth century. It plays variations on the clicking of typewriters, of telegraphic Morse code, telephone receivers and exchanges, sewing machines, cash registers, calculators, tickertape, and the ticking of the time bomb (a word that is first recorded in print in 1893). It evokes the rattle of railway tracks, the clicking of switches and operating devices of all kinds, most notably the clicking of the camera shutter, and anticipates the eras of Geiger counters and mouse clicks. Its speed reminds us of the many forms of rotary motion that accelerate the click into the whirr or rattle, the pleasantly rasping dials of telephones, or in fans, propellers, or cinema projectors. The increasing commonness of precisely engineered artefacts, like buttons and boxes, and locks and catches that snapped open or shut, and materials like plastic that clicked easily together, made the click stand for the sense of rightness or exactness of fit. Yeats wrote in 1935 that, 'the correction of prose, because it has no fixed laws, is endless, a poem comes right with a click like a closing box'.[31] But clicking also suggests accident, maladjustment or damage, whether in the clicks of radio interference, usually caused by the sparking of electrical equipment like the connectors of trams or lightning, or in the click of the damaged record or broken gramophone. The shufflings of tap are perhaps allotropes of the 'chuff chuff chuff' of the idling gramophone in Woolf's *Between the Acts* (1941).[32]

The confluence of music, timing and number is registered in an oblique way in Joyce's novel written at the dawn of the jazz age, *Ulysses*, which features Tom Rochford's mechanical gadget for automatically displaying the number of a turn at the music hall for latecomers, literalising the idea of a musical 'number':

> Tom Rochford took the top disk from the pile he clasped against his claret waistcoat.
> – See? he said. Say it's turn six. In here, see. Turn Now On.
> He slid it into the left slot for them. It shot down the groove, wobbled a while, ceased, ogling them: six . . .
> – See? he said. See now the last one I put in is over here: Turns Over. The impact. Leverage, see?
> He showed them the rising column of disks on the right.
> – Smart idea, Nosey Flynn said, snuffling. So a fellow coming in late can see what turn is on and what turns are over.[33]

This scene occurs in the episode known as 'Wandering Rocks', in which Joyce coordinates the movements across Dublin of a number of characters. Famously, he asked friends to pace out certain routes through Dublin to time them, and is said to have written the chapter with a stopwatch at his side. In fact, the whole of *Ulysses* might be regarded

not just as 'manipulating a continuous parallel between contemporane-
ity and antiquity', as Eliot famously said, but as an exercise in orches-
trating complex synchronicities – centred on the newspaper, that great
synchronising device beloved of kidnappers.[34] *Ulysses* parallels the odys-
seys of its two characters with the irregular passage out to sea of a flyer
advertising the arrival of an evangelical preacher that Bloom tosses into
the river Liffey, but it plays similar games of pooh-sticks with the different itineraries of persons and objects through the day. What is more,
Ulysses might be said to feature its own version of the click-track, in the
regular tippings and tappings that seem to mark off the passage of time
through the novel. Some of them are associated with the 'blind stripling'
whose cane is heard and imagined tapping his way through the streets
of Dublin: 'Queer idea of Dublin he must have, tapping his way round
by the stones', thinks Bloom when he first sees him (173). He, or rather
the sound of his progress, is used to synchronise the music in the 'Sirens'
episode of the novel, in which Bloom sits in the Ormond Bar listening
to music – 'Tap blind walked tapping by the tap the curbstone tapping,
tap by tap' (276). In fact, forty-four of the one hundred or so appearances of the word 'tap' in *Ulysses* occur in these rhythmic punctuations
of the 'Sirens' episode, culminating in a Lear-like sequence of eight of
them in a paragraph of its own – 'Tap. Tap. Tap. Tap. Tap. Tap. Tap.
Tap' (277). These sounds also modulate in the 'Sirens' episode into the
sexually predatory rat-a-tat of Blazes Boylan on the door of Eccles Street
– 'One rapped on a door, one tapped with a knock, did he knock Paul
de Kock with a loud proud knocker with a cock carracarracarra cock.
Cockcock' (271) – as well as into Bloom's conjugations of erotic tipping
and tupping – 'Tipping her tepping her tapping her topping her. Tup'
(273). There is a great deal of tapping elsewhere in the novel, including
tapping with a fan and rolled up newspaper, as well as the heeltaps of
Bella dancing in the brothel. Bloom has a fondness for this elementary
sound-particle, using the expression 'tiptop' for example, repeatedly
through the novel. It is a fondness which Joyce seems to have shared,
for he punctuates the text of *Finnegans Wake* with the word 'tip', which
often seems to indicate the mechanical pecking of a hen, for example in
the jaunty, jiggerpokery rhythms of a passage describing the unearthing
of a document or photograph (as it might be, the *Wake* itself) from a
midden:

> Well, almost any photoist worth his chemicots will tip anyone asking him
> the teaser that if a negative of a horse happens to melt enough while drying,
> well, what you do get is, well, a positively grotesquely distorted macromass of
> all sorts of horsehappy values and masses of meltwhile horse. Tip. Well, this
> freely is what must have occurred to our missive (there's a sod of a turb for

you! please wisp off the grass!) unfilthed from the boucher by the sagacity of a lookmelittle likemelong hen. Heated residence in the heart of the orangeflavoured mudmound had partly obliterated the negative to start with, causing some features palpably nearer your pecker to be swollen up most grossly while the farther back we manage to wiggle the more we need the loan of a lens to see as much as the hen saw. Tip.[35]

If tap dance may perhaps be regarded as another of the forms of automatism that so fascinated psychologists in the late nineteenth and early twentieth centuries, it may also be associated with the more spasmodic kinds of click involved in the Touretter's tic. The association of dance and mania is, of course, strongly established, for example in the epidemic of tarantella that swept across Europe in the sixteenth century, and the forms of dyskinesia, or uncontrolled but rhythmic movement, characteristic of different forms of what is medically known as chorea, such as Sydenham's Chorea, or St Vitus Dance. The style of grotesque dancing, as practised by performers such as Henry 'Rubberlegs' Williams, which involved unpredictable movements of legs, and evolved into forms like the Charleston, was often called 'legomania' (and, oddly, came to be associated with Russian and Hungarian dancing). Though behavioural automatisms like humming, clapping and twitching of limbs have frequently been observed in epileptic seizures, it is perhaps surprising that no explicit association between tapping and epilepsy has been made until a paper of 2011 by a group of physicians at the Royal Hallamshire hospital in Sheffield, Yorkshire. The authors report that a 60-year-old, right-handed woman with a history of temporal lobe epilepsy developed a pattern of behaviour during seizures that included 'stereotyped and extremely complex musical automatisms in the form of tap dancing. Interestingly, there was no social history of learned dancing; dance had never been a hobby or pastime to any significant degree in earlier life.'[36] There is no suggestion of elaborate routines being danced, and the tap dancing really seems to have consisted in nothing more developed than 'rhythmic leg and foot tapping' (151).

Tap dance is possessed of an energy and a joyous vitality that few dances can match. The underlying principle of tap, says Joseph Epstein 'was solely joie de vivre, simple happy bloody joy in living . . . The physical delight in dance was the thing, and to hell with the conscience of the king.'[37] But the infectiousness of this energy is a sign also of its strange rootlessness, the fact that it circulates so ceaselessly between bodies, objects, mechanisms, sounds and images, coming to rest nowhere. The energy of which tap is possessed possesses and dispossesses it. Tap is an image and enactment of our manifold forms of entanglement with modern machineries of ardour, labour and delight.

Notes

1. Ames and Siegelman, *The Book of Tap*, p. x.
2. Eliot, *Complete Poems and Plays*, p. 178.
3. Draper, *On Tap Dancing*, p. 12.
4. Quoted in Slide, *The Vaudevillians*, p. 128.
5. Adorno, *Prisms*, p. 14.
6. Greenberg, 'Avant-Garde and Kitsch', p. 51.
7. Ames and Siegeleman, p. xii.
8. Gunning, 'The Cinema of Attractions', pp. 63–70; Strauven, *The Cinema of Attractions Reloaded*.
9. Quoted in Hill, *Tap Dancing America*, p. 155.
10. 'tap-dancing, n.', *OED Online*. June 2016. Oxford University Press, available at: <http://www.oed.com/view/Entry/197655> (last accessed 14 June 2016).
11. Epstein, *Fred Astaire*, p. 63.
12. Knowles, *Tap Roots*, p. 138.
13. Hill, p. 186.
14. Stearns, *Jazz Dance*, p. 226.
15. Ames and Siegelman, p. 20.
16. Dinerstein, *Swinging the Machine*, pp. 221–2.
17. Dinerstein, p. 224.
18. Quoted in Stearns, p. 224.
19. Hill, p. 129.
20. Delamater, *Dance in the Hollywood Musical*, p. 98.
21. Eustis, 'Fred Astaire', p. 381.
22. Mueller, *Astaire Dancing*, p. 26.
23. Eustis, pp. 378–9.
24. Chion, 'Silence of the Loudspeakers', p. 153.
25. Bergson, *Creative Evolution*, pp. 305, 306.
26. Frank, *Tap!*, p. 246.
27. Hill, p. 143.
28. Benjamin, *Illuminations*, p. 236.
29. James, 'The Feeling of Effort', p. 111.
30. Russell, *ABC of Relativity*, p. 39.
31. Yeats to Dorothy Wellesley, 8 September 1935, *Letters on Poetry*, p. 24.
32. Woolf, *Between the Acts*, p. 110.
33. Joyce, *Ulysses* (2008), pp. 222–3.
34. Eliot, *Selected Prose*, p. 177.
35. Joyce, *Finnegans Wake* (1971), pp. 111–12.
36. Barker, 'Tap Dancing in Epilepsy', p. 151.
37. Epstein, p. 175.

Contributors

Debra Rae Cohen is Associate Professor in the Department of English Language and Literature at the University of South Carolina. She is the author of *Remapping the Home Front* (2002) and co-editor of *Broadcasting Modernism* (2009), and co-editor of the journal *Modernism/modernity*.

Steven Connor is Grace 2 Professor of English at the University of Cambridge and a Fellow of Peterhouse. His most recent books are *Paraphernalia: The Curious Lives of Magical Things* (2011), *A Philosophy of Sport* (2011), *Beyond Words: Sobs, Hums, Stutters and Other Vocalizations* (2014) and *Beckett, Modernism and the Material Imagination* (2014).

Lisa Gitelman is Professor of Media and English at New York University. Her most recent books are *Paper Knowledge: Toward a Media History of Documents* (2014) and *Always Already New: Media, History, and the Data of Culture* (2006), and the co-editor of *'Raw Data' is an Oxymoron* (2013).

Kristin Grogan is a DPhil student in English Literature at the University of Oxford, Exeter College. Her doctoral work examines the concept of labour in modernist poetry.

Helen Groth is Professor of English in the School of the Arts and Media at UNSW Australia. She is the author of *Victorian Photography and Literary Nostalgia* (2003), *Moving Images: Nineteenth-Century Reading and Screen Practices* (2013), (with Natalya Lusty) *Dreams and Modernity: A Cultural History* (2013), and the co-editor of *Mindful Aesthetics: Literature and the Science of Mind* (2014).

Penelope Hone recently completed her PhD in English at UNSW Australia. Her research concentrates on the novel in the nineteenth century, with a particular interest in changing conceptions of the literary voice, noise and new media. She has previously published on George Eliot.

Laura Marcus is Goldsmith's Professor of English at Oxford University and a Fellow of New College. She is the author of *Dreams of Modernity: Psychoanalysis, Literature, Cinema* (2014), *The Tenth Muse: Writing about Cinema in the Modernist Period* (2007) and *Autobiographical Discourses* (1994), and the co-editor of *The Cambridge History of Twentieth-Century Literature* (2004).

Julian Murphet is Scientia Professor of English and Film Studies in the School of the Arts and Media at UNSW Australia. He is the author of *Multimedia Modernism* (2009) and *Literature and Race in Los Angeles* (2001), and the co-editor of *William Faulkner in the Media Ecology* (2015).

Julie Beth Napolin is Assistant Professor of Digital Humanities at The New School. She is the author of a range of articles on sound, resonance and voice in Conrad and Faulkner. She is currently completing a monograph entitled *The Fact of Resonance: Transnational Sound in the Modernist Novel*.

John Plotz, Professor of English at Brandeis University, is the author of *The Crowd* (2000) and *Portable Property* (2008) and a young-adult novel, *Time and the Tapestry: A William Morris Adventure* (2014). His current project is 'Semi-Detached: The Aesthetics of Partial Absorption'.

Sean Pryor is a Senior Lecturer in English in the School of the Arts and Media at UNSW Australia. He is the author of *W. B. Yeats, Ezra Pound, and the Poetry of Paradise* (2011) and many essays on modernism and poetry.

Helen Rydstrand recently completed her PhD in English at UNSW Australia. Her thesis examined concepts of rhythm in the modernist short stories of Katherine Mansfield, Virginia Woolf and D. H. Lawrence. Her article, 'Ordinary Discordance: Katherine Mansfield and the First World War', appeared in a collection on *Katherine Mansfield and World War One*, published by Edinburgh University Press (2014).

Tom Vandevelde recently completed his PhD in Literature and Culture at KU Leuven. He has published articles on aspects of sound and reading in the work of Samuel Beckett, Ford Maddox Ford and Paul van Ostaijen.

Bibliography

'A Yorkshire Spade Club', *Listener* (27 January 1932), p. 144.

Abraham, Nicholas, *Rhythms: On the Work, Translation, and Psychoanalysis* (Stanford: Stanford University Press, 1995).

Adorno, T. W., *Negative Dialectics*, trans. Dennis Redmond, 2001, available at: <http://members.efn.org/~dredmond/ndintro.PDF> (last accessed 30 May 2016).

——, *Negative Dialektik* (Frankfurt am Main: Suhrkamp Verlag, 1970).

——, *Prisms*, trans. Samuel and Shierry Weber (Cambridge, MA: MIT Press, 1983).

Adorno, T. W. and Max Horkheimer, *Dialectic of Enlightenment*, ed. Gunzelin Schmid Noerr, trans. Edmund Jephcott (Stanford: Stanford University Press, 2002).

Ahearn, Amy, 'Full-Blooded Writing and Journalistic Fictions: Naturalism, the Female Artist and Willa Cather's *The Song of the Lark*', *American Literary Realism*, 33:2 (Winter 2001), pp. 143–56.

Albright, Daniel, 'Modernist Poetic Form', in Neil Corcoran (ed.), *The Cambridge Companion to Twentieth-Century English Poetry* (Cambridge: Cambridge University Press, 2007), pp. 24–41.

Allen, Grant, *Physiological Aesthetics* (New York: Garland, 1877).

Ames, Jerry and Jim Spiegelman, *The Book of Tap: Recovering America's Long Lost Dance* (New York: David McKay Co., 1977).

Andem, James L., *A Practical Guide for the Use of the Edison Phonograph* (Cincinnati: North American Phonograph Company, 1892).

Anderson, Sherwood, *Mid-American Chants* (Niantic, CT: Quale Press, 2006).

Armstrong, Julie Buckner, *Mary Turner and the Memory of Lynching* (Athens: The University of Georgia Press, 2011).

Armstrong, Tim, *Modernism, Technology, and the Body* (Cambridge: Cambridge University Press, 1998).

Attridge, Derek, 'Joyce's Noises', *Oral Tradition*, 24:2 (2009), pp. 471–84.

——, *Moving Words: Forms of English Poetry* (Oxford: Oxford University Press, 2013).

Augustine, *De doctrina christiana*, ed. and trans. R. P. H. Green (Oxford: Clarendon Press, 1995).

Bacigalupo, Massimo, *The Forméd Trace: The Later Poetry of Ezra Pound* (New York: Columbia University Press, 1980).

Badiou, Alain, *The Century*, trans. Alberto Toscano (Oxford: Polity, 2007).

Bainton, George (ed.), *The Art of Authorship: Literary Reminiscences, Methods of Work, and Advice to Young Beginners. Personally Contributed by Leading Authors of the Day* (New York: D. Appleton and Co., 1890).

Bal, Mieke, *Narratology: Introduction to the Theory of Narrative* (Toronto: University of Toronto Press, 1985).

—, *Narratology: Introduction to the Theory of Narrative* (1985), 3rd edn (Toronto: University of Toronto Press, 2009).

—, 'Visual Narrativity', in David Herman, Manfred Jahn and Marie-Laure Ryan (eds), *The Routledge Encyclopedia of Narrative Theory* (London: Routledge, 2005), pp. 629–33.

Baldwin, Dean, *Virginia Woolf: A Study of the Short Fiction* (New York: Twayne, 1989).

Barker, A. St. J. E., J. R. C. Bowen, Basil Sharrack and P. G. Sarrigiannis, 'Tap Dancing in Epilepsy', *Epilepsy and Behavior*, 20:1 (2011), pp. 151–2.

Barthes, Roland, *A Lover's Discourse: Fragments* (London: Jonathan Cape, 1978).

—, 'Death of the Author', in *Image, Music, Text*, trans. Stephen Heath (New York: Hill and Wang, 1977), pp. 142–8.

—, 'Listening', in *The Responsibility of Forms: Critical Essays on Music, Art, and Representation* (1982), trans. Richard Howard (Berkeley: University of California Press, 1985), pp. 245–60.

—, *The Neutral: Lecture Course at the Collège de France (1977–1978)*, trans. Rosalind E. Krauss and Denis Hollier (New York: Columbia University Press, 2005).

—, *The Responsibility of Forms: Critical Essays on Music, Art, and Representation*, trans. Richard Howard (Berkeley: University of California Press, 1991).

BBC Handbook 1929, The (London: BBC, 1929).

Beach, Joseph Warren, *The Method of Henry James* (New Haven: Yale University Press, 1918).

Beach, Sylvia, *Shakespeare and Company* (London: Faber and Faber, 1959).

Beckett, Samuel, *All That Fall*, in *The Complete Dramatic Works* (London: Faber and Faber, 1986).

—, 'Company' (1980), in *Nohow On: Company, Ill Seen Ill Said, and Worstward Ho* (New York: Grove Press, 2014).

—, 'Texts for Nothing', in *The Grove Centenary Edition: Volume IV Poems, Short Fiction, Criticism*, ed. Paul Auster (New York: Grove Press, 2006), pp. 295–339.

Bell, Michael, 'The Metaphysics of Modernism', in Michael Levenson (ed.), *The Cambridge Companion to Modernism*, 2nd edn (Cambridge: Cambridge University Press, 2011), pp. 9–32.

Benjamin, Walter, *Illuminations*, ed. Hannah Arendt, trans. Harry Zohn (London: Fontana, 1969).

—, 'Paris, the Capital of the Nineteenth Century', in *The Work of Art in the Age of Its Technological Reproducibility and Other Writings on Media*, ed. Michael W. Jennings, Brigid Doherty and Thomas Y. Levin, trans. Edumund Jephcott, Rodney Livingstone, Howard Eiland, et al. (Cambridge: Harvard University Press, 2008), pp. 96–115.

Benson, Alex, 'Gatsby's Tattoo: Gesture, Tic, and Description', *Criticism* 56:4 (23 July 2016), pp. 725–59, available at *Project Muse*, <https://muse.jhu. edu/>.

Bentley, Phyllis, *The English Regional Novel* (1941) (New York: Haskell House, 1966).

Benveniste, Emile, 'The Notion of Rhythm in its Linguistic Expression', in *Problems in General Linguistics*, trans. Mary Elizabeth Meek, *Miami Linguistic Series No. 8* (Coral Gables: University of Miami Press, 1971), pp. 281–8.

Bergson, Henri, *Creative Evolution*, trans. Arthur Mitchell (New York: Henry Holt, 1911).

Bernstein, Charles (ed.), *Close Listening: Poetry and the Performed Word* (New York: Oxford University Press, 1998).

——, 'Objectivist Blues: Scoring Speech in Second-Wave Modernist Poetry and Lyrics', *American Literary History*, 20:1–2 (Spring–Summer 2008), pp. 346–68.

Besnault-Levita, Anne, '"– Ah, what is it? – that I heard": Voice and Affect in Katherine Mansfield's Short Fictions', in Janet Wilson, Gerri Kimber and Susan Reid (eds) *Katherine Mansfield and Literary Modernism* (London: Continuum, 2011), pp. 89–100.

Blanchot, Maurice, *The Infinite Conversation* (1969), trans. Susan Hanson (Minneapolis: University of Minnesota Press, 1993).

Blasing, Mutlu Konuk, *Lyric Poetry: The Pain and the Pleasure of Words* (Princeton: Princeton University Press, 2007).

Bluemel, Kristin, 'Rural Modernity and the Wood Engraving Revival in Interwar England', *Modernist Cultures*, 9:2 (2014), pp. 233–59.

Bolton, Thaddeus L., 'Rhythm', *The American Journal of Psychology*, 6:2 (January 1894), pp. 145–238.

Bonadei, Rossana, 'Glimpses into a System', *TEXTUS – Rivista dell'Associazione Italiana di Anglistica*, 2 (2006), available at: <http://www00.unibg.it/dati/corsi/3009/14840-glimpses%20into%20a%20system.pdf> (last accessed 15 June 2016).

Brantlinger, Patrick, *The Reading Lesson: The Threat of Mass Literacy in Nineteenth-Century British Fiction* (Bloomington: Indiana University Press, 1998).

Briggs, Asa, *The Golden Age of Wireless: The History of Broadcasting in the United Kingdom Volume II* (London: Oxford University Press, 1965).

Brooks, Tim, 'Columbia Records in the 1890s: Founding the Record Industry', *Journal of the Association for Recorded Sound Collections* 10 (1978), pp. 4–35.

Browning, Robert, *The Complete Works of Robert* Browning, ed. John C. Berkey, Allan C. Dooley and Susan E. Dooley, vol. 6 (Athens: Ohio University Press, 1996).

Brownlow, Kevin, *The Parade's Gone By*, new edn (Berkeley: University of California Press, 1992).

Bücher, Karl, *Arbeit und Rhythmus* (Leipzig: Teubner, 1902).

Bull, Michael, 'Thinking about Sound, Proximity, and Distance in Western Experience: The Case of Odysseus' Walkman', in Veit Erlmann (ed.), *Hearing Cultures: Essays on Sound, Listening and Modernity* (Oxford: Berg, 2004), pp. 173–90.

Burckhardt, Sigur, 'The Poet as Fool and Priest', *ELH*, 23:4 (December 1956), pp. 279–98.

Bush, Ronald, 'Confucius Erased: The Missing Ideograms in *The Pisan Cantos*', in Zhaoming Qian (ed.), *Ezra Pound and China* (Ann Arbor: University of Michigan Press, 2003), pp. 163–92.

Butler, Judith, 'Endanger/Endangering: Schematic Racism and White Paranoia', in Robert Gooding-Williams (ed.), *Reading Rodney King/Reading Urban Uprising* (New York: Routledge, 1993), pp. 15–22.

——, *Giving an Account of Oneself* (New York: Fordham University Press, 2005).

——, *The Psychic Life of Power* (Palo Alto: Stanford University Press, 1997).

Castle, Pat, 'Where to Fish Sea-Trout', *Listener* (29 June 1932), pp. 949–50.

Cather, Willa, 'A Wagner Matinée', in *Early Novels and Stories* (New York: Library of America, 1987), pp. 102–10.

——, *My Antonia*, in *Early Novels and Stories* (New York: Library of America, 1987), pp. 707–938.

——, *O Pioneers!*, in *Early Novels and Stories* (New York: Library of America, 1987), pp. 133–290.

——, 'On *The Professor's House*', in *On Writing: Critical Studies on Writing as Art* (New York: Knopf, 1949), pp. 31–2.

——, 'The Novel Démeublé', in *Not Under Forty* (Lincoln: University of Nebraska, 1988), pp. 43–51.

——, *The Professor's House*, in *Later Novels* (New York: Library of America, 1990), pp. 99–272.

——, *The Selected Letters of Willa Cather*, ed. Andrew Jewell and Janis Stout (New York: Alfred A. Knopf, 2013).

——, *The Song of the Lark*, in *Early Novels and Stories* (New York: Library of America, 1987), pp. 291–606.

——, 'Three American Singers', *McClure's Magazine*, 42 (December 1913), pp. 33–48.

——, 'Two Friends', *Woman's Home Companion* (July 1932), pp. 673–90; repr. in *Stories Poems and Other Writings* (New York: Library of America, 1992), pp. 673–90.

——, *World and the Parish: Willa Cather's Articles and Reviews, 1893–1902*, ed. William M. Curtin, 2 vols (Lincoln: University of Nebraska Press, 1970).

Cavarero, Adriano, *For More Than One Voice: Toward a Philosophy of Vocal Expression*, trans. Paul A. Kottman (Stanford: Stanford University Press, 2005).

Cendrars, Blaise, *Complete Poems*, trans. Ron Padgett (Berkeley: University of California Press, 1992).

——, *Moravagine* (New York: New York Review Books, 2004).

——, *Selected Writings* (New York: New Directions, 1966).

——, *The Astonished Man*, trans. Nina Rootes (London and Chester Springs: Peter Owen, 1970).

Chatman, Seymour Benjamin, 'Characters and Narrators: Filter, Center, Slant, and Interest Focus', *Poetics Today*, 7:2 (1986), pp. 189–204.

Chion, Michel, 'The Silence of the Loudspeakers, or Why With Dolby Sound It is the Film That Listens to Us', trans. John Howe, in *Soundscape: The School of Sound Lectures, 1998–2001*, ed. Larry Sider, Jerry Sider, Diane Freeman (London: Wallflower Press, 2003), pp. 150–4.

Clegg, R. I., 'Slot Machinery', *American Machinist*, 14 (September 1890), pp. 869–70.

Cohen, Debra Rae, 'Intermediality and the Problem of the *Listener*', *Modernism/modernity*, 19:3 (2012), pp. 569–92.

Colvin, Sidney, Preface to *Selections from the Writings of Walter Savage Landor* (1882), ed. Sidney Colvin (London: Macmillan and Co., 1920), pp. v–xxx.

Connor, Steven, *Beckett, Modernism and the Material Imagination* (Cambridge: Cambridge University Press, 2014).

—, *Dumbstruck: A Cultural History of Ventriloquism* (Oxford: Oxford University Press, 2012).

—, 'The Modern Auditory I', in Roy Porter (ed.), *Rewriting the Self: Histories From the Renaissance to the Present* (London: Routledge, 1996), pp. 203–23.

Cook, Nicholas, *Music: A Very Short Introduction* (Oxford: Oxford University Press, 1998).

Copenhafer, David, 'Invisible Man (Ellison)', in Sylvia Mieszkowski, Joy Smith, Marijike de Valck (eds), *Sonic Interventions* (Amsterdam: Rodopi B.V., 2007), pp. 171–92.

Corbin, Alain, *Village Bells: Sound and Meaning in the Nineteenth-Century French Countryside*, trans. Martin Thom (New York: Columbia University Press, 1998).

Coustillas, Pierre, '"A Voice that Spoke Straight and Shapely Words": Gissing in the Works and Papers of Virginia Woolf', *The Gissing Newsletter* 13:3 (July 1987), pp. 1–29.

Coustillas, Pierre and Colin Partridge (eds), *George Gissing: The Critical Heritage* (London: Routledge and Kegan Paul, 1972).

Coustillas, Pierre and Patrick Bridgewater (eds), *George Gissing at Work, George Gissing at Work: A Study of His Notebooks, Extracts from My Reading* (Greensboro: ELT Press, 1988).

Cox, Christoph and Daniel Warner (eds), *Audio Culture: Readings in Modern Music* (New York: Continuum, 2004).

Croffut, W.A., *Current Literature*, 3 (September 1889), p. 223.

Cuddy-Keane, Melba, 'Modernist Soundscapes and the Intelligent Ear: An Approach to Narrative through Auditory Perception', in James Phelan and Peter Rabinowitz (eds), *A Companion to Narrative Theory* (Oxford: Blackwell, 2005), pp. 382–98.

—, 'Virginia Woolf, Sound Technologies, and the New Aurality', in Pamela Caughie (ed.), *Virginia Woolf in the Age of Mechanical Reproduction* (London: Routledge, 1999), pp. 69–96.

—, *Virginia Woolf, the Intellectual, and the Public Sphere* (Cambridge: Cambridge University Press, 2003).

Culler, Jonathan, *Theory of the Lyric* (Cambridge, MA: Harvard University Press, 2015).

Cummings, Brian (ed.), *The Book of Common Prayer: The Texts of 1549, 1559, and 1662* (Oxford: Oxford University Press, 2011).

Cummings, E. E., *Complete Poems: 1904–1962*, ed. George James Firmage, rev. edn (New York: Liveright, 1994).

Curtin, Adrian, 'Hearing Joyce Speak: the Phonograph Recordings of "Aeolus" and "Anna Livia Plurabelle" as Audiotexts', *James Joyce Quarterly*, 46:2 (Winter 2009), pp. 269–84.

Dames, Nicholas, *The Physiology of the Novel: Reading, Neural Science, and the Form of Victorian Fiction* (Oxford: Oxford University Press, 2007).

Danius, Sara, *The Senses of Modernism: Technology, Perception, and Aesthetics* (Ithaca, NY: Cornell University Press, 2002).

Delamater, Jerome, *Dance in the Hollywood Musical* (Ann Arbor: UMI Research Press, 1981).

Deleuze, Gilles, *Foucault*, trans. S. Hand (Minneapolis: University of Minnesota Press, 1988).

Derrida, Jacques, *Of Grammatology* (1967), trans. Gayatri Spivak (Baltimore: The Johns Hopkins University Press, 1974).

—, *Speech and Phenomena* (1967), trans. David B. Allison (Evanston: Northwestern University Press, 1973).

—, 'Ulysses Gramophone: *Hear say yes in Joyce*', in Bernard Benstock (ed.), *James Joyce: The Augmented Ninth* (New York: Syracuse University Press, 1988), pp. 27–75.

Dinerstein, Joel, *Swinging the Machine: Modernity, Technology, and African American Culture Between the World Wars* (Amherst: University of Massachusetts Press, 2003).

Dizikes, John, *Opera in America: A Cultural History* (New Haven: Yale University Press, 1993).

Dobrée, Bonamy, *Modern Prose Style*, 2nd edn (Oxford: Oxford University Press, 1964).

Dolan, Emily, *The Orchestral Revolution: Haydn and the Technologies of Timbre* (New York: Cambridge University Press, 2013).

Dolar, Mladen, *A Voice and Nothing More* (Cambridge, MA: MIT Press, 2006).

Donoghue, Denis, 'The Vigour of Its Blood: Yeats's "Words for Music Perhaps"', *Kenyon Review*, 21:3 (Summer 1959), pp. 376–87.

Draper, Paul, *On Tap Dancing*, ed. Fran Avallone (New York: Marcel Dekker, 1978).

Duff, J. Wight, and Arnold M. Duff (trans.), *Minor Latin Poets, Volume II*, Loeb Classical Library 434 (Cambridge, MA: Harvard University Press, 1935).

Duncan, Robert, 'Four Pictures of the Real Universe', in *The Collected Later Poems and Plays*, ed. Peter Quartermain (Berkeley: University of California Press, 2014), pp. 34–5.

Dworkin, Craig, and Marjorie Perloff (eds), *The Sound of Poetry/The Poetry of Sound* (Chicago: Chicago University Press, 2009).

Eliot, T. S., *Collected Poems, 1909–1962* (London: Faber and Faber, 1974).

—, *Complete Poems and Plays* (London: Faber and Faber, 1969).

—, *Introducing James Joyce: A Selection of Joyce's Prose* (London: Faber and Faber, 1942).

—, *Selected Prose* (London: Faber and Faber, 1975).

—, 'The Approach to James Joyce', *The Listener* (14 October 1943), pp. 446–7.

—, *The Complete Poems and Plays* (London: Faber and Faber, 1969).

—, *The Letters of T. S. Eliot*, ed. Valerie Eliot and John Haffenden, 5 vols (London: Faber and Faber, 2014).

Ellison, Ralph, *Invisible Man* (1947) (New York: Vintage Books, 1980).

Ellmann, Richard, *James Joyce* (Oxford: Oxford University Press, 1982).

Epstein, Joseph, *Fred Astaire* (New Haven: Yale University Press, 2008).

Esty, Jed, *A Shrinking Island: Modernism and National Culture in England* (Princeton: Princeton University Press, 2004).

Eustis, Morton, 'Fred Astaire: The Actor-Dancer Attacks His Part', *Theatre Arts Monthly*, 21 (May 1937), pp. 371–86.

Fanon, Frantz, *Black Skin, White Masks* (1952), trans. Charles Lam Markmann (New York: Grove Press, 1967).

Farquhar, George, *Sir Harry Wildair: Being the Sequel of the Trip to the Jubilee* (London: Printed for James Knapton, 1701).

Fenollosa, Ernest, *The Chinese Written Character as a Medium for Poetry: A Critical Edition*, ed. Lucas Klein, Haun Saussy and Jonathan Stalling (New York: Fordham University Press, 2008).

Fitts, Dudley, 'Prelude to Conclusion', repr. in Betsy Erkkila (ed.), *Ezra Pound: The Contemporary Reviews* (Cambridge: Cambridge University Press, 2011), pp. 355–6.

Flint, F. S., 'Presentation: Notes on the Art of Writing; on the Artfulness of Some Writers; and on the Artlessness of Others', *Chapbook*, 2:9 (March 1920), pp. 17–24.

Frank, Rusty E., *Tap! The Greatest Tap Dance Stars and Their Stories, 1900–1955* (New York: Morrow, 1990).

Frattarola, Angela, 'Developing an Ear for the Modernist Novel: Virginia Woolf, Dorothy Richardson and James Joyce', *Journal for Modern Literature*, 33:1 (2009), pp. 132–53.

Freud, Sigmund, *The Complete Letters of Sigmund Freud to Wilhelm Fliess, 1887–1904*, ed. and trans. Jeffrey Moussaieff Masson (Cambridge, MA: The Belknap Press of Harvard University Press, 1986).

——, 'Three Essays on Sexuality', in Sigmund Freud, *The Standard Edition of the Complete Psychological Works of Sigmund Freud*, vol. 7 (London: Hogarth Press, 1953).

Friedman, Norman, 'Point of View in Fiction: The Development of a Critical Concept', *PMLA* 70: 5 (December 1955), pp. 1160–84.

Friedwald, Will, *Stardust Melodies: The Biography of Twelve of America's Most Popular Songs* (New York: Pantheon Books, 2002).

Gallagher, Catherine, 'The Rise of Fictionality', in Franco Moretti (ed.), *The Novel. Vol. 1: History, Geography and Culture* (Princeton: Princeton University Press, 2006), pp. 336–63.

Gates, Jr, Henry Louis, *The Signifying Monkey: A Theory of African American Literary Criticism* (New York: Oxford University Press, 1988).

Genette, Gérard, *Figures III* (Paris: Seuil, 1972).

——, *Narrative Discourse Revisited*, trans. Jane E. Lewin (Ithaca, NY: Cornell University Press, 1990).

——, *Narrative Discourse: An Essay in Method* (1972), trans. J. E. Lewin (Ithaca, NY: Cornell University Press, 1972).

Gigante, Denise, *Taste: A Literary History* (New Haven: Yale University Press, 2005).

Gilbert, Sandra M., *Acts of Attention: The Poems of D. H. Lawrence* (Carbondale: Southern Illinois University Press, 1990).

Gilbert, Stuart, 'Homage to James Joyce', *transition*, 21 (1932), pp. 247–9.

Gissing, George, *Charles Dickens: A Critical Study* (1898) (Stroud: Nonsuch, 2007).

——, *New Grub Street* (1891) (New York: The Modern Library, 2002).

——, 'The Place of Realism in Fiction', *The Humanitarian* (May 1895); reprinted in *George Gissing on Fiction*, ed. Jacob and Cynthia Korg (London: Enitharmon Press, 1978), pp. 84–6.

——, 'The Pronunciation Of Greek', *The Times* (Wednesday, 25 February 1891), p. 13.

Gitelman, Lisa, *Always Already New: Media, History, and the Data of Culture* (Cambridge, MA: MIT Press, 2006).

Golston, Michael, *Rhythm and Race in Modernist Poetry and Science* (New York: Columbia University Press, 2007).

Gosse, Edmund, *Questions at Issue* (London: William Heinemann, 1893).

Gray, Nancy, 'Un-Defining the Self in the Stories of Katherine Mansfield', in Janet Wilson, Gerri Kimber and Susan Reid (eds) *Katherine Mansfield and Literary Modernism* (London: Continuum, 2011), pp. 78–88.

Greenberg, Clement, 'Avant-Garde and Kitsch', in Francis Frascina (ed.), *Pollock and After: The Critical Debate*, 2nd edn (London: Routledge, 2000), pp. 48–59.

Grusin, David and Richard Bolter, *Remediation: Understanding New Media* (Cambridge, MA: MIT Press, 1999).

Guido, Laurent, '"The Supremacy of the Mathematical Poem": Jean Epstein's Conceptions of Rhythm', in Sarah Keller and Jason N. Paul (eds), *Jean Epstein: Critical Essays and New Translations* (Amsterdam: Amsterdam University Press, 2012), pp. 143–60.

Gunning, Tom, 'The Cinema of Attractions: Early Film, Its Spectator and the Avant-Garde', *Wide Angle*, 8 (1986), pp. 63–70.

Hacking, Ian, *The Taming of Chance* (Cambridge: Cambridge University Press, 1990).

Hajkowski, Thomas, *The BBC and National Identity in Britain, 1922–53* (Manchester: Manchester University Press, 2010).

Hall, Jason David, 'Materializing Meter: Physiology, Psychology, Prosody', *Victorian Poetry*, 49:2 (Summer 2011), pp. 179–97.

——, 'Mechanized Metrics: From Verse Science to Laboratory Prosody, 1880–1918', *Configurations*, 17:3 (Fall 2009), pp. 285–308.

Halliday, Sam, *Sonic Modernity: Representing Sound in Literature, Culture and the Arts* (Edinburgh: Edinburgh University Press, 2013).

Hardy, Thomas, *Tess of the d'Urbervilles* (1892) (Oxford: Oxford University Press, 1998).

Haslam, Sara, '"The moaning of the world" and the "words that bring me peace": Modernism and the First World War', in Adam Piette and Mark Rawlinson (eds), *The Edinburgh Companion to British and American War Literature* (Edinburgh: Edinburgh University Press, 2012), pp. 47–57.

Hazen, Margaret Hindle and Robert M. Hazen, *The Music Men: An Illustrated History of Brass Bands in America, 1800–1920* (Washington: Smithsonian Institution Press, 1987).

Hegel, G. W. F., *Aesthetics: Lectures on Fine Art*, trans. T. M. Knox, 2 vols (Oxford: Clarendon Press, 1975).

Heidegger, Martin. *Being and Time*, trans. Joan Stambaugh (Albany: State University Press of New York, 1996).

——, *Parmenides* (1942–3), trans. Andre Schuwer and Richard Rojcewicz (Bloomington: Indiana University Press, 1992).

Helsinger, Elizabeth K., *Poetry and the Thought of Song in Nineteenth-Century Britain* (Charlottesville: University of Virginia Press, 2015).

Hemingway, Ernest, interview by George Plimpton in *The Paris Review*, 18 (1958), available at: <http://www.theparisreview.org> (last accessed 23 July 2016).

——, *The Sun Also Rises* (1926) (New York: Scribner, 2006).

Hill, Constance Valis, *Tap Dancing America: A Cultural History* (New York: Oxford University Press, 2010).

Holtby, Winifred, *South Riding* (1936) (London: BBC Books, 2011).

——, 'The Ruin of Mr. Hilary', Undated ms, Winifred Holtby Collection, Hull History Centre, WH/1/1.3/08/01a; published as 'A Littlepuddle Saga: The Ruin of Mr. Hilary or the Sad Tale of a Village Running Commentary', *Radio Times* (2 August 1929), p. 219.

Holtby, Winifred and Stephen Tallents, 'Two Resounding Arguments in the Great Controversy over the B.B.C', *Nash's Magazine* (November 1935), pp. 13–14.

Homberger, Eric (ed.), *Ezra Pound: The Critical Heritage* (London: Routledge & Kegan Paul, 1972).

Homer, *The Iliad*, trans. A. T. Murphy, rev. William F. Wyatt, 2 vols, Loeb Classical Library (Cambridge, MA: Harvard University Press, 1999).

Howkins, Alun, 'Death and Rebirth? English Rural Society, 1920–1940', in Paul Brassley, Jeremy Burchardt and Lynne Thompson (eds), *The English Countryside between the Wars: Regeneration or Decline?* (Woodbridge, Sussex: Boydell, 2006), pp. 10–25.

——, 'The Discovery of Rural England', in Robert Colls and Philip Dodd (eds), *Englishness: Politics and Culture 1880–1920* (London: Croon Helm, 1986), pp. 62–88.

——, *The Death of Rural England: A Social History of the Countryside Since 1900* (London: Routledge, 2003).

——, '"The Land of Lost Content": Ruralism, Englishness and Historical Change in the Countryside, 1890–1990', in Jeremy Burchardt and Philip Conford (eds), *The Contested Countryside: Rural Politics and Land Controversy in Modern Britain* (London: I. B. Tauris, 2008), pp. 187–201.

Hughes, Langston, *The Collected Poems of Langston Hughes*, ed. Arnold Rampersand and David Roessel (New York: Vintage Classics, 1995).

Huizinga, Johan, *Homo Ludens: A Study of the Play-element in Culture* (London: Routledge & Kegan Paul, 1949).

Icart, Roger, *Abel Gance, ou, Le Prométhée foudroyé* (Lausanne: l'Age d'homme, 1983).

Irwin, John, *Doubling and Incest / Repetition and Revenge: A Speculative Reading of Faulkner* (1975) (Baltimore: Johns Hopkins University Press, 1996).

Iser, Wolfgang, *The Act of Reading: A Theory of Aesthetic Response* (Baltimore: The Johns Hopkins University Press, 1978).

Jackson, Shannon, 'White Noises: On Performing White, On Writing Performance', *The Drama Review*, 42:1 (Spring 1998), pp. 49–65.

Jaffe, Aaron, *Modernism and the Culture of Celebrity* (Cambridge: Cambridge University Press, 2005).

Jahn, Manfred, 'Focalisation', in David Herman, Manfred Jahn and Marie-Laure Ryan (eds), *The Routledge Encyclopaedia of Narrative Theory* (London: Routledge, 2005), pp. 173–7.

——, 'Windows of Focalisation: Deconstruction and Reconstructing a Narratological Concept', *Style* 30:2 (1996), pp. 241–67.

James, Henry, *The Ambassadors. The Novels and Tales of Henry James*, vols 21–2 (New York: Scribners, 1909).

——, 'The House of Fiction' (1881), in *Theory of the Novel*, Philip Stevick (ed.) (New York: Free Press, 1967), pp. 58–62.

James, William, 'The Feeling of Effort' (1880), *Essays in Psychology* (Cambridge, MA: Harvard University Press), pp. 83–124.

Jameson, Fredric, *The Political Unconscious: Narrative as a Socially Symbolic Act* (1981) (London: Routledge, 2010).

Jarvis, Simon, 'Musical Thinking: Hegel and the Phenomenology of Prosody', *Paragraph*, 28:2 (July 2005), pp. 57–71.

John, Richard, *Network Nation: Inventing American Telecommunications* (Cambridge, MA: Harvard University Press, 2010).

Jolas, Eugene, 'Homage to James Joyce', *transition* 21 (1932), pp. 246–82.

Jost, François, *L'Oeil-Caméra: Entre Film Et Roman* (Lyon: Presses Universitaires de Lyon, 1987).

Joyce, James, *Finnegans Wake* (London: Faber and Faber, 1971).

——, *Finnegans Wake*, ed. Finn Fordham (Oxford: Oxford University Press, 2012).

——, *James Joyce's Letters to Sylvia Beach: 1921–1940*, ed. Melissa Banta and Oscar A. Silverman (Bloomington: Indiana University Press, 1987).

——, *Ulysses* (New York: Vintage, 1961).

——, *Ulysses*, ed. Hans Walter Gabler (London: The Bodley Head, 1986).

——, *Ulysses*, ed. Jeri Johnson (New York: Oxford University Press, 2008).

Kafka, Franz, *Metamorphosis and Other Stories*, trans. Michael Hofmann (London: Penguin, 2007).

——, *Metamorphosis and Other Stories*, trans. Willa and Edwin Muir (London: Vintage, 2012).

——, *The Basic Kafka*, trans. Willa and Edwin Muir (New York and London: Pocket Books, 1979).

Kahn, Douglas, 'Introduction: Histories of Sound Once Removed', in Douglas Kahn and Gregory Whitehead (eds), *Wireless Imagination: Sound, Radio and the Avant-Garde* (Cambridge, MA: MIT Press, 1992), pp. 1–29.

——, *Noise, Water, Meat: A History of Sound in the Arts* (Cambridge, MA: MIT Press, 1999).

Kaplan, Sydney Janet, *Katherine Mansfield and the Origins of Modernist Fiction* (Ithaca, NY: Cornell University Press, 1991).

Keats, John, *The Complete Poems*, 2nd edn, ed. John Barnard (London: Penguin, 1978).

Kenner, Hugh, *The Pound Era* (Berkeley: University of California Press, 1971).

King, Norman, *Abel Gance* (London: BFI Publishing, 1984).

Kittler, Friedrich A., *Discourse Networks 1800/1900*, trans. Michael Meteer, with Chris Cullens (Stanford: Stanford University Press, 1990).

——, *Gramophone, Film, Typewriter*, trans. Geoffrey Winthrop-Young and Michael Wutz (Stanford: Stanford University Press, 1999).

Klages, Ludwig, *Vom Wesen des Rhythmus* (Kampen auf Sylt: Kampmann, 1934).

Kleist, Heinrich von, *The Marquise of O – and Other Stories*, trans. David Luke and Nigel Reeves (London: Penguin, 1978).

Knowles, Marc, *Tap Roots: The Early History of Tap Dancing* (Jefferson, NC: McFarland and Co., 2002).

Knowles, Sebastian D. G., 'Death by Gramophone', *Journal of Modern Literature*, 27:1–2 (Autumn 2003), pp. 1–13.

Kobler, J. F., *Katherine Mansfield: A Study of the Short Fiction*, Twayne Studies in Short Fiction (Boston: Twayne Publishers, 1990).

Kreitner, Kenneth, *Discoursing Sweet Music: Town Bands and Community Life in Turn of the Century Pennsylvania* (Urbana: University of Illinois Press, 1990).

Lacan, Jacques, *The Four Fundamental Concepts of Psychoanalysis: Book XI*, ed. Jacques-Alain Milner, trans. Alan Sheridan (New York: Norton, 1998).

Langland, William, *The Vision of Piers Plowman*, ed. A. V. C. Schmidt, 2nd edn (London: J. M. Dent, 1995).

Lanz, Henry, *The Physical Basis of Rime* (1931); reprinted (New York: Greenwood, 1968).

Lawrence, D. H., *Apocalypse and the Writings on Revelation*, ed. Mara Kalnins (Cambridge: Cambridge University Press, 2001).

——, *Studies in Classic American Literature*, ed. Ezra Greenspan, Lindeth Vasey and John Worthen (Cambridge: Cambridge University Press, 2003).

——, *Study of Thomas Hardy and Other Essays*, ed. Bruce Steele (Cambridge: Cambridge University Press, 1985).

——, *The Letters of D. H. Lawrence*, vol. 2. *June 1913–October 1916*, ed. George J. Zytaruk and James T. Boulton (Cambridge: Cambridge University Press, 1981).

——, *The Poems*, ed. Christopher Pollnitz, 2 vols (Cambridge: Cambridge University Press, 2013).

Leavis, Q. D., 'Regional Novels', *Scrutiny*, 4:4 (March 1936), p. 440.

Lee, Hermione, *Willa Cather: A Life Saved Up* (London: Virago, 1989).

Lefebvre, Henri, *Critique of Everyday Life*, vol. 3, trans. Gregory Elliott (London: Verso, 2005).

——, *Rhythmanalysis: Space, Time and Everyday Life* (1992), trans. Stuart Elden and Gerald Moore (New York: Continuum, 2004).

Levin, Harry, *James Joyce: A Critical Introduction* (London: Faber and Faber, 1960).

Levitin, Daniel, *This is Your Brain on Music* (New York: Dutton, 2006).

Levy, Michelle, 'Virginia Woolf's Shorter Fictional Explorations of the External World: "closely united . . . immensely divided"', in Kathryn N. Benzel and Ruth Hoberman (eds), *Trespassing Boundaries: Virginia Woolf's Short Fiction* (Palgrave Macmillan, 2004), pp. 139–56.

Levy, Pierre, *Becoming Virtual: Reality in the Digital Age*, trans. Robert Bononno (New York: Plenum Trade, 1998).

Lewes, G. H., 'Dickens in Relation to Criticism', *Fortnightly Review* 11:62 (February 1872), pp. 141–54.

Liu, Haoming, '"Pharmaka and Volgar" Eloquio: Speech and Ideogrammic Writing in Ezra Pound's Canto xcviii', *Asia Major*, 22:2 (2009), pp. 179–214.

Lloyd James, A., 'Extremes of Pronunciation', *Listener* (22 June 1932), p. 901.

——, 'Is There a Standard Pronunciation?', *Listener* (15 June 1932), p. 867.

——, 'Speech Today and Tomorrow', *Listener* (6 July 1932), pp. 15–16.

——, *The Broadcast Word* (London: Kegan Paul & Trench Trubner, 1935).

Loukopoulou, Eleni, 'Joyce's Progress Through London: Conquering the English Publishing Market', *James Joyce Quarterly*, 48:4 (Summer 2011), pp. 683–710.

——, 'Upon Hearing James Joyce: The *Anna Livia Plurabelle* Gramophone Disc (1929)', in Sarah Posman, et al. (ed.), *The Aesthetics of Matter* (Berlin: De Gruyter, 2013), pp. 118–27.

Lovecraft, H. P., *The Call of Cthulhu and Other Weird Tales* (London: Vintage, 2011).

Loy, Mina, *The Lost Lunar Baedeker*, ed. Roger L. Conover (New York: Farrar, Straus and Giroux, 1996).

Lubbock, Percy, *The Craft of Fiction* (London: Cape, 1921).

'Ludwig Koch and the Music of Nature', available at: <http://www.bbc.co.uk/archive/archive_pioneers/6505.shtml> (last accessed 21 May 2016).

Lupton, Christina and Tilman Reitz, '*New Grub Street*'s Self-Consciousness', in Martin Ryle and Jenny Bourne Taylor (eds), *George Gissing: Voices of the Unclassed* (Aldershot: Ashgate, 2005), pp. 133–44.

McCracken, Scott, 'George Gissing Urban Modernity and Modernism', in *Masculinities, Modernist Fiction and the Urban Publish Sphere* (Manchester: Manchester University Press, 2007), pp. 13–20.

McDonald, Peter, *British Literary Culture and Publishing Practice, 1880–1914* (Cambridge: Cambridge University Press, 1997).

Mandelstam, Osip, *Modernist Archaist: Selected Poems*, ed. Kevin Platt, trans. Charles Bernstein, et al. (Santa Monica: Whale and Star, 2008).

——, *The Selected Poems of Osip Mandelstam*, trans. Clarence Brown and W. S. Merwin (New York: New York Review Books, 2004).

Manning, Frederic, 'Poetry in Prose', *The Chapbook*, no. 22 (1921), pp. 10–15.

Mansfield, Katherine, 'Miss Brill', in *The Collected Works of Katherine Mansfield*, ed. Gerri Kimber and Vincent O'Sullivan, 3 vols (Edinburgh: Edinburgh University Press, 2012), vol. 2, pp. 250–5.

——, *The Collected Letters of Katherine Mansfield*, ed. Vincent O'Sullivan and Margaret Scott, 5 vols (Oxford: Clarendon Press, 1984–2008).

Marcus, Laura, *Dreams of Modernity: Psychoanalysis, Literature, Cinema* (Oxford: Oxford University Press, 2014).

Marcus, Phillip L., 'Lawrence, Yeats, and "the Resurrection of the Body"', in Peter Balbert and Phillip L. Marcus (eds), *D. H. Lawrence: A Centenary Celebration* (Ithaca, NY: Cornell University Press, 1985), pp. 210–36.

Marinetti, F. T. and Pino Masnata, 'La Radia' (1933), trans. Stephen Sartorelli, in Douglas Kahn and Gregory Whitehead (eds), *Wireless Imagination* (Cambridge, MA: MIT Press, 1992), pp. 265–8.

Martin, William, *Joyce and the Science of Rhythm* (New York: Palgrave Macmillan, 2012).

Matheson, Hilda, *Broadcasting* (London: Thornton Butterworth, 1933).

Matz, Aaron, *Satire in an Age of Realism* (Cambridge: Cambridge University Press, 2010).

——, 'Some Versions of Vitriol (the Novel circa 1890)', *Novel: A Forum on Fiction* 42:1 (Spring 2009), pp. 23–39.

Meynell, Alice, *The Rhythm of Life* (London: J. Lane, 1905).

Michaels, Walter Benn, 'The Gold Standard and the Logic of Naturalism', *Representations* 9 (1985), pp. 105–32.

Milton, John, *The Complete Poetry and Essential Prose of John Milton*, ed. William Kerrigan, John Rumrich and Stephen M. Fallon (New York: Modern Library, 2007).

Moretti, Franco, *The Way of the World: The Bildungsroman in European Culture*, trans. Albert Sbragia (London: Verso, 2000).

'Mr. Love, the Polyphonist', *Illustrated London News* (25 March 1843), pp. 214–15.

Mueller, John, *Astaire Dancing: The Musical Films* (London: Hamish Hamilton, 1986).

Murray, Albert, *Stomping the Blues* (New York: Da Capo, 1976).

Murry, John Middleton, *Between Two Worlds: An Autobiography* (London: Jonathan Cape, 1935).

——, *Defending Romanticism: Selected Criticism of John Middleton Murry*, ed. Malcolm Woodfield (Bristol: Bristol Press, 1989).

Nancy, Jean-Luc, *Listening*, trans. Charlotte Mendel (New York: Fordham University Press, 2007).

——, *The Inoperative Community* (1986), trans. Peter Connor (Minneapolis: The University of Minnesota Press, 1991).

Nash, John, *James Joyce and the Act of Reception* (Cambridge: Cambridge University Press, 2006).

Nelles, William, *Frameworks: Narrative Levels and Embedded Narrative* (New York: Lang, 1997).

Nicholas, Siân, *The Echo of War: Home Front Propaganda and the Wartime BBC, 1939–45* (Manchester: Manchester University Press, 1996).

Nicholls, Peter, 'Lost Object(s): Ezra Pound and the Idea of Italy', in Richard Taylor and Claus Melchior (eds), *Ezra Pound and Europe* (Amsterdam: Rodopi, 1993), pp. 165–76.

Norris, Frank, *A Novelist in the Making: A Collection of Student Themes and the Novels* Blix *and* Vandover and the Brute, ed. James D. Hart (Cambridge, MA: Harvard University Press, 1970).

——, *The Pit* (New York: Doubleday, 1903).

North, Michael, *The Dialectic of Modernism: Race, Language, and Twentieth-Century Literature* (New York: Oxford University Press, 1998).

Novak, David and Matt Sakakeeny (eds), *Keywords in Sound* (Durham, NC: Duke University Press, 2015).

Nowell Smith, David, *Sounding/Silence: Martin Heidegger at the Limits of Poetics* (New York: Fordham University Press, 2013).

Nysembaum, Sylvie, 'Une pensée qui va et vient', quoted in J-B. Pontalis, *Ce temps qui ne passe pas, suivi de Le Compartiment de Chemin de fer* (Paris: Gallimard, 1997).

O'Brien, Sharon, *Willa Cather: The Emerging Voice* (Cambridge, MA: Harvard University Press, 1997).

O'Connor, Margaret Anne (ed.), *Willa Cather: The Contemporary Reviews* (Cambridge: Cambridge University Press, 2001).

Ogden, C. K., 'James Joyce's Anna Livia Plurabelle. In Basic English', *transition* 21 (1932), pp. 259–62.

—, 'Orthological Institute, International Orthophonic Archives', *Psyche* 10 (1929) p. 111.

—, 'The Orthological Institute', *Psyche* 1 (July 1930), pp. 95–7.

Otto, Peter, *Multiplying Worlds: Romanticism, Modernity, and the Emergence of Virtual Reality* (Oxford: Oxford University Press, 2011).

Outka, Elizabeth, *Consuming Traditions: Modernity, Modernism, and the Commodified Authentic* (New York: Oxford University Press, 2009).

Pater, Walter, *Studies in the History of the Renaissance* (Oxford: Oxford University Press, 2010).

—, *The Renaissance: Studies in Art and Poetry*, ed. Donald L. Hill (Berkeley: University of California Press, 1980).

Perloff, Marjorie, *Rhyme and Meaning in the Poetry of Yeats* (The Hague: Mouton, 1970).

Phelan, James, 'Why Narrators Can Be Focalisers – and Why It Matters', in Willie van Peer and Seymour Chatman (eds), *New Perspectives on Narrative Perspective* (Albany: SUNY Press, 2001), pp. 51–64.

Picker, John M., *Victorian Soundscapes* (Oxford: Oxford University Press, 2003).

Plotz, John, '"On the Spot": Willa Cather's Remarkable Quotation Marks', *Willa Cather Newsletter and Review*, 56:2 (Spring 2013), pp. 20–1.

—, 'Overtones and Empty Rooms: Willer Cather's Semi-Detached Modernism', *Novel* (forthcoming, 2017).

—, *Semi-Detached: The Aesthetic of Partial Absorption* (forthcoming, Princeton: Princeton University Press, 2017).

Poole, Adrian, *Gissing in Context* (London: The MacMillan Press Ltd, 1975).

Pope, Alexander, *Minor Poems*, ed. Norman Ault and John Butt, The Twickenham Edition of the Poems of Alexander Pope, vol. 6 (London: Methuen, 1954).

—, *The Correspondence of Alexander Pope*, ed. George Sherburn, 5 vols (Oxford: Clarendon Press, 1956).

Postgate, R. W., 'A Listener's Commentary', *Listener* (12 February 1930), p. 284.

—, *What to Do with the BBC*, Day to Day Pamphlets No. 28 (London: Hogarth Press, 1935).

Pouillon, Jean, *Temps et Roman* (Paris: Galimard, 1946).

Pound, Ezra, *ABC of Reading* (London: Faber and Faber, 1979).

—, 'Debabelization and Ogden', *The New English Weekly* (28 February 1935), p. 411.

—, *Ezra Pound's Chinese Friends: Stories in Letters*, ed. and intro. Zhaoming Qian (Oxford: Oxford University Press, 2008).

—, *Ezra Pound and Music: The Complete Criticism*, ed. R. Murray Schafer (New York: New Directions, 1977).

—, *Gaudier-Brzeska: A Memoir* (New York: New Directions, 1970).

—, *Machine Art and Other Writings: The Lost Thought of the Italian Years*, ed. Maria Louisa Adrizzone (Durham, NC: Duke University Press, 1996).

—, *Selected Letters 1907–1941* (New York: New Directions, 1971).

—, *The Cantos* (New York: New Directions, 1996).

Price, Leah, *The Anthology and the Rise of the Novel From Richardson to George Eliot* (Cambridge: Cambridge University Press, 2000).

Prins, Yopie, 'Metrical Translation: Nineteenth-Century Homers and the Hexameter Mania', in Sandra Bermann and Michael Wood (eds), *Nation, Language, and the Ethics of Translation* (Princeton: Princeton University Press, 2005), pp. 229–56.

Pryor, Sean, '"Particularly Dangerous Feats": The Difficult Reader of the Difficult Late Cantos', *Paideuma* 36 (2007–9), pp. 27–45.

Puffer, Ethel D., *The Psychology of Beauty* (1905) (Whitefish: Kessinger Publishing, 2004).

Rainey, Lawrence, Christine Poggi and Laura Wittman (eds), *Futurism: An Anthology* (New Haven: Yale University Press, 2009).

Rancière, Jacques, *The Future of the Image*, trans. Gregory Elliott (London: Verso, 2007).

—, *The Politics of Aesthetics* (2000), trans. Gabriel Rockhill (New York: Bloomsbury, 2004).

Rangan, Pooja, *Immediations* (Durham, NC: Duke University Press, forthcoming).

Read, Herbert, *English Prose Style*, new rev. edn (London: G. Bell and Sons, 1956).

Reed, Christopher (ed.), *A Roger Fry Reader* (Berkeley: University of Chicago Press, 1996).

Riley, Denise, 'The Voice Without A Mouth: Inner Speech', *qui parle*, 14:2 (Spring/Summer 2004), pp. 57–104.

Rilke, Rainer Maria, 'Die Sonette an Orpheus', Sonett 1, *Spiegel Online*, available at: <http://gutenberg.spiegel.de/buch/rainer-maria-rilke-sonette-5562/1> (last accessed 30 May 2016).

Roberts, Morley, *The Private Life of Henry Maitland: A Record Dictated by J. H.*, 2nd edn (London: Eveleigh Nash & Grayson Ltd, 1912).

Rose, Sonya O., *Which People's War? National Identity and Citizenship in Wartime Britain 1939–1945* (Oxford: Oxford University Press, 2003).

Ross, Stephen M., *Fiction's Inexhaustible Voice: Speech and Writing in Faulkner* (Athens, GA: University of Georgia Press, 1989).

Russell, Bertrand, *ABC of Relativity* (London: Routledge, 2005).

Ryan, Mary P., 'The American Parade: Representations of the Nineteenth-Century Social Order', in Lynn Hunt (ed.), *The New Cultural History* (Berkeley: University of California, 1989), pp. 131–53.

Ryle, Martin, '"To Show a Man of Letters": Gissing, Cultural Authority and Literary Modernism', in Martin Ryle and Jenny Bourne Taylor (eds), *George Gissing: Voices of the Unclassed* (Aldershot: Ashgate, 2005), pp. 119–32.

Saddlemyer, Ann, 'Poetry of Possession: Yeats and Crazy Jane', *Yeats: An Annual of Critical and Textual Studies*, 9 (1991), pp. 136–58.

Sagar, Keith M., *D. H. Lawrence: Poet* (London: Troubadour, 2008).

Saintsbury, George, *Essays in English Literature 1780–1860. Second Series* (London: J. M. Dent & Co., 1895).

Saler, Michael, *As If: Modern Enchantment and the Literary Prehistory of Virtual Reality* (New York: Oxford University Press, 2012).

Sandburg, Carl, *Smoke and Steel* (New York: Harcourt, Brace and Howe, 1920).

Scannell, Paddy, *Radio, Television, and Modern Life* (Oxford: Blackwell, 1996).

Schafer, Murray, *The Soundscape: Our Sonic Environment and the Tuning of the World* (New York: Knopf, 1977).

Schlickers, Sabine, 'Focalisation, Ocularisation and Auricularisation in Film and Literature', in Peter Hühn, Wolf Schmid and Jörg Schönert (eds), *Point of View, Perspective and Focalisation: Modeling Mediation in Narrative* (Berlin: Walter de Gruyter, 2009), pp. 243–58.

Schlickers, Sabine, *Verfilmtes Erzählen* (Frankfurt: Vevuert, 1997).

Schuchard, Ronald, *The Last Minstrels: Yeats and the Revival of the Bardic Arts* (Oxford: Oxford University Press, 2008).

Schwartz, Hillel, *Making Noise: From Babel to the Big Bang and Beyond* (Cambridge, MA: MIT Press, 2011).

Scientific American. 'Invention in 1889' (14 February 1891), p. 105.

'Should Dialect Survive?', *Listener* (6 May 1931), p. 758.

Sieburth, Richard, 'The Sound of Pound: A Listener's Guide', PEPC digital edition, published in conjunction with PennSound at: <http://writing.upenn.edu/pennsound/x/text/Sieburth-Richard_Pound.html> (last accessed 10 May 2016).

Simmel, Georg, *The Philosophy of Money*, trans. Tom Bottomore and David Frisby (London: Routledge & Kegan Paul, 1978).

Skrabanek, Petr, '*Finnegans Wake*: Night Joyce of a Thousand Tiers', in Augustine Martin (ed.), *James Joyce: The Artist and the Labyrinth* (London: Ryan, 1990), pp. 231–42.

Skrbic, Nena, *Wild Outbursts of Freedom: Reading Virginia Woolf's Short Fiction* (London: Praeger, 2004).

Slide, Anthony, *The Vaudevillians: A Dictionary of Vaudeville Performers* (New Rochelle, NY: Arlington House, 1981).

Smith, Mark M., 'Introduction', in Mark M. Smith (ed.), *Hearing History: A Reader* (Athens, GA: University of Georgia Press, 2004), pp. ix–xxii.

——, *The Smell of Battle, The Taste of Siege: A Sensory History of the Civil War* (Oxford: Oxford University Press, 2014).

Sousa, John Philip, 'Menace of Mechanical Music', *Appleton's Magazine* 8 (August 1906), pp. 278–84.

Spencer, Herbert, *First Principles*, 2nd edn (London: Williams and Norgate, 1867).

Stadler, Gustavus, 'Never Heard Such a Thing: Lynching and Phonographic Modernity', *Social Text* 102 (Spring 2010), pp. 87–105.

Stead, Christina, *A Web of Friendship. Selected Letters (1928–1973)* (Sydney: Angus & Robertson, 1992).

Stearns, Marshall and Jean, *Jazz Dance: The Story of American Vernacular Dance* (New York: Schirmer Books, 1979).

Stein, Gertrude, 'If I Told Him: A Completed Portrait Of Picasso' (1923) in Stein, *A Gertrude Stein Reader*, ed. Ulla E. Dydo (Evanston: Northwestern University Press, 1993, p. 464.

Steiner, Wendy, *The Colors of Rhetoric: Problems in the Relation between Modern Literature and Painting* (Berkeley: University of Chicago Press, 1982).

Stephenson, Ryan, 'Mr. Baker and Miss Yule: Mass Literacy and the Complexity of Reading and Writing in George Gissing's *New Grub Street*', *The Gissing Journal* 43:3 (July 2007), pp. 3–26.

Sterne, Jonathan, *MP3: The Meaning of a Format* (Durham, NC: Duke University Press, 2012).

——, *The Audible Past: Cultural Origins of Sound Reproduction* (Durham, NC: Duke University Press, 2003).

Stevens, Wallace, *Collected Poetry and Prose*, ed. Frank Kermode and Joan Richardson (New York: Library of America, 1997).

Stewart, Garrett, *Dear Reader: The Conscripted Audience in Nineteenth Century British Fiction* (Baltimore: The Johns Hopkins University Press, 1996).

——, *Reading Voices: Literature and the Phonotext* (Berkeley: The University of California Press, 1990).

Stoicheff, Peter, *The Hall of Mirrors: Drafts & Fragments and the End of Ezra Pound's Cantos* (Ann Arbor: University of Michigan Press, 1998).

Stopes, Marie, *Married Love* (London: Putnam, 1917).

Strauven, Wanda (ed.), *The Cinema of Attractions Reloaded* (Amsterdam: Amsterdam University Press, 2006).

Street, A. G., *A Crook in the Furrow* (London: Faber and Faber, 1940).

——, *Already Walks To-Morrow* (London: Faber and Faber, 1938).

——, *Country Days: A Series of Broadcast Talks* (London: Faber and Faber, 1933).

——, *Farmer's Glory* (London: Faber and Faber, 1932).

——, 'Haymaking', *Listener* (22 June 1932), pp. 912–13.

——, *Hedge-Trimmings* (London: Faber and Faber, 1933).

——, 'Machinery and the Farm-hand', 'Microphone Miscelllany', *Listener* (1 August 1934), p. 201.

——, 'Old Hands and New Ways', *Listener* (6 July 1932), p. 33.

——, *Strawberry Roan* (London: Faber and Faber, 1932).

——, 'The Art of Coversation', *Listener* (24 May 1933), pp. 831–2.

——, 'The Countryman's View', in Clough Williams-Ellis (ed.), *Britain and the Beast* (London: J. M. Dent, 1937), pp. 122–32,

——, *The Endless Furrow* (London, Faber and Faber, 1934).

——, *The Gentleman of the Party* (London: Faber and Faber, 1936).

——, *Thinking Aloud* (London: Faber and Faber, 1934).

——, *Wessex Wins* (London: Faber and Faber, 1941).

Street, Pamela, *My Father, A. G. Street* (1969) (London: Robert Hale, 1984).

Suarez, Juan. A., *Pop-Modernism: Noise and the Reinvention of the Everyday* (Urbana: University of Illinois Press, 2007).

Taft, Joshua, '*New Grub Street* and the Survival of Realism', *ELT* 54:3 (2011), pp. 362–81.

Terrell, Carroll F., *A Companion to the Cantos of Ezra Pound*, vol. 2 (Berkeley: University of California Press, 1984).

Thomas A. Edison Papers Digital Edition, ed. Paul Israel, et al., available at: <http://edison.rutgers.edu> (last accessed 21 March 2016).

Thompson, Emily, *The Soundscape of Modernity: Architectural Acoustics and the Culture of Listening in America, 1900–1933* (Cambridge, MA: MIT Press, 2002).

Thompson, Gordon E., 'Introduction: Lyrical Aesthetics in African American Poetry', in Gordon E. Thompson (ed.), *Black Music, Black Poetry: Blues and Jazz's Impact on African American Versification* (Farnham: Ashgate, 2014), pp. 1–16.

Thoreau, Henry David, *Walden and Other Writings* (New York: Barnes and Noble, 1993).

——, *Walden and Other Writings* (New York: The Modern Library, 2000).

Toomer, Jean, *Cane* (1923) (New York: Liveright, 2011).

Trotter, David, *Literature in the First Media Age: Britain Between the Wars* (Cambridge, MA: Harvard University Press, 2013).

Turner, Victor, *Forest of Symbols: Aspects of Ndembu Ritual* (Ithaca, NY: Cornell University Press, 1967).

Van Ghent, Dorothy, *Willa Cather* (Minneapolis: University of Minnesota Press, 1964).

Vendler, Helen, *Our Secret Discipline: Yeats and Lyric Form* (Cambridge, MA: The Belknap Press of Harvard University Press, 2007).

Wagner, Birgit, *Technologie und Literatur im Zeitalter der Avantgarden. Ein Beitrag zur Geschichte des Imaginären* (Munich: Fink, 1996).

Wakelin, Martyn F., *The Southwest of England*, Varieties of English Around the World, vol. T5 (Amsterdam: John Benjamins, 1986).

Warner, Michael, *The Letters of the Republic: Publication and the Public Sphere in Eighteenth-Century America* (Cambridge, MA: Harvard University Press, 1990).

Watson, E. L. Grant, 'Foxes, Geese and Ducks', *Listener* (27 January 1932), p. 144.

'Week by Week', *Listener* (9 November 1932), p. 657.

Weheilye, Alexander, *Phonographies: Grooves in Sonic Afro-Modernity* (Durham, NC: Duke University Press, 2005).

Wellbery, David, Foreword to Kittler, *Discourse Networks 1800/1900*, trans. Michael Meteer, with Chris Cullens (Stanford: Stanford University Press, 1990), pp. vii–xxxiii.

Weiner, Martin J. *English Culture and the Decline of the Industrial Spirit 1850–1980* (Cambridge: Cambridge University Press, 1981).

Wesley, John, and Charles Wesley, *The Poetical Works of John and Charles Wesley: Reprinted from the originals, with the last corrections of the authors; together with the poems of Charles Wesley not before published*, ed. G. Osborn, 13 vols (London: Wesleyan-Methodist Conference Office, 1868–72).

Wesling, Donald, *The Chances of Rhyme: Device and Modernity* (Berkeley: University of California Press, 1980).

White, Gilbert, *The Natural History of Selbourne*, ed. Richard Mabey (London: Penguin, 1977).

Whitman, Walt, *Leaves of Grass* (Brooklyn, New York, 1855).

Williams, R. John, *The Buddha in the Machine: Art, Technology, and the Meeting of East and West* (New Haven: Yale University Press, 2014).

Williams, William Carlos, 'Overture to a Dance of Locomotives', in Leonidas Warren Payne (ed.), *Selections from American Literature, Part 2* (Chicago: Rand McNally, 1919), p. 873.

Wilson, Peter, *A Preface to Ezra Pound* (London: Routledge, 2014).

Winnicott. D. W., *Playing and Reality* (New York, Basic Books, 1971).

Woolf, Virginia, *Between the Acts* (London: Granada, 1980).

——, 'George Gissing', in *The Common Reader: Second Series*, available at: <https://ebooks.adelaide.edu.au/w/woolf/virginia/w91c2/chapter18.html> (last accessed 1 June 2016).

——, 'In the Orchard' (1923), in *The Complete Shorter Fiction of Virginia Woolf: Second Edition*, ed. Susan Dick (London: Harcourt Books, 1989), pp. 149–52.

——, *The Complete Shorter Fiction of Virginia Woolf: Second Edition*, ed. Susan Dick (London: Harcourt Books, 1989).

——, 'The Novels of George Gissing', *The Living Age*, 272 (January–March 1912), pp. 675–80.

Yeats, W. B., *Early Essays*, ed. George Bornstein and Richard J. Finneran (New York: Scribner, 2007).

——, *Letters on Poetry from W. B. Yeats to Dorothy Wellesley* (London: Oxford University Press, 1940).

——, *The Collected Letters of W. B. Yeats*, gen. ed. John Kelly (Oxford: Oxford University Press; InteLex Electronic Edition, 2002).

——, *The Variorum Edition of the Poems of W. B. Yeats*, ed. Peter Allt and Russell K. Alspach, corrected 3rd printing (New York: Macmillan, 1966).

——, *Words for Music Perhaps and Other Poems: Manuscript Materials*, ed. David R. Clark (Ithaca, NY: Cornell University Press, 1999).

Zilliacus, Clas, *Beckett and Broadcasting: A Study of the Works of Samuel Beckett for and in Radio and Television* (Åbo: Åbo Akademi, 1976).

Index